ACADEMIC DEPENDENCY IN THE SOCIAL SCIENCES

Academic Dependency in the Social Sciences

Structural Reality and Intellectual Challenges

Edited by

KATHINKA SINHA-KERKHOFF
SYED FARID ALATAS

SEPHIS

Asian Development Research Institute

MANOHAR
2010

First published 2010

ISBN 978-81-7304-894-4

Published by
Ajay Kumar Jain *for*
Manohar Publishers & Distributors
4753/23 Ansari Road, Daryaganj
New Delhi 110 002

Typeset by
Kohli Print
Delhi 110 051

Printed at
Salasar Imaging Systems
Delhi 110 035

In Memoriam
Dr Tharcisse Nsabimana (1954–2009)

Contents

II. MOUNTING CHALLENGES TO ACADEMIC DEPENDENCY

Acknowledgements

This volume is the outcome of an international conference at Patna in 2008 on 'Coping with Academic Dependency: How?' organized by the Asian Development Research Institute (ADRI), the South-South Exchange Programme for Research on the History of Development (SEPHIS) and the Indian Council of Social Science Research (ICSSR). Among our colleagues at ADRI we would specially like to thank Dr Shaibal Gupta, Dr P.P. Ghosh, Dr Sunita Lall, Dr. Chirashree Dasgupta, Dr Ratnakar Tripathy, Mr Md. Masoom Reza and Mr Suryakant Kumar who were very active during the conference in different capacities.

We also acknowledge the invaluable contributions made by Dr Marina de Regt (SEPHIS Coordinator), Dr Maria Serena I. Diokno (SEPHIS Steering Committee) and Ms Jacqueline Rutte (SEPHIS Secretariat). Without the support of Dr Ulbe Bosma, Professor Willem van Schendel and Dr Lakshmi Subramaniam during the conception of this project, this volume would never have seen the light of the day. We specially thank Dr T.C.A. Anant of ICSSR for his personal interest and participation in the conference.

We are very grateful to other conference participants whose contributions are not included in this book but whose participation nevertheless was of great value including Dr D.N. Jha (former Professor of History, University of Delhi), Dr Monica Hirst (Programa de Estudios Internacionales, Argentina) and discussant-in-absentia Dr Alpa Shah (Goldsmiths, University of London). We are particulary indebted to Prof. Dr Sujata Patel (Head, Dept. of Sociology, University of Pune). Apart from delivering a public lecture on 'The Challenges to Academic Dependency in the Global World', she also volunteered as chairperson and discussant during the conference. We are also greatly indebted to Ms. Radhika Borde (proprietor, The Little Tradition, Ranchi, India) and acknowledge her valuable editorial contributions, though we alone are answerable for the final results, of course.

We are obliged to mention the immense enthusiasm for the project displayed by late Dr Tharcisse Nsabimana of the Kigali Institute of Education in Rwanda. Most unfortunately, he passed away in August 2009 not having been able to revise his conference paper for publication in this volume. We nevertheless decided to publish his more or less unmodified paper adding only a few editorial changes. We remember Dr Nsabimana with fond memories and were shocked when informed about his untimely death, which remains a great loss. The shocking news of the sudden demise of Dr Anjan Ghosh in June 2010 reached us when this book was about to be printed. Anjan Ghosh's article in this book is an unequivocal testimony to his concern with the cause of academic independence in the South.

Finally, the publication of this volume is wholly sponsored by SEPHIS, an initiative that certainly helps to lessen academic dependency.

EDITORS

Introduction: A Common Pool of Knowledge or Academic Dependency?

KATHINKA SINHA-KERKHOFF
SYED FARID ALATAS

D.N. Jha, an eminent historian of India, made a provocative point during the inaugural session of the international workshop on 'Coping with Academic Dependency: How?'[1] Jha asserted that knowledge is not monopolized by a few privileged in the world but belongs to all mankind. Once it becomes part of the public domain it can be used by all and is independent of the place of residence. Jha denied there is such a thing as the academic dependency of scholars residing in the South and he did not understand why so much was being made out of it. Jha strongly believes that knowledge is individual. The proposition that certain individuals are excluded from the pool of knowledge is according to him an insult to us as 'we are intelligent people and can criticize what others want to impose upon us'. In his talk he illustrated how some Indian historians who influenced him intellectually had been able to reject 'a European view of Indian history' and 'were not dependent on the West'. There is a lot of truth in what Jha said. There are many examples in India and elsewhere in the South of historians and other social scientists overcoming the problems of intellectual imperialism and academic dependency. Nevertheless, in the opinion of many, including the other participants of the workshop, academic dependency is still to be considered as a central problem characterizing the state of knowledge in the South.

In fact, none of the other around twenty-five workshop participants, almost all social scientists based in the South, agreed with Jha on the idea of a common pool of knowledge. Sabo Bako, a postdoctoral researcher at the Department of Political Science of the Ahmadu Bello University in Zaria, Nigeria, suggested that the whole idea of a 'common pool of knowledge' was a myth. He opinionated that 'knowledge in the world is not commonly owned, not commonly produced and not commonly applied'. He added there would not have been any need for an international workshop like this one that took place in Patna, an intellectually peripheral area within India, if such a pool of common knowledge indeed existed. All other participants shared his opinion and welcomed the opportunity to voice their opinion during the three-day workshop. As P.P. Ghosh, Director of the Asian Development Research Institute (ADRI) put it during his vote of thanks on the first day, 'many times things are done that are immediate but not those things that are important. We have now organized a workshop that is important for us and we thank the South-South Exchange Programme for Research on the History of Development (SEPHIS) for making this possible.' His remark set the tone of the deliberations on academic dependency that followed.

As Anjan Ghosh of the Centre for Studies in Social Sciences (CSSS) and SEPHIS Coordinator formulated it, the workshop asked:

> Is academic dependency extant in countries of the South in an era of neo-liberal globalization? Electronic and digital technology has interconnected and integrated the world into a 'global village'. But has this incorporation diminished the unilateral flow of information and the 'consumption' of the periphery by the metropolis?

Clearly, participants agreed with Ghosh who described during his valedictory speech on 'Local Scholars, Global Academy'[2] how neo-liberal globalization has created conditions in many parts of the South leading to the evacuation of advanced research and higher studies. He also explained how this has further concentrated the knowledge economy in the North leading to a unilateral flow of educated manpower from the South. As a consequence, Ghosh argued, homegrown scholars are marginalized and largely confined to teaching, owing to resource constraints and lack of academic infrastructure. One objective of the workshop was therefore to get people to think about developing a flexible career model that would guide these 'marginalized scholars in the South' to cope and possibly reduce academic dependency.

A 2002 report on 'Social Science Research Capacity in South Asia' published in the *Economic and Political Weekly* (2002: 3604–61) argued that the assignment of national identities has become very complicated in the contemporary world in which various categories of globally mobile people are able to lay claim to—and are being claimed by—more than one national context. Indeed, the existence of a category of the so-called globalized academy is now acknowledged by many scholars who also argue that the internet and other communication technologies have 'levelled the playing field' for participation in the global academia. Yet, some, however, feel that, in theory, these technologies could 'perpetuate or exacerbate the inherent positional inequalities in the system of global academia and scholarly production of knowledge' (Thompson, 2006: 55). In other words, although that these scholars acknowledge that place might play a different role in the contemporary world, the location of people has not yet become irrelevant. However, there is limited knowledge of the costs and benefits of academic globalization. More so because not much is known about the impact of place among academicians located in the South and there seems to be an urge to know more about the net result of such a calculus today for various regions in the South.

Syed Farid Alatas has argued that in international social science scholarship an academic division of labour exists between those who produce ideas and theory, on the one hand, and those who engage primarily in empirical work, on the other. He describes global academia as characterized by a 'centre-periphery continuum or structure of academic dependency', particularly in—but not limited to—the social sciences and humanities (Alatas, 2003: 610, n. 5; 2006: 70–3). From the few empirical studies carried out so far we learn that in some regions in the South the best students who are interested in an academic career invariably leave for Western universities. What is more, in these regions and unlike twenty or thirty years ago, those who obtain doctoral degrees abroad do not want to come back. Reasons given for this are first, the shrinking of employment in the higher education sector, and second, the intellectually deadening atmosphere in most universities and even research institutions in the regions in the South. Generally, even among those who have obtained their doctoral degrees locally, there is little incentive to excel, except as a means to move out of the system—into a non-academic career or simply to go abroad. The result is not only a shortage of high standard published research studies but also a shortage of researchers who are located in one of these countries belonging to the South.[3]

Although the problem seems particularly acute in the field of economics, among many historians in the South who go abroad to get advanced research degrees, there is also a tendency not to come back or to come back and choose other employment or select teaching rather than research posts at home. In general, the number of historians located in the South seems to be shrinking and so is their research output in terms of publications. However, there seems to be great intra-regional as well as intra-national variation in these, what Thompson (2006: 41) calls, academically 'peripheral' nations.

Although the participants at the workshop and the papers collected in this volume acknowledge the centrality of academic dependency as a problem, there are differences of opinion as to what constitutes academic dependency, what its manifestations are, and how we may cope with academic dependency. Alatas expressed his concern on the matter during his keynote address at the workshop:

Imagine that a scholar in India [for instance], let's say an expert of Christianity, is invited to Oxford to talk about Christianity in Europe. Now also imagine she/he only speaks about Christianity using the vocabulary of Hinduism (let's say) without employing the terminology belonging to Christianity. Now such a scholar would first of all in all probability never be invited to Europe to give such a talk or she would be laughed out of the lecture hall. But indeed this is what is happening in much of the world. In the Muslim world, for example, Americans, Dutch, Australians, etc., give lectures about Islam. But Islam for them is just an object of study not the source of theoretical ideas or concepts. So this is the kind of problem we are facing in academic dependency.

The papers presented at the workshop and published in this volume in revised form deal with two major dimensions or levels of the problem of academic dependency, that is, the theoretical and practical. It is essential that academic dependency be understood and dealt with at these two levels in order for us to appreciate the magnitude of the problem and seriously consider the options available to us as we consider measures to overcome academic dependency.

THE MAGNITUDE OF THE PROBLEM: THE MEANING OF ACADEMIC DEPENDENCY

The precarious position of social scientists residing in the South is not independent from what is done or not done by scholars in the North. Though it should be recognized that there is variation within the North (as there is in the South), generally the problems faced by social scientists in the North are of a different nature than those described above. Besides, those who migrated from the South may often continue to work on the South, but few have an inclination to return once they have obtained prestigious positions in academic institutions in the North. What is more, work and fame of those who migrated is much more acclaimed than those who stayed behind, or returned, as vividly described by Ramachandra Guha in a recent article. Guha also shows, however, that the position of social scientists, who resided and worked in, for instance, India during the 1960s and the 1970s, enjoyed a much higher status than their colleagues in India now.

The present problems of social scientists in the South are the result of the fact that they have gradually become (though some more than others) institutionally and theoretically dependent on the North. The phenomenon of academic dependency has been discussed in great detail by Alatas who concluded that this dependence has resulted in, 'an uncritical and imitative approach to ideas and concepts' from the West. We argue that this dependence has resulted in the above-described general regression among social scientists based in the South and in a marginalization of their works. Scholars based in the South are therefore challenged to prove themselves (once again) as internationally established first-rate scholars equipped with journals in which scholars of the North wish to publish their best works (and not the other way round as is the case at present). They can only do this by liberating themselves from the Northern way of defining problem areas, methods, and standards of excellence.

As against Jha's notion referred to at the outset of this introduction, according to Alatas there is no *pool*, let alone a common pool, but an *ocean* of knowledge. Parts of this ocean are polluted while others are clean. Now he feels we cannot swim the whole ocean and do not always have the choice to select the part we will swim in. Alatas, in his keynote address on 'Intellectual and Structural Challenges to Academic Dependency'[4] referred to the work of his late father, the noted social scientist Syed Hussein Alatas, on 'Academic Imperialism' (1969, 2000) and the 'Captive Mind' (1972, 1974) and explained that the problem of academic dependency was not a new one. It originated during the first phase of globalization during the colonial days of the nineteenth century. This point was elaborated on by Sujata Patel[5] in her public lecture on 'Challenges to Academic Dependency in the Global World'. Patel explained how colonized people had inherited an entire matrix of binaries that created hierarchies, social exclusions and inequalities. Patel also felt that though efforts had been made, academic dependency was, even in post-colonial times, evident in the everyday life of scholars as well as in the way disciplinary divisions are constituted in the South. In fact, Patel explained that academic dependency has become reformulated in the context of globalization as some participants like Ayokunle Olumuyiwa Omobowale and late Tharcisse Nsabimana personally experienced. They suggested that globalization along with structural adjustment had made things worse in their countries. Another participant, Hetukar Jha concurred with them that there now is a clear distinction and hierarchy between the 'centre' and the 'periphery' within their own countries and regions as well. There exists a dialectical relation between the periphery and the metropolis, Anjan Ghosh explained, and added that we should ask ourselves who is dependent on what. T.C.A. Anant[6] in his inaugural speech at the workshop emphasized that the reality of academic dependency in present-day life has also implications for public policies. He showed for instance how mistaken notions of property that were borrowed from the West, negatively impacted present-day life in India.

Alatas emphasized that academic dependency is also a problem faced by scholars living in countries that were never formally colonized. Such countries may not be in the South economically but are in the South academically. Nevertheless, Alatas and many other participants asserted that academic dependency is not to be equated with a 'South-North' division. Shaibal Gupta[7] pointed to the 'periphery within the periphery' and thereafter quipped, 'there also is a South in the North and a North in the South'. Maria Serena I. Diokno[8] accurately summarized that special categories of the North and the South really shift on the basis of how the question of academic dependency is approached, that is, either as an epistemological problem or as a structural problem. In short, all agreed that academic dependency is a reality for many scholars in the world and in particular, though not exclusively, for those residing in what is commonly referred to as the South. Though some of the paper presenters such as Fernanda Beigel and Carlos P. Tatel showed in their papers that one could, under certain circumstances, bypass academic dependency, they all agreed that academic dependency existed and manifested itself on the practical or structural as well as theoretical levels. Participants also agreed that it was high time to tackle this geopolitics of knowledge on both levels.

ACADEMIC DEPENDENCY AT THE THEORETICAL LEVEL

While it was apparent during the workshop that academic dependency was experienced on two levels, the theoretical or intellectual (the level of knowledge/ideas) and the practical or structural level, most of the papers presented and collected in this volume addressed academic dependency on the theoretical level. Syed Farid Alatas explained that for the understanding of academic dependency on that level it is important to take the idea of intellectual imperialism as a starting point.[9] Drawing from his father's work on intellectual imperialism, he notes that intellectual imperialism is analogous to political and economic imperialism in that it refers to the 'domination of one people by another in their world of thinking'(Alatas, 2000: 24). Intellectual imperialism was more direct in the colonial period, whereas today it has more to do with the West's control of and influence over the flow of social scientific knowledge rather than its ownership and control of academic institutions. Indeed, this form of hegemony was 'not imposed by the West through colonial domination, but accepted willingly with confident enthusiasm, by scholars and planners of the former colonial territories and even in the few countries that remained independent during that period' (Alatas, 2006: 7–8).

The ideological context within which academic dependency

is to be understood is that of Eurocentrism. While the critique of Eurocentrism in the social sciences is well known (Amin, 1989; Alatas, 2006), this has yet to be translated into the teaching of basic and mainstream social science courses in universities around the world to the extent that the canon can be influenced. Foundational and introductory courses and textbooks in the social sciences are generally biased in favour of American or British theoretical perspectives, illustrations and reading materials. The logical consequence of the critique of Eurocentrism in the social sciences is the development of alternative concepts and theories that are not restricted to Western civilization as the main source. This can only happen if the critique of Eurocentrism becomes an important theme in the teaching of the social sciences.

If we take the example of sociology, a survey of course syllabi for sociological theory will show the prevalence of Eurocentrism. In most sociological theory textbooks as well as other writings on the history of social theory, it is mainly Americans and Europeans who do the thinking and writing, they are the social theorists and social thinkers, that is, the knowing subject. When non-Europeans do appear in the texts they are invariably the objects of study of European thinkers and not knowing subjects. They are rarely considered as sources of sociological theories and ideas. This is what can be referred to as the subject-object dichotomy (Alatas, 2007: 271). If we take the nineteenth century as an example, the impression is given that it is only Europeans such as Marx, Weber and Durkheim who were thinking about the nature of society and its development, and that there were no thinkers in Asia, Africa or South America doing the same.

The absence of non-European thinkers in the standard works on social thought and theory is inexcusable when we know that many non-Europeans had actually influenced the development of social thought. For example, Ibn Khaldun[10] is occasionally referred to in histories of social thought but is rarely seen as a source of relevant sociological theories and concepts. He is merely regarded as a precursor or prototype of modern sociology and other social sciences.

Some have argued that the relations of power between the colonialists and their subjects have not fundamentally changed and that such relations of power between nations were transposed to within nations and that 'the international division of intellectual labour was maintained through the presence of the metropolis in the periphery itself' (Ghosh, 1991: 72). These unequal relations of dominance between and within nations must therefore be altered and not only for reasons of personal benefit of individual historians in the so-called periphery. Their silencing also poses a problem for others as it leaves history writing in the hands of a few bureaucrats, politicians and a handful of academics in the 'centres' who write history of all others and therefore decide on the future course of the lives of these 'others'. Globally, the voices of 'others' are not heard, the periphery does not hear each other and at times not even the voices of the centre, as the past and future of many people in the South is not conceptualized in the South but in the North. Finally, until this inequality is somehow redressed, history writing in all nations remains poorly developed and untransformed causing a lack of alternative paths, which tell people all over the world where they still can go and what they still can be.

Coming to a more formal definition of academic dependency, Syed Farid Alatas stated that:

Academic dependency theory is a dependency theory of the global state of the social sciences. It defines academic dependency as a condition in which the knowledge production of certain scholarly communities is conditioned by the development and growth of knowledge of other scholarly communities to which the former is subjected. Then relations of interdependence between two or more scientific communities, and between these and global transactions in knowledge, assumes the form of dependency when some scientific communities (those located in the knowledge powers) can expand according to certain criteria of development and progress, while other scientific communities (such as those in developing societies) can only do this as a reflection of that expansion, which generally has negative effects on their development according to the same criteria. The psychological dimension to this dependency [. . .] is such that the dependent scholar is more a passive recipient of research agendas, theories and methods from the knowledge powers [which in today's world encompasses three core countries, namely the United States, Great Britain and France].[11]

Academic dependency on the intellectual level, Alatas clarified, is determined by the dimensions on which it operates. These are (1) dependence on ideas; (2) dependence on the media of ideas; (3) dependence on the technology of education; (4) dependence on aid for research and teaching; (5) dependence on investment in education; and (6) dependence of scholars in developing societies on demand in the knowledge powers for their skills. Moreover what is very crucial about the structure of academic dependency Alatas reminds us, is the knowledge division of labour which is founded on a three-fold division as follows: (1) the division between theoretical and empirical intellectual labour; (2) the division between other country and own country studies; and (3) the division between comparative and single case studies.[12]

With reference to foreign aid in science, Singh Uberoi emphasized that it 'upholds the system of foreign dominance in all matters of scientific and professional life and organization. . . . It subordinates the national science of the poor to the national and international science of the rich. It confirms our dependence [. . .]' (Singh Uberoi, 1969: 120). Developing countries, therefore, find themselves at the periphery of the world social science system in which intellectual and educational power is concentrated in the core. Thus, as Altbach (1977: 188) felt, 'industrialized nations dominate the world's research production, mass media, information systems, and advanced training facilities'.

How academic dependency is understood was clearly described in most of the papers presented during the workshop, some of which are after revision included in this volume. Omobowale, for instance, concluded his paper on 'Academic Dependency and Sociological Theorizing in the Third World: The Case Study of Akiwowo's *Asuwada* Theory of Sociation' as follows:

> Conclusively, inasmuch as Akiwowo attempted providing an African sociological-theoretical perspective to the understanding of contextual social relations in Africa, his theory has remained largely obscured in Nigeria's academic environment. This is not unconnected to the preference for Western sociological theories even among scholars who accept the relevance of Akiwowo's theory to sociological applications in Nigeria. This is a classic evidence of the disadvantaged position of African scholarship vis-à-vis Western scholarship, not only among Westerners, but even among indigenous scholars in Nigerian universities. For as long as this persists, it may be difficult for Africa to channel an independent course to development as it remains dependent on the West in an ever increasingly globalizing world where the West has remained dominant at the expense of Third World nations.[13]

In a similar vein, Sabo Bako in his paper[14] entitled 'Colonial Dependency and the Study of the Sokoto Caliphate in West Africa' examined the travails of doctorate students working under colonial dependency in transition to independence in Nigeria, and how that affected the construction and de-construction of paradigms among history career building academics in their universities.

ACADEMIC DEPENDENCY OF THE PRACTICAL LEVEL

Shaibal Gupta of ADRI in his vote of thanks at the end of the workshop mentioned that bringing people from the South together is not an easy proposition. It is, Gupta believed, much easier to get people from the North to the South [though not always vice versa!] than from the South to the South. And right he is. Apart from the sheer distance between Argentina and India for instance, trying to get somebody from Burundi to India, to give another example, is difficult and expensive, as the former country does not offer Indian visa facilities. An extreme example manifested itself during the workshop when we got the news that Samuel Nilimi Nkumbaan, a lecturer in Archaeology at the University of Ghana in Legon, who had a ticket and visa for India, had been refused passage, as he could not produce a transit visa for Germany where he was to change planes. Such a visa had not been deemed necessary at the time of booking.

While discussing in absentia Nkumbaan's paper entitled 'Defining Archaeology in Ghana: A Historical Interpretation', Ratnakar Tripathy[15] pointed to many more examples of this level of academic dependency. The paper examines the beginning of Archaeology in Ghana in the 1930s and its association with the West. It also looks at the development of the discipline thereafter in terms of research, research funding, and publications, most of which are not without Western influence of a kind. Nkumbaan also mentions in his paper that many skeletal remains and other artefacts recovered from excavations in Ghana and sent to various countries abroad for specialist analysis have since not been returned though some publications on them [written by archaeologists in the West] exist. Other forms of dependency on this practical level are examined by Nkumbaan in his paper in the light of post-Second World War affluent tourism and the consequent looting and trafficking of antique materials, migrated archives, and brain drain or migration.

Other scholars in their papers, but more during the discussions thereof, pointed to the fact that they often had little or no access to local theories in the periphery itself though those located in the knowledge centres did have such access. Besides, these local knowledges known outside their country were not read/taught/known in their own country. Omobowale complained that in Nigeria too much value was attached to publications in the West whereas, publications in Nigerian journals were rarely read. He was also critical of the fact that degrees from abroad provided more life chances in Nigeria than degrees locally procured. Hetukar Jha discussed the factors afflicting the course of social sciences in the universities and colleges of India, focusing on Bihar. In this context, the phenomenon of hierarchization of universities/institutes appeared to be quite visible.[16] Likewise, in his paper 'The Institutions of Higher Education in Burundi and Rwanda: Facing the Challenges of Post-Conflict Societies', late Tharcisse Nsabimana analysed the situation through which the institutions of higher education from the African Great Lakes region went through from the 1990s onwards. Nsabimana mentioned that the higher education system in the region is devastated due to neo-liberalization. He added that old universities nowadays face many problems such as economic, insufficient infrastructure, and shortages of human resources (academic staff, lack of teaching and learning material). As a result private institutions have mushroomed and have increased pressure on the academic staff at the expense of quality teaching and research. The outcome of all this is, he concluded that, 'the institutions of higher education in the Great Lakes region are heavily depending on each other and on international donors. This leads to academic dependency.'[17]

COPING WITH ACADEMIC DEPENDENCY

Given the various problems resulting from academic dependency, what did the participants at the workshop whose revised papers are collected in this volume have to say about dealing with the problem? There was much discussion around the need for the generation and promotion of alternative discourses. Alatas defined these in the following manner:

> [Alternative discourses are those which] are informed by local/regional historical experiences and cultural practices in the same way that the

Western social sciences are. Being alternative means a turn to philosophies, epistemologies, histories, and the arts, other than those of the Western tradition.[18]

Following Alatas, Bako in his paper (not included in this volume), examined the possibility of developing 'an objective scientific approach', which could be constructed in order to facilitate some mutual but independent academic dialogue between established historians in the North and emerging local historians on the history, development, conquest and legacy of the Sokoto Caliphate. Mario Rufer followed suit. In his paper 'Evidence, Temporality, Analytical Frameworks: Categories, Writing Procedures and Academic Dependency', he sets out to discover alternative discourses and propagates an emic approach as a mode of history writing. He asks:

> How can we deal with alternative forms of production when the *alternative* is many times formatted in terms of a fixed category, socialized by first-world chains of intellectual diffusion? Is a South-South exchange effectively possible in terms of consolidation of projects/discussion and production of knowledge from south(ern) institutional locations? If the answer is yes, and taking into consideration these general *geo-politics of knowledge,* what are precisely the *disciplinary politics of knowledge* we must discuss in history, in terms of teaching and doing research from southern positions/institutions/real locations?[19]

Discussing a flexible model for historians residing in the South(s) and doing research from/on South(s), which would help them cope with academic dependency, Rufer discussed three points in his paper: (1) the construction of evidence, its powerful grammar and its implication for southern intellectual locations; (2) the re-emergence of heterogeneous temporality and its potential to a situated historical discipline; and (3) the consideration of analytical unities in historical discourse involving what Rufer considers as *memories without warranty.*

However, as Alatas mentioned, coping we all do. Yet, participants did feel that 'just coping' was not enough. Alatas suggested that the term 'coping' had a pessimistic connotation. Rather than speak about coping with academic dependency we should be striving to reduce this academic dependency and perhaps even dismantle its structures. Alatas, for example, argued that alternative discourses:

> [. . .] are all to be considered as potential sources of social science theories and concepts, which would decrease academic dependence on the world social science powers. Therefore, it becomes clear that the emergence and augmentation of alternative discourses is identical to the process of universalizing and internationalizing the social science. It should also be clear that alternative discourses refer to good social science because they are more conscious of the relevance of the surroundings and the problems stemming from the discursive wielding of power by the social sciences. As such, alternative discourses could be advocated for Western social science itself.[20]

An example of doing alternative social science is given by the Malaysian geographer, Abdul Samad Hadi. Referring to the field of migration studies, Abdul Samad Hadi suggested that Western theories of internal migration are predominantly based on the idea that the movement of people involves a change in residence from one administrative unit to another. The movement is unidirectional with a tendency not to return to the place of origin. In the Third World, however, there are also other kinds of movements. Internal migration tends to be circular and migration to urban areas is often temporary (Abdul Samad, 1983: 64–5). Furthermore, such information cannot be derived from reports and census data. Abdul Samad urges us to think about local concepts of migration such as the Malay *pindah* or *hijrah* (permanent migration), and *merantau* (leaving the state to earn a living with eventual return) (ibid.: 74–5) which refer to the circular nature of internal migration.

MOUNTING CHALLENGES TO ACADEMIC DEPENDENCY

The objectives of the workshop had been formulated as follows: (1) We should develop a flexible career model for social scientists (and in particular for historians) residing in the South that can be appropriated in different contexts; and (2) the aim of this new career model is to breed social scientists in the South who can cope with academic dependency in its various manifestations and possibly reduce this dependency.

Now, participants argued, we should reflect on developing a flexible career model for social scientists in the South to transcend academic dependency today. Muchkund Dubey,[21] in his presidential speech, was of the opinion, however, that this effort to try and reduce or even overcome academic dependency is an uphill task as it involves the dismantling of a paradigm based on an unequal world order, which the dominant powers seek to maintain. In this regard he narrated his failed effort to introduce a new concept of education in Geneva, which should not mean, he had pleaded at the time, the acquiring of literacy skills only, but the development of skills to comprehend, contest and transform knowledge. Other participants also expressed their pessimism, such as Nsabimana, who felt we can never overcome academic dependency. Others were more optimistic for instance. Beigel who cited in her paper 'The Chilean Circuit (1957–73): The Emergence of Chile as a Centre of Internationalization and Regionalization of Social Knowledge', as an example of the possibility of transcending academic dependency. Her research is part of an effort to make a contribution to affront academic dependency today and her paper was a first stage of a necessary investigation on the history of the institutionalization of the academic field in South America that shows the main structural processes that are involved in academic development.[22] Carlos P. Tatel shared her optimism. In his paper on 'Anthropology at the University of the Philippines Examining

Institutional History and Academic Dependency in a Southeast Asian University', he referred to the 'challenge to the current generation of 'home-grown' anthropologists to finally break from the academic/colonial bondage'.[23]

Alatas, however, felt that scholars have more autonomy and control where overcoming academic dependency at the intellectual level is concerned. At the structural level much of the solution, Alatas argued, has to do with the awareness, will and resolve of politicians, bureaucrats and administrators, without which the structure of academic dependency cannot be dismantled. T.C.A. Anant agreed and therefore advised that in order to reverse academic dependency two key partners are involved: the academic community and the state. According to him both have to be addressed in order to transcend academic dependency. Furthermore, it is not sufficient to discuss coping. It was also necessary to talk about academic freedom and autonomy thus addressing change and the political. Yet, Alatas believes that 'we as scholars can not do much on the structural (material) level of academic dependency as we are neither in charge of institutions nor are we the state but our fight will be more at the intellectual/theoretical level'. Besides it was recognized that different countries faced different problems and that for some the practical level of academic dependency was more urgent while for others the theoretical or intellectual level. Both Alatas and Anant recognized, however, that concepts and theories are never completely independent and that we therefore can only strive at 'relative autonomy'.

Alatas also emphasized the need to avoid nativism. The extent to which attempts to overcome academic dependency, particularly at the level of theories and concepts, are informed by ethnocentrism as problematic as the Eurocentrism they criticize must be examined. The vast majority of proponents of alternative discourses would distance themselves from what has been referred to as nativism, or orientalism in reverse (al-'Azm, 1984; Moghadam, 1989; Abaza & Stauth, 1990), or academic nationalism (van Dijk, 1994). The call for alternative discourses should be indistinguishable from calls for universal or internationalized social science. Therefore, the so-called 'dilemma of two alternative "calls": to maintain international standards of scholarship by focusing on internationally recognized methodologies and theory-building orientations; and to do work relevant to the daily lives of their own peoples' (Quah, 1993: 95), does not or should not exist.

Nativism refers to the positing of an absolute opposition between 'Western' and 'Eastern' culture, and may result in the wholesale and irrational rejection of Western thought. The call for alternative discourses, on the other hand, is simultaneously a call for the universalization of the social sciences. It is conscious of the need to avoid creating mirror opposites (Moghadam, 1989: 82) of Eurocentric scholarship.

The idea of Orientalism in reverse was elaborated by the Syrian thinker, Sadiq Jalal al-'Azm. He refers to the work of another Syrian, Georges Saddikni, on the concept of man (Ar. *insan*):

> The philosophy of Hobbes is based on his famous saying that 'every man is a wolf unto other men', while, on the contrary, the inner philosophy implicit in the word *insan* preaches that 'every man is a brother unto other men. (Saddikni, cited in al-'Azm, 1984: 368)

Al-'Azm then critiques Saddikni:

> I submit that this piece of so-called analysis and comparison contains, in a highly condensed form, the entire apparatus of metaphysical abstractions and ideological mystifications so characteristic of Ontological Orientalism and so deftly and justly denounced in Said's book. The only new element is the fact that the Orientalist essentialist ontology has been reversed to favour one specific people of the Orient. (al-'Azm, 1984: 368)

Orientalism in reverse is informed by an essentialist approach to both 'Oriental' and 'Occidental' civilizations and is, therefore, a form of auto-Orientalism, which is explained with reference to the Japanese case. The *nihonjinron* (theories of Japanese people) tradition in Japanese sociology is founded on essentialized views on Japanese society, with emphasis on cultural homogeneity and historical continuity and was heavily influenced by the Western Orientalist scholarship on Japan. The difference, however, is that the knowing subjects this time are the Japanese themselves (Lie, 1996: 5).

At the end of the very successful workshop in Patna, which also received tremendous attention of the local media (newspapers as well as television in Patna) all seemed to agree with Mahatma Gandhi who had during a conference in New Delhi in 1946 expressed his dislike of having, as recalled by Muchkund Dubey in his speech, to live in a world that was no 'world-world'. Or, as Anjan Ghosh in his paper included in the present volume stated,[24] Gandhi clearly understood that 'the eviction of the British from India would not necessarily lead to the rejection of the values and institutions of Western civilization'. It was against this Ghosh argues that Gandhi wanted, 'to exert his moral force' and, 'subsequently the notion of *swaraj* would be deployed by Indian philosophers and social scientists to mark their distance from the West'. All workshop participants therefore supported actual globalization of knowledge while denouncing ethnocentric knowledge. They all aspired at formulating a model that could help transcend academic dependency at the two levels and would make the 'pool of knowledge' truly 'common' (thus gain *swaraj* in ideas as well as practice). Anjan Ghosh warned, however, that we have no readymade answers but only speculations. In his valedictory speech he clearly stated that, we generally try to overcome intellectual domination not in a prescriptive but speculative manner. Self-rule in social science is still to be achieved in the South. We should be constructing new theories, teaching them and including them in the canon. In doing so, we should be setting new standards and try to have them universally established.

AN AGENDA FOR OVERCOMING ACADEMIC DEPENDENCY

At the valedictory session of the workshop the following unilaterally proposed the following measures that could function as the 'flexible career model' that they desired to develop:[25]

- A journal should be established in order to get our alternative discourses heard. The journal could first function as an annual review and may include new theories and alternative thinkers and include work of marginalized traditions in the West. Also, there should be a consortium of existing journals in the South.
- We should not 'mirror the Western mirror' but set our own agenda. We should do away with 'spurious and inauthentic knowledge' and we might like to go for new forms of validation. Beigel proposed an international agreement in the South in this regard.
- We should formulate our own new paradigms based on the 'provincialization of Europe' (and other dominant powers) but reject essentialism. In other words, alternative discourses should be accepted as mainstream universal theories.
- We should establish a new epistemic community through networks of knowledge production in terms of institutions, geographical level or level of space, culture and profession. These networks (or links of connectivity) that go beyond the local, regional, national and international should displace the binaries we inherited and which causes academic dependency. These networks should be careful not to become new hierarchies.
- There should be some kind of exchange between South within North and South within South.
- There are our stories told by others and our stories told by us and we should relate these with each other and try to understand why other people tell the kind of stories about

us as this may be the only way to become an expert on ourselves.

- We should decide on a common language to understand different local knowledges and to communicate with each other and 'the other'.
- Funding should not be tied exclusively to the interests of donors but also to the interests of those who receive funds/scholarships.
- The importance of individuals could be emphasized but should also be cautioned.
- In their efforts to transcend academic dependency scholars in the South should be honest, determined, self-reflexive, self-confident and self-critical.
- Language is important but we will not solve the problems of academic dependency by just writing in the local language. Rather, we should confront concepts designed in the West, analyse them and come up with alternative concepts if deemed necessary.
- We should strive for more academic autonomy, which in some places might mean getting more involved on the political level whereas in other places it might mean less political involvement.
- We have to go beyond the binary opposition of 'sociology of the vernacular' and 'sociology of the universal'.
- We should not reject the state as the state could function as intermediary and provide material and theoretical resources. Maria Hirst, guest participant from Argentina with a special contribution on the 'IBSA Ford Foundation Fellowship Progamme in Brazil, its Academic Results and Challenges' emphasized the role of the State and its connection with the private sector to counter pressures that come from outside.
- Whereas, scholars in the South should go against accepting only going after 'useable (marketable) knowledge', that is, knowledge that enhances their career, 'body shoppers' should not go for mechanical skills only but also search for scholars with theoretical knowledge.

- We should care for strong institution building in our own regions.
- There should be a democratic use of the World Wide Web that reduces its function as a marginalizing technology. It is important to realize that it is not only access to the web that we are concerned with here. We are equally or even more interested in the right outlook to the web (what is on the web and in which way: classification, sourcing of information and search agents). 'Grey' literature could be put on the website but should be used also by scholars in the South themselves and not only by Western scholars (as empirical fieldwork material).
- Sites such as JSTOR should be made available to all institutions, also those located in the South.
- Instead of using the universal as a dominant way of understanding the particular we should proceed to universalization from the particular.
- As the politics of the day make something a universal social theory or not we should address these politics, as academic freedom is related to political freedom.
- We no longer strive for endogenous knowledge but for parity of thought. Our way of thinking in the South is often defined as 'endogenous knowledge' and separated from and subdued by knowledge produced in the North. We want parity of thought. All knowlege formation should be invaded in one truly universal theory.
- We should address the politics of access and issues of library resources.
- Manuscripts, archaeological artefacts exported to the 'North' should either be returned to the country of origin or made available to scholars in that country.
- A policy should be introduced where the North should 'pay' the South for the services or materials provided. Alternative 'payments' should be devised.
- We as scholars and the state should reject stipulations that come with aid and that increase our academic dependency.
- We should address the external aspects of academic depend-

ency but also the internal aspects and related to the latter we should not forget the ethical foundations of universities.

- We should have scholarships for students in the South to come up with their own proposals after they receive some training in alternative concepts and theories during a workshop.
- We should not only write new textbooks but also create a demand for these different types of textbooks.
- We should aim at collaboration between universities in different regions and between regions and seek alliance with European and American scholars who also face the problem of marginalization in their own country.
- We should have a dialogue between different generations of scholars in different countries.
- Scholarships should be made available that allow scholars in the South to carry out comparative research and study other countries than their own. This might stimulate reversed anthropology for instance where a scholar from the South studies Western society.
- There should be more South-South exchange but one should be careful that such exchange does not support new kinds of hegemonic power in the South. Besides, the sponsor should not become the 'Big Brother'. Chirashree Dasgupta[26] therefore proposed discussions on how to evolve different South-South collaborations that could confront the hegemonic powers (in the North as well as in the South). Sponsored in this way, scholars in the South could try and come up with alternative discourses that if not transcend then at least can reduce academic dependency. In this regard one workshop participant Mario Rufer wrote at the beginning of his paper:

Almost all my academic life and objectives have to do with academic dependency. I was 24 years old when, holding a B.A. in History (from the interior of Argentina) I decided to pursue an M.A. in African Studies, but in Mexico. Why? Because I thought—as an intuitive knowledge at that time—that learning about other places in the 'global South' (and *from* those places) could encourage a change in a disciplinary regime so rooted in Western epistemologies and methodologies.

CONCLUSION

The original formulation of the central problem of the workshop that is 'academic dependency and how to cope with it' was based on the idea that the problem is widely recognized in the South. The discussions on the phenomenon during the workshop and in the revised versions of the workshop papers that are published in this volume collectively make a few important points. Alternative discourses or the search for autonomous social science is a universal response of those who critique the structures of academic dependency. Nevertheless, the alternatives that are imagined are to be understood in radically different ways in different countries. For example, in Taiwan it is understood more in the context of Chinese and then Taiwanese nationalism, whereas in the Philippines and India the notion is less tied to the nation state.

Also, by alternative discourse is meant that there must be conscious attempts to engage in social scientific activity with a view to taking into account the world-views, socio-historical contexts, cultural practices, and scholarship of the indigenous societies so that alternative concepts and theories can be generated.

Finally, the point must be made that the call for alternative discourses is not simultaneously a call for nativism or reverse orientalism. It is not, in other words, a call for 'Occidentalism'. This refers to the trend of 'going native' among both Western and local scholars and constitutes an almost total and wholesale rejection of Western social science. The search for alternative discourses is to be seen as a simultaneous call to internationalization as long as the latter is understood not as a one-sided process but rather as one emanating from developing societies while incorporating selectively the Western social sciences. 'Alternative' here is not to be understood as something that replaces Western social science but rather adds to the plurality of social science voices.

The obstacles to the emergence of alternative discourses in the social sciences are varied but there are at least two which are universal. One is the structure of academic dependency, which is the focus of discussion in this volume. The other refers to the cultural environment of academic discourse.

As far as the intellectual culture in Asia, Africa and South America is concerned, what is needed is consciousness of the problem of Eurocentrism, the captive mind and the problems of an uncritically applied social science tradition. This consciousness can be spread through publications, seminars, public lectures and teaching in the universities. The effort to dismantle the structure of academic dependency must be accompanied by a change in the intellectual culture of social science communities in the South as well as the North. This can only be brought about through a process of conscientizing via the various media of intellectual socialization, including the schools, universities and other institutions of higher learning.

Workshop participants thought that though workshops such as the one we organized in Patna are extremely helpful in reducing academic dependency, we should not only 'talk to the converted' but try to get our ideas 'globally accepted'. We therefore agreed that the papers of the workshop should be revised and presented in the form of the book now before you.

NOTES

1. Jointly organized by the South-South Exchange programme for research on the History of Development (SEPHIS) and the Asian Development Research Institute (ADRI), Patna, 4–7 February 2008. The Indian Council for Social Science Research (ICSSR) also contributed to the workshop in a limited way.
2. Ghosh's paper in this volume (Chapter 7) is, however, specially written for this volume.
3. See also Sinha-Kerkhoff in this regard, Chapter 11. This paper was specially written for this volume and was not presented during the workshop.
4. See Alatas, Chapter 2.
5. Head of Department, Department of Sociology, University of Pune. Unfortunately, Patel's paper could not be included in this volume yet see Sujata Patel (ed.), *The ISA Handbook of Diverse Sociological Traditions*, London: Sage, 2009.
6. Member of the ICSSR and a well-known Indian economist.
7. Member Secretary, ADRI.
8. Prominent historian from the Philippines and member of the SEPHIS Steering Committee.
9. See Alatas, Chapter 2.
10. 'Abd al-Rahman Abu Zayd ibn Muhammad ibn Muhammad ibn Khaldun was born on 1 Ramadan/5 May AH 732/AD 1332. After receiving a customary education in the traditional sciences ibn Khaldun held posts in various courts in North Africa and Spain. After a number of unsuccessful stints in office he withdrew into seclusion to write his *Muqaddimah*, a prolegomenon to the study of history which was completed in AD 1378 and which introduces his *'ilm al-'umran* (science of society).
11. See Alatas, Chapter 2.
12. Ibid.
13. See Omobowale, Chapter 6.
14. Though Sabo Bako worked on a complete revision of his paper, it did not reach the editors in time. His paper therefore unfortunately could not be included in this volume. Political problems in Nigeria during the last couple of weeks seem also to have affected internet facilities in the country and therefore did play a part in the delay.
15. Senior Research Fellow, ADRI.

16. See Hetukar Jha, Chapter 5.
17. See Tharcisse Nsabimana, Chapter 4.
18. See Alatas, Chapter 2.
19. See Mario Rufer, Chapter 10.
20. See Alatas, Chapter 2.
21. Chairman of ADRI and President of the Council for Social Development in New Delhi. After the workshop, Prof. Dubey wrote his paper specially for inclusion in this volume, see Chapter 1.
22. See Fernanda Beigel, Chapter 8.
23. See Carlos Tatel, Chapter 9.
24. See Anjan Ghosh, Chapter 7.
25. See also Sinha-Kerkhoff's paper in this regard, Chapter 11.
26. Assistant Professor in ADRI.

REFERENCES

Abaza, Mona and Georg Stauth (1990), 'Occidental Reason, Orientalism, Islamic Fundamentalism: A Critique', in Martin Albrow and Elizabeth King (eds.), *Globalization, Knowledge and Society: Readings from International Sociology*, London: Sage, pp. 209–30.

Abdul Samad, Hadi (1983), 'Mengkonsepsi Mobiliti Penduduk Semasa Urbanisasi di Semenanjung Malaysia: Satu Perbincangan Berasaskan Pengalaman di beberapa buah Kampung di Negeri Sembilan', in *Akademika* 22, pp. 63–81.

Alatas, Syed Farid (2003), 'Academic Dependency and the Global Division of Labour in the Social Sciences', in *Current Sociology*, 51 (6), November, pp. 599–613.

——— (2006), *Alternative Discourses in Asian Social Science: Responses to Eurocentrism*, New Delhi: Sage.

——— (2007), 'The Historical Sociology of Muslim Societies: Khaldunian Applications', in *International Sociology* 22 (3), pp. 267–88.

Alatas, Syed Hussein (1969), 'Academic Imperialism', *Lecture* delivered to the History Society, University of Singapore, 26 September.

——— (1972), 'The Captive Mind in Development Studies', in *International Social Science Journal* 34 (1), pp. 9–25.

——— (1974), 'The Captive Mind and Creative Development', in *International Social Science Journal* 36 (4), pp. 691–9.

——— (2000), 'Intellectual Imperialism: Definition, Traits, and Problems', in *Southeast Asian Journal of Social Science* 28 (1), pp. 23–45.

——— (2006), 'The Autonomous, the Universal and the Future of Sociology', in *Current Sociology* 54 (1), pp. 7–23.

Altbach, Philip G. (1977), 'Servitude of the Mind? Education, Dependency, and Neocolonialism', in *Teachers College Record*, 79 (2), pp. 187–204.

Amin, Samir (1989), *Eurocentrism*, London: Zed Books.

al-'Azm, Sadiq Jalal (1984), 'Orientalism and Orientalism in Reverse', in John Rothschild (ed.), *Forbidden Agendas: Intolerance and Defiance in the Middle East*, London: Al Saqi Books, pp. 349–76.

van Dijk, Teun A. (1994), 'Academic Nationalism', in *Discourse and Society* 5 (3), pp. 275–6.

Ghosh, Anjan (1991), 'The Stricture of Structure, or the Appropriation of Anthropological Theory', in *Review* XIV, pp. 55–7.

Guha, Ramachandra (2003), 'The Ones Who Stayed Behind', in *Economic and Political Weekly*, XXXVIII (12, 13), March and April, pp. 1121–4.

Lie, John (1996), 'Sociology of Contemporary Japan', in *Current Sociology* 44 (1), pp. 1–95.

Moghadam, Val (1989), 'Against Eurocentrism and Nativism', in *Socialism and Democracy* 9, pp. 81–104.

Quah, Stella (1993), 'The Native Sociologist and the Challenge of Science: National, Indigenous and Global Sociologies', in *Current Sociology* 41 (1), pp. 95–106.

Report (2002), 'Social Science Research Capacity in South Asia', in *Economic and Political Weekly* XXXVII (35), 31 August to 6 September, pp. 3604–61.

Thompson, Eric C. 2006, 'Internet-Mediated Networking and Academic Dependency in Indonesia, Singapore and the United States', in *Current Sociology*, 54 (1), pp. 41–61.

Uberoi, J.P. Singh (1968), 'Science and Swaraj', in *Contributions to Indian Sociology* 2, pp. 119–23.

I. DIFFERENT DIMENSIONS OF ACADEMIC DEPENDENCY

CHAPTER 1

Academic Dependency: Some Reflections[1]

MUCHKUND DUBEY

GLOBALIZATION AND DEPENDENCY

Academic dependency has not been a subject of my specialization, but both in my diplomatic and academic careers, I have felt the impact of and been subjected to academic dependency from time to time. Some of the very important papers—at least I thought they were very important—written by me and presented at international seminars, were ignored because they did not conform to the mainstream thinking on the subject concerned in the countries exercising dominant academic power, particularly the USA and the UK. Similarly, I have found in seminar after seminar that Third World[2] scholars have taken the theories propounded by scholars in academic power centres as axiomatic or as final wisdom, without even testing them on the touchstone of empirical evidence.

One would have thought that academic dependency would decline after the end of colonialism. Unfortunately, nothing of this sort has happened. In fact, dependency has become deeper and the situation of dependency far worse now than during the colonial period. This is mainly because of the co-option on a massive scale of scholars and thinkers from the Third World, particularly the best minds among them, into the dominant theories and ideas originating in academic power centres. In fact, these scholars and thinkers from the

Third World are more ardent adherents and greater champions of these theories and ideas than the scholars in the Western countries from where they originate. As in the international economic order, there is a kind of Centre/Periphery relationship in the international academic order also.

The theories and ideas coming from the Centre hold sway in teaching, research and even in policy formulation in the countries at the Periphery. Academics and scholars in the latter countries suffer from an intellectual inferiority complex in the presence of well-known theorists and thinkers of Western countries whom they regard as the ultimate authority for authenticating their work, which is of crucial importance for advancing their career. They also look upon the patronage of these scholars from the West for getting fellowships or scholarships for advanced studies in Western academic institutions. It is also the highest ambition of scholars from the Third World to get recognition for their work by social scientists of repute from the West. The former also regard it as a great academic honour to get published in the research, academic and other eminent journals in Western countries. As a matter of fact, their ability to get recognition in their own countries depends heavily on the recognition of their work in the centres of academic power. I have also repeatedly seen that applicants for academic posts who have got published only in local journals or by local publishers are brushed aside and generally rejected in interviews for faculty positions in important academic institutions in India.

Globalization has been a major factor responsible for deepening academic dependency in recent times. Globalization itself is derived from the neo-classical economic theory developed in the West, which believes in the efficacy of the free market forces to achieve equilibrium and maximize welfare. Liberalization, therefore, is one of the instruments through which globalization is promoted. The advocates of globalization argue that if liberalization does not work then it does not mean that there is anything wrong with the theory; it is simply because it has not been applied rigorously enough.

Thomas Friedman has compared globalization to a golden jacket that is prescribed for all countries irrespective of their size or stage of development. If it hurts, then it should be worn more tightly.[3] It is now widely recognized that the current phase of globalization is not only an irreversible process brought about by the inexorable march of science and technology, but it is also a project deliberately designed and promoted by major economic powers, who also happen to be 'social science powers'.[4] Thomas Friedman refers to them as the 'movers and shakers' of globalization. He states that globalization is spreading in the rest of the world not only because of the power of the idea but also through the navy and air force of the United States.

There is no doubt that ideas, theories and policies based thereon, played an important role in the spread of colonialism. But colonialism advanced mainly by the strength of force; by invasions and conquests. Today, globalization, which, in a sense is a form of neo-colonialism, is advancing by the combination of the same forces, i.e. of the idea and military might. The main motive behind the dismembering of Yugoslavia and dismantling its infrastructure during the Kosovo War and behind the more recent attack on Iraq was to make these two recalcitrant but economically and militarily significant powers, i.e. Yugoslavia and Iraq, to conform to the dominant ideology of globalization and liberalization. When the force of the idea failed, military force followed. The purpose was to transform the socio-economic systems of these countries in order to pave the way for the free play of market forces, which is synonymous with the free play of multinational corporations of the major powers.

COMMODIFICATION OF EDUCATION

One of the insidious forms that globalization has taken in the Third World is the commodification of education. The main goal of education is taken to be to make its recipients marketable. This has resulted in an emphasis on literacy rather than education; on acquiring functional skills rather than developing the capacity to comprehend, contest and transform. It also implies teaching of subjects and courses which can be readily marketable and ignoring those designed to advance knowledge for the sake of knowledge, explore natural phenomena and social relationships for their better understanding, and satisfy urges other than commercial, i.e. philosophical, aesthetic, artistic and literary urges.

As a part of the logic of globalization and liberalization, universities and other academic institutions are being prevailed upon in this country [India] and may be in other Third World countries also, to give preference to teaching subjects and courses which can be self-financing, in which business is interested and, therefore, willing to finance or which can be afforded by those students whose parents have the capacity to pay. In the process, teaching of and research in humanities is suffering in our academic institutions. This aggravates academic dependency, as it forces greater reliance on institutions in academic power centres as the source of knowledge in social sciences.

The dominant academic powers have harnessed international organizations, particularly the financial agencies like the World Bank and the IMF which they control, in order to propagate the theories and impose policies which have the effect of perpetuating academic dependency in the Third World. In the field of education, these institutions have used aid conditionality to prevail upon recipient developing countries to substitute education by literacy, underline the functional role of education at the cost of its philosophical purpose, and push to the background the goal of the universalizing of school education. They have cited budgetary constraints of the aid-receiving countries as the justification for not pursuing the goal of universalizing of school education, which is a right and instead imparting education for enabling students to enter the marketplace, which remains limited in most developing countries. As a result, a huge number of children remain out of school in these countries. Nothing has contributed more to the deepening of academic dependency than this phenomenon of massive exclusion of children from the school system.

INTERNATIONAL DIVISION OF LABOUR

In some of his papers on this subject, Dr Syed Farid Alatas[5] has referred to the international division of labour in social sciences having the effect of perpetuating conditions of academic dependency. This division of labour is in terms of (1) division between theoretical and empirical intellectual labour; (2) the division between other country studies and own country studies; and (3) the division between comparative and single case studies. I have come across some very interesting examples of the second kind of division, i.e. scholars from developing countries being confined to the study of their own countries while pursuing higher education in the centres of academic power.[6] One of the very renowned professors in the Hindi Department of the University where I was educated, i.e. Patna University, took his PhD degree from London University on the Bhojpuri language, the language spoken in the region of Bihar from where the distinguished professor hailed. When I was in Oxford University as part of my training in the Indian Foreign Service, I met a Sri Lankan Tamil girl who was doing her research on 'The Legend of Parasuram in the Mahabharata'.

In economics, which has been my field of specialization, I found during my university days that most of my Indian teachers and the scholars whose books were prescribed readings, had got their PhD degrees from British universities on subjects like the monetary and fiscal policies and planning in India, and different periods and aspects of Indian economic history. Only one Indian scholar, Professor A.K. Dasgupta, worked on an aspect of economic theory, i.e. 'The Concept of Surplus in Theoretical Economics', which was later published as a book that was on our reading list. Most of the theories of development also, which is primarily the concern of developing countries, came from the centres of academic powers. These included the theories of Regnar Nurske, O.A. Hirschman, Hans Singer, Dudley Seers, etc. Prof. Amartya Sen and Prof. Jagdish Bhagwati were the only exceptions. But their theoretical contributions were developed as a part of the mainstream thinking on development in the Centre. They only made a limited contribution to the creation of capacity in India for alleviating academic dependency.

POWER AND THEORIES

It is widely recognized that theories in social sciences are value-loaded.[7] They are developed to justify or rationalize a particular system, or are used as a basis for policy prescription designed to serve the interest of a particular class or power. The main interest of the dominant power centres is to preserve the existing world order, which serves their interests very well. They, therefore, resist all efforts to bring about a systemic change in the world order. Policy-makers in major power centres also think that their interest lies in keeping the Third World weak, unstable and divided. Therefore, theories are propounded and disseminated to serve these interests. Here are some examples of such theories drawn from the disciplines of security studies, international relations and political science, with which I have been familiar:

SECURITY STUDIES AND STUDIES ON INTERNATIONAL RELATIONS[8]

The following are some of the reigning theories in this discipline, propounded in dominant academic centres:

1. The international political system is in the nature of anarchy. Anarchy is implicit in the very nature of an inter-

national system consisting of sovereign states. If units are sovereign, then their system of association must be anarchic; otherwise units will lose their sovereignty.

2. The alternative to international anarchy is either no international system or a unitary system, i.e. world government. A unitary system is not possible. At the same time, we cannot dispense with the international system. Therefore, we must get reconciled to an international system in the form of international anarchy.
3. A unitary system or world government is not possible because:

   (a) there is an uneven distribution of power in the system;
   (b) there is no sufficient political consensus for it; and
   (c) there is no organizing principle for it.

4. In the absence of a world government, security and stability of the international system is ensured by hegemony in the form of a single state, like the United States or a group of states like the Permanent Members of the Security Council.
5. Weak states are mainly responsible for instability and turmoil in the world. Their instability threatens neighbours and their vulnerability offers temptation to intervene, which makes for instability. The global security and stability can be enhanced best by bringing them into alliance with the hegemonic state.

The assumptions underlying theories one to three are either incorrect or misleading. For example, there is an uneven distribution of power even within the state system and yet we have states endowed with sovereignty. Therefore, there is no reason why we cannot have an international system endowed with sovereignty. Similarly, if there is no sufficient political consensus for a world government, the task is to build one rather than giving it up right from the beginning, almost as a matter of convenience. Moreover, it is not impossible to conceive of or evolve consensus on an organizing principle for a world government. The principles which will figure prominently for contention in this context will obviously be peace, development, universal brotherhood and the inevitability of cooperation to ensure human survival and welfare.

The main purpose of the theories four and five is to justify the hegemony of major powers and provide a justification for resisting efforts to bring about changes in the existing world order in order to make it just and equitable.

The academics in the Third World take these theories for granted and seldom make efforts to propound theories based on different historical evidence and a different vision for the future which can justify a different world-view and a different international order.

Political Theory

Following are the current versions of the theories of nationalism, federalism and self-determination, developed by scholars in academic power centres and taken as received wisdom by Third World academics:

1. Nationalism is an outmoded and undemocratic concept.
2. All forms of unitarism constitute derogation from the democratic principle. Federalism is the prescribed form of government for all developing countries.
3. Self-determination of a part of a sovereign state should be an essential ingredient of a democratic system.

In the immediate post-Second World War period until the early 1960s, the notions of nationalism, unitarism and self-determination propounded in the centres of academic power were entirely different from the above formulations. Until that period, the nation state was the foundation of the international system and nationalism was universally eulogized as a great cementing force and a potent means of bringing about enlightenment and development. Some of the most interesting books that I read during that period were in the nature of a eulogy for nationalism. The United Nations was based on the principle that national boundaries as they emerged from the post-Second World War settlements were sacrosanct. Therefore, there was no question of the self-determination of a part of a sovereign State.

Now all these notions have undergone a change as in (1) to (2) above because they apply in actual practice to only Third World countries and only theoretically to the major power centres. There is no threat to the nationalism of any of the major powers. They have long resolved the issue of unitarism *vs.* federalism and there is no significant movement or agitation for self-determination by a group or a region, in any of these countries.

These paradigmatic shifts in the notion of nationalism, federalism and self-determination may be justified on empirical grounds in certain circumstances and may very well provide an answer to some of the problems facing the Third World countries, in holding their pluralistic societies together. But the perception of the need to change must be home-grown and the changes to be brought about must be suited to the conditions prevailing in individual Third World countries. These cannot be derived from theorems propounded in the Western countries and handed down to the academics in the Third World countries.

Dr Syed Farid Alatas (2003) in his paper: 'Academic Dependency and the Global Division of Labour in Social Sciences' has suggested a number of measures for getting out of the prevailing academic dependency. He has in particular emphasized that 'there has to be a conscious effort on the part of the social scientists and administrators of research and teaching institutions to formulate and implement policies designed to help social science communities break out of the current division of labour'. This calls for the development of new courses and methodology and new approaches to research and teaching through collaborative effort of the academic community in the Third World countries. This also requires academic institution building in these countries on a massive scale involving the assembly of not only bricks and mortars but also capable faculty members. The experience of Japan, and recently of China, has shown that enhanced availability of resources alone is not going to be of much help in reducing academic dependency. The availability of resources is, of course, a pre-condition, but ultimately there has to be a change in attitude. Academics in the Third World must be made attentive to the continuing prevalence and the deepening of the phenomenon of academic dependency. They must have the will to come together to build vibrant and creative social science communities of their own. They must get out of the intellectual servility of the theories and ideas propounded in and received from the centres of academic power and consciously plan and mobilize academic resources for re-modelling courses and re-orienting research in order to develop theories and ideas of their own based on their experience, historical perspective, intellectual heritage and vision of the world order.

NOTES

1. This paper is a revised version of Muchkund Dubey's 'Presidential Speech' delivered on the first day of the workshop in Patna (see Introduction, this volume).
2. I have deliberately used the term 'Third World' in this paper. This has all along been a contested concept and it is still used to connote a sense of dependency. I, therefore, think that in the context of 'economic dependency' it is better to use the term 'Third World' than 'developing countries'. The term 'Third World' has neither been rejected officially nor has it disappeared from the vocabulary of social science. Many of the groupings representing the 'Third World' are still in existence today like the G-77, Non-aligned Group, etc., even though they have today become much weaker and less cohesive.

3. T.L. Friedman (2001), *The Lexus and the Olive Tree,* New York: Simon and Schuster.
4. This term is used in S.F. Alatas (forthcoming), 'Eurocentrism, Academic Dependency and the Role of the Social Sciences in the Dialogue Among Civilizations', in Itty Abraham and Seteney Shami (eds), *Global Perspectives on the United States*, New York: New Press.
5. S.F. Alatas (2003), 'Academic Dependency and the Global Division of Labour in the Social Sciences', in *Current Sociology*, 51 (6): pp. 599–613.
6. It is relevant to add here that scholars going to academic power centres are rarely encouraged to investigate into what is happening in the countries within these power centres.
7. See G. Myrdal (1953), *The Political Element in the Development of Economic Theory*, London and New York: Routledge; E. Roll (1956), *A History of Economic Thought*, New Jersey: Prentice-Hall; and J.V. Robinson (1962), *Economic Philosophy*, Harmondsworth, Middlesex: Penguin Books.
8. B. Buzan (1983), *People, States and Fear: The National Security Problem in International Relations*, Chapel Hill, N.C.: University of North Carolina Press.

CHAPTER 2

Intellectual and Structural Challenges to Academic Dependency

SYED FARID ALATAS

DEFINING ACADEMIC DEPENDENCY

The problem of academic dependency presents itself to us at two levels. At the structural level much of the solution has to do with the awareness, will and resolve of politicians, bureaucrats and administrators, without which the structures of academic dependency cannot be dismantled. Scholars have more autonomy and control where overcoming academic dependency at the intellectual level is concerned. The intellectual activity of generating alternative discourses at several levels with a view towards creating an autonomous social science tradition is discussed in this paper.

My main concern as far as the state of the social sciences in developing societies or the South is the problem of Eurocentrism and the context within which this exists, that is, academic dependency. I owe my interest in these topics to the life-long intellectual concerns of my father, Syed Hussein Alatas (1928–2007) who wrote on, among other things, the captive mind (Alatas, 1969a, 1972, 1974) and on intellectual imperialism (1969b, 2000). The idea of intellectual imperialism is an important starting point for the understanding of academic dependency. Intellectual imperialism is analogous to political and economic imperialism in that it refers to the 'domination of one people by another in their world of thinking' (ibid., 2000: 24). Intellectual imperialism was more direct in the colonial period, whereas today it has more to do with the West's control of and influence over the flow of social scientific knowledge rather than its ownership and control of academic institutions. Indeed, this form of hegemony was 'not imposed by the West through colonial domination, but accepted willingly with confident enthusiasm, by scholars and planners of the former colonial territories and even in the few countries that remained independent during that period' (Alatas, S.H., 2006: 7–8).

Intellectual imperialism is the context within which academic dependency exists. Academic dependency theory is a dependency theory of the global state of the social sciences. It defines academic dependency as a condition in which the knowledge production of certain scholarly communities are conditioned by the development and growth of knowledge of other scholarly communities to which the former is subjected. Then relations of interdependence between two or more scientific communities, and between these and global transactions in knowledge, assumes the form of dependency when some scientific communities (those located in the knowledge powers) can expand according to certain criteria of development and progress, while other scientific communities (such as those in the developing societies) can only do this as a reflection of that expansion, which generally has negative effects on their development according to the same criteria. The psychological dimension to this dependency, captured by the notion of the captive mind (ibid., 1969a, 1972, 1974), is such that the dependent scholar is more a passive recipient of research agenda, theories and methods from the knowledge powers (Alatas, 2003: 603).

Today's knowledge powers constitute a kind of 'world system' of knowledge in which the three core countries, i.e. the United States, Great Britain and France, determine the nature of the discourse (Kuwayam & Bremen, 1997: 54). According to Garreau and Chekki, it is no coincidence that the great economic powers are also the great social science powers (Garreau, 1985: 64, 81, 89; see also Chekki, 1987). This is only partially true as some economic powers are actually very peripheral as knowledge producers, Japan being an interesting example.

The mode of conditioning of the captive mind in academically-dependent social science communities is determined by the dimension of academic dependency that is operating. These are (1) dependence on ideas; (2) dependence on the media of ideas; (3) dependence on the technology of education; (4) dependence on aid for research and teaching; (5) dependence on investment in education; and (6) dependence of scholars in developing societies on demand in the knowledge powers for their skills (Alatas, 2003: 604).

What is very crucial about the structure of academic dependency is the global knowledge division of labour which is founded on a threefold division as follows: (1) the division between theoretical and empirical intellectual labour; (2) the division between other country and own country studies; and (3) the division between comparative and single case studies.

I have elaborated on this and given empirical examples elsewhere (ibid., 2003: 607). While there has been recognition of the phenomenon of academic dependency, there have been few attempts to delineate its structure. Among the exceptions are the works of Altbach (1975, 1977) and Garreau (1985, 1988, 1991).

In the section which follows, I shall discuss the first dimension of academic dependency in the context of the related problem of Eurocentrism in the social sciences.

ACADEMIC DEPENDENCY AT THE LEVEL OF IDEAS: EUROCENTRISM IN THE CURRICULA

Academic dependency at the level of ideas is the general condition of knowledge in the South. Although scholarly communities in developing societies have tirelessly pointed out ethnocentric biases in the Western social sciences, the emergence of autonomous, alternative theoretical traditions has yet to be seen, and the dependence on theories and concepts generated in the context of Western historical backgrounds and cultural practices continues. This problem of dependence is linked to the pervasiveness of imitation, a condition conceptualized by Syed Hussein Alatas as 'mental captivity'.

Alatas originated and developed the concept of the captive mind to conceptualize the nature of scholarship in the developing world, particularly in relation to Western dominance in the social sciences and humanities. The captive mind is defined as an 'uncritical and imitative mind dominated by an external source, whose thinking is deflected from an independent perspective' (Alatas, 1974: 692). The external source is Western social science and humanities and the uncritical imitation influences all the constituents of scientific activity such as problem-selection, conceptualization, analysis, generalization, description, explanation, and interpretation (ibid., 1972: 11). Among the characteristics of the captive mind are the inability to be creative and raise original problems, the inability to devise original analytical methods, and alienation from the main issues of indigenous society. The captive mind is trained almost entirely in the Western sciences, reads the works of Western authors, and is taught predominantly by Western teachers, whether in the West itself or through their works available in local centres of education. Mental captivity is also found in the suggestion of solutions and policies. Furthermore, it reveals itself at the levels of theoretical as well as empirical work.

Alatas elaborated the concept in the 1972 and 1974 papers, but had raised the problem in the 1950s referring to the 'wholesale importation of ideas from the Western world to Eastern societies' without due consideration of their socio-historical context, as a fundamental problem of colonialism (ibid., 1956). He had also suggested that the mode of thinking of colonized peoples paralleled political and economic imperialism. Hence, the expression 'academic imperialism' (ibid., 1969b; 2000: 23–45), the context within which the captive mind appears.

Academic dependency at the level of ideas should be seen in terms of the domination of social science teaching and research by the captive mind, the consequence of which is the persistence of Eurocentrism as an outlook and orientation as well as a condition. In teaching, for example, a survey of course syllabi for the history of sociological theory in general will reveal a number of characteristics of Eurocentrism. These are the subject–object dichotomy, Europeans in the foreground, Europeans as originators, and the dominance of European categories and concepts.

In most sociological theory textbooks or writings on the history of social theory, the subject–object dichotomy is a dominant, albeit unarticulated principle of organization. Europeans are the ones that do the thinking and writing, they are the social theorists and social thinkers, what we might call the 'knowing subject'. If at all non-Europeans appear in the texts they are objects of study of the European theorists featured and not as knowing subjects, that is, as sources of sociological theories and ideas. If we take the nineteenth century as an example, the impression is given during the period that Europeans such as Marx, Weber and Durkheim were thinking about the nature of society and its development, there were no thinkers in Asia and Africa doing the same. Therefore, the only non-Europeans that appear in these works are those usually nameless ones, anonymous ones mentioned or referred to by the European thinkers whose ideas are being discussed.

The absence of non-European thinkers in these accounts is particularly glaring in cases where non-Europeans had actually influenced the development of social thought. Typically, a history of social thought text or a course on social thought and theory would cover theorists such as Montesquieu, Vico, Comte, Spencer, Marx, Weber, Durkheim, Simmel, Toennies, Sombart, Mannheim, Pareto, Sumner, Ward, Small, and others. Generally, non-Western thinkers are excluded. Even when they are, they tend to be cited out of historical interest rather than as sources of ideas. For example, Ibn Khaldun[1] is occasionally referred to in histories of social thought but is rarely seen as a source of relevant sociological theories and concepts. He is merely regarded as a precursor or proto-sociologist.

What the subject–object dichotomy does is to place Europeans and later, North American scholars, in the foreground in the social sciences. One interesting exception, as far as sociology is concerned, is the work of Becker and Barnes in their *Social Thought from Lore to Science*. This was first published in 1938 and contains several pages discussing the ideas of Ibn Khaldun (Becker & Barnes, 1961, vol. I: 266–79). It is said that the first writer after Polybius to apply modern-like ideas in historical sociology was not a European but Ibn Khaldun (ibid.: 266). A few scholars like Becker and Barnes in the nineteenth and early twentieth century were responsible for making Ibn Khaldun known in the West. Becker and Barnes also discussed the influence of Ibn Khaldun's ideas on some European thinkers. Although these influences have been recognized these ideas are hardly discussed in mainstream sociological theory textbooks and courses.

The consequence of this is that the West, particularly the Americans, British, French and Germans, are seen as the sole originators of ideas in the social sciences. The question of the multicultural origins of the social sciences is not raised. Many social thinkers from India, China, Japan, and South-East Asia during the nineteenth and early twentieth century who were contemporaneous with Marx, Weber and Durkheim are either only briefly mentioned in works on the history of sociology or totally ignored. Examples of such thinkers are José Rizal

(Philippines, 1861–96), Benoy Kumar Sarkar (India, 1887–1949), and Yanagita Kunio (Japan, 1875–1962).

A more serious consequence of all of this is that what dominates in the social sciences are theories, concepts and categories in social sciences that were developed in Europe and North America. This domination has been at the expense of non-European ideas and concepts. I had mentioned earlier that interest in Ibn Khaldun tends to be historical. There has never been much interest in studying his concepts with a view to developing a theoretical perspective for sociological studies. While there are some exceptions, that is, attempts to develop a neo-Khaldunian sociology, they remain marginal to mainstream social science teaching and research.[2] Another example, comes from the study of religion. It is astonishing that the social scientific study of religion does not take into account the conceptual vocabulary of the various religions in its presentation of concepts. Rather, it draws for its concepts almost exclusively from thc Christian Western tradition with the belief that these concepts are of universal value. While that may be true, it is equally true that the concepts of Islam, Buddhism and Hinduism have the same potential to be universalized and brought into the social sciences.

REVERSING ACADEMIC DEPENDENCY VIA WRITING AND RESEARCH

The logical consequence of the critique of Eurocentrism in the social sciences is to urge and agitate for a kind of intellectual movement that would eventually result in an autonomous tradition of the social sciences. This tradition would generate and apply universal social science thinking in an autonomous fashion to specific problems in a way that is not imitative and uncritical conceptually and methodologically (Alatas, S.H., 2006: 9). It would result in what I have called alternative discourses in the social sciences. Alternative discourses is defined as:

those which are informed by local/regional historical experiences and cultural practices in the same way that the Western social sciences are. Being alternative means a turn to philosophies, epistemologies, histories, and the arts, other than those of the Western tradition. These are all to be considered as potential sources of social science theories and concepts, which would decrease academic dependence on the world social science powers. Therefore, it becomes clear that the emergence and augmentation of alternative discourses is identical to the process of universalizing and internationalizing the social science. It should also be clear that alternative discourses refer to good social science because they are more conscious of the relevance of the surroundings and the problems stemming from the discursive wielding of power by the social sciences. . . . As such, alternative discourses could be advocated for Western social science itself. (Alatas, S.F., 2006: 82–3)

The practice of alternative discourses in the social sciences stands for universalization at varying degrees of universality:

1. At the simplest level, relevant social science would insist on a cautious application of Western theory to the local situation. An example of this would be the economic dependency theory.
2. At a higher level of universality, both indigenous and Western theory are applied to the local context.
3. At yet another level of universality, local, Western and other indigenous theories and concepts (that is, indigenous to other non-Western societies) are applied to the local setting. I have in mind as an example, the application of Ibn Khaldun's theory of state formation to the Mongol conquest of China.
4. The highest level of universality refers to the application of indigenous theory from within and without one's own society to areas outside of one's own area.

Levels two to three require increasing degrees of creativity. Our success with reversing academic dependency will be determined by our ability, not merely as individuals but as collectivities and institutions, to push the limits and boundaries of such creativity.

Consider as an example the study of religion. Social scientific concepts originate from cultural terms in everyday language. As such they present problems when brought into scientific discourse and used to talk about areas and periods outside of those of their origins. The result is a distortion of the phenomena that they are applied to. By the eighteenth century 'religion', from the Latin *religio*, came to be used as a scientific concept, referring to belief systems other than Christianity. When 'religion' is applied to beliefs other than Christianity, for example, Islam or Hinduism, there is an implicit or explicit comparison with Christianity, which results in an elision of reality and a cultural Christianization of these other belief systems in the sense that it is the characteristics of Christianity which are attributed to these other 'religions'. This has become a problem in the social sciences because of the fact that it was European Christendom that became dominant culturally, resulting in the cognitive hegemony of European knowledge. This does, however, suggest the possibility of alternative constructions of other religions and would require the study of the various and not just Christian-originated constructs of different belief systems.

According to Smith, Hinduism is a particularly false conceptualization, one that is conspicuously incompatible with any adequate understanding of the religious outlook of the Hindus. Even the term 'Hindu' (an Indian or non-Muslim inhabitant of India) was unknown to the classical Hindus. 'Hinduism' as a concept they certainly did not have (Smith, 1964: 61, cited in Frykenberg, 1989: 102, n. 3). The term 'Hindu' has its origins in antiquity as the Indo–Aryan name of the river Indus, which is its Greek transliteration (ibid.: 249, n. 46, cited in ibid.: 83).[3] It is from this usage that the terms 'Hindu' and 'Hinduism' gradually acquired their descriptive and geographical denotations. Muslim scholars such as al-Biruni (AD 973–1048), writing in Arabic, used the term *al-Hind* to refer to the Indian subcontinent, but when they referred to the people of that subcontinent or aspects thereof they were referring to what they considered the indigenous and non-Muslim inhabitants of India. In Persian and Urdu the corresponding geographical term to *al-Hind* was *Hindustan*. Things *Hindustani* referred to whatever that was indigenous to India and non-Muslim (Frykenberg, 1989: 84). The English 'Hindu' probably derived from the Persian. The term 'Hindu' appears in the *Gaudiya Vaishnava* texts of the sixteenth century (O'Connell, 1973: 340–3, cited in Frykenberg, 1989: 84), probably as a result of Muslim influence. The usage here is consistent with that in the Muslim texts of the pre-modern Arabs and Persians. Even in the modern period, this negative definition of Hinduism is found evident in the Hindu Marriage Act. The Act defines a Hindu, among other things, as one 'who is not a Muslim, Christian, Parsi or Jew by religion . . .' (Derret, 1963: 18–19).

The terms 'Hindu' and 'Hinduism' in reference to religion, and a unitary one at that, was for the most part, a modern development. In the eighteenth century it began to be used to denote an Aryan, Brahmanical or Vedic-based high culture and religion by European Orientalists such as Halhed, Jones and Müller (Frykenberg, 1989: 85–6). It is this usage that was adopted by the early Indian nationalists themselves like Rammohun Roy, Gandhi and Nehru (ibid.: 86). This 'new' religion was founded on the ontology and epistemology contained in the *Varnashramadharma* and encompassed the entire cosmos, detailing as part of its vision a corresponding stratified social structure (ibid.: 86).

What is important in these developments as far as the intellectual Christianization of Indian beliefs systems is concerned is that (1) the belief systems of the inhabitants of the Indian subcontinent (excluding Muslims, Jews, Christians and Parsis) came to be regarded as religion; (2) these beliefs systems were seen to constitute a single religion; and (3) were founded on a system of Brahmanical doctrines based on the *Catur-Veda*

(Four Vedas) (ibid.: 86). It is in these senses that characteristics of Christianity were read into Indian beliefs.

Gradually, the newly-christened Hinduism also came to encompass the 'low' tradition or what is nowadays referred to as 'popular', 'temple', 'bhakti', 'village', or 'tribal' Hinduism (ibid.: 87).

This is a construction at odds with indigenous thinking and experience as there was never such a thing as a single all-encompassing religion (or *dharma*, for that matter) called Hinduism or any other name that can be traced to the Vedas and which characterize the beliefs of the non-Muslim, non-Jewish, non-Christian, non-Parsi population of India. Instead, what happened was a process of reification, that is, an ideal type of the 'Hindu' religion was constructed and assumed to be a description of the real Indian society. As Deshpande suggests, this is a 'case of simulated identity which over the years has been accepted as true identity' (Deshpande, 1985, cited in Frykenberg, 1989: 101).

Looking at south Indian examples, Frykenberg tells us how this happened in practical terms beginning in the nineteenth century. Modern Hinduism is a

> form of corporate and organized and 'syndicated' religion which arose in south India and by which highly placed and influential groups of Brahmans, supported by Brahmanized non-Brahmans, did most of the defining, the manipulating, and the organizing of the essential elements of what gradually became, for practical purposes, a dynamic new religion. Moreover, this process of reification, this defining and organizing of elements which they did, occurred with the collaboration, whether witting or unwitting, with those who governed the land.
> (Frykenberg, 1989: 89)

This was facilitated by the process of centralization, rationalization, and bureaucratization of information (Dykes, 1853: 232, cited in Frykenberg, 1989: 89) which had two bases. One was the interaction between local officials and the rulers, examples of which are the patronage of cultural events and the policy with respect to temples and their administration.

The latter entailed the collection and preservation of information (historical, archaeological, artistic) (Frykenberg, 1989: 89, 91, 92, 94) that served to concretize a concept that was gradually developing in the minds of colonial scholars and administrators, and local elites.

In the previous section it was suggested that the intellectual Christianization of 'religion' is a special case of the application of an exclusive definition of religion. The exclusivity of the definition is smuggled into the concept unwittingly. The result is a specific type of construction of religion determined in the first place by the elements smuggled into the concept of religion to begin with. I have argued that the elements smuggled into the understanding of Islam and 'Hinduism' are derived from Christianity.

The application of a universal concept of religion would not result in such constructions of individual religions because the elements that make up the universal concept of religion are derived from all religions, apply to all of them with varying degrees of significance and are, therefore, neutral, in the sense that one is not led by the very concept of religion to read into a particular religion the traits of another. The neutrality of the universal concept of religion would extend to all related concepts in the study of religion. A universal concept of religion implies neutrality for all other concepts applied in the description and analytical study of religion. The reverse is also true. A non-universal concept of religion, such as an exclusive one, would render all other concepts in the study of religion non-universal.

Therefore, the use of the conceptual vocabulary of one religion to talk about another is not in itself a problem if the concept of religion in operation is the universal one. For example, in the sociology of religion, concepts such as sect and denomination are defined in terms of another concept, that of the church. Since the idea of the church as a religious organization does not exist in other religions, the use of concepts like denomination and sect for other religions runs the risk of resulting in an intellectual Christianization of these religions.

We may, however, go beyond the critique of the intellectual Christianization of Islam or Hinduism and study alternative constructions of these religions. An example would be al-Biruni on what is now called 'Hinduism'. Abu al-Rayhan Muhammad bin Ahmad al-Biruni aimed to provide a comprehensive account of the civilization of India, including the religion, philosophy, literature, geography, science, customs and laws of the Indians. This section concentrates on al-Biruni's construction of the religions of India.[4]

The work of al-Biruni that can be considered as sociological is his study of India. His *Kitab ma li al-Hind* (*The Book of What Constitutes India*) aimed to provide a comprehensive account of what he called 'the religions of India and their doctrines'. This included the religion, philosophy, literature, geography, science, customs and laws of the Indians. Of special interest to sociology is al-Biruni's construction of the religions of India. Al-Biruni considered what we call 'Hinduism' as religion, centuries before Europeans recognized Hinduism as not mere heathenism.

In attempting a reconstruction of al-Biruni's construction of 'Hinduism' it is necessary to point out that it is inadequate to rely on Sachau's English translation of the Arabic original. The translation, which was undertaken in the late nineteenth century, reads into Arabic terms, nineteenth-century European ideas about what Hinduism was. For example, in his preface in the Arabic original, al-Biruni refers to 'the religions of India' (*adyan al-Hind*) (al-Biruni, 1377/1958 [*c*.1030]: 4) while this is translated by Sachau as 'the doctrines of the Hindus' (Sachau, 1910: 6), leading one to assume that al-Biruni conceived of a single religion called Hinduism.[5] As we shall see, this was not the case.

We begin our reconstruction of al-Biruni's construction of the religions of India with the title of his work: *Kitab al-Biruni fi tahqiq ma li al-Hind min maqbulat fi al-'aql aw mardhulat.*

This can be translated as *The Book of What Constitutes India as Derived from Discourse which is Logically Acceptable or Unacceptable*. As noted by Sachau (1910: xxiv), al-Biruni's method was to allow Indians to speak in order to present Indian civilization as understood by Indians themselves (Sachau, 1910: 25; al-Biruni, 1377/1958: 19).[6] Al-Biruni quotes extensively from Sanskrit texts which he had either read himself or which were communicated to him.[7]

The second chapter of the *Tahqiq ma li al-Hind* was translated by Sachau as 'On the Belief of the Hindus in God', whereas the Arabic original has it as 'On their Beliefs in God, Praise be to Him'. Moreover, the term Hindu does not appear in the Arabic text and the term *hind* does not have religious connotations. Sachau writes 'the Hindu religion' in his translation (Sachau, 1910: 50), whereas the Arabic original has no equivalent (al-Biruni, 1377/1958: 38).

The account of the creed of the Indians begins in Chapter Two with an exposition of their belief in God, by which al-Biruni means the same God that is worshipped by Jews, Christians and Muslims. The exposition begins with an account of the nature of God, with reference to his speech, knowledge and action (Sachau, 1910: 27–30; al-Biruni, 1377/1958: 20–2).

We are then told that this is an account of the belief in God among the elite. Here al-Biruni is making a distinction between ideas associated with a high tradition and ideas held by the common people, as far as the conception of God is concerned (Sachau, 1910: 31–2; al-Biruni, 1377/1958: 23–4).

What we get so far is a picture of a monotheistic religion based on a determinate number of books, the *Patañjali, Veda* and *Gita* (Sachau, 1910: 27, 29; al-Biruni, 1377/1958: 20–1). The Veda was 'sent down' to Brahma (*anzalahu 'ala Brahma*) (Sachau, 1910: 29; al-Biruni, 1377/1958: 21), which al-Biruni understands as the First Power (*al-quwwah al-awwali*) (Sachau, 1910: 94; al-Biruni, 1377/1958: 71). Al-Biruni draws an analogy between the Christian trinity and the three forces of Brahma, Narayana (second force) and the Rudra (third force). The unity of these three forces is called Vishnu, sometimes called the middle force and sometimes conflated with the first force (Sachau, 1910: 94).

Sociologically speaking, a distinction has to be made between the abstract, metaphysical ideas of the high tradition and the literalist, anthropomorphic ideas of the common people.

Al-Biruni is, therefore, referring to a specific Vedic-Sanskritic religion that revolved around the worship of Brahma, which today in retrospect is often seen as a branch or sect within Hinduism, and which was historically a minor tradition among the more major traditions of Vaishnavism, Shaivism and Shaktism (Klostermaier, 1989: 53). Al-Biruni refers to the tradition around Brahma as a *dharma*. *Dharma* refers to, among other things, a system of socio-ethical laws and obligations, including a system of social classification based on the division of society into *varnas* (castes) (Klostermaier, 1989: 46). To the extent that the Islamic concept, *din*, approximates 'religion', al-Biruni would have understood *dharma* as religion as he translates *dharma* as *din* (al-Biruni, 1377/1958: 30; Sachau, 1910: 40).

Clearly, the task for those concerned with the problem of the neglect of ideas emanating from non-Western societies, and for those concerned with a more universalistic approach to knowledge, is to counteract Eurocentrism in the social sciences by reversing the subject–object dichotomy, bringing in non-Europeans into the foreground, recognizing non-Europeans as originators, and turning attention to the non-European concepts and categories. This should be done not with the idea of displacing modern social science but to truly universalize. The task should not be to develop a social scientific tradition that is equally parochial as the one being critiqued here.

It is theoretical work that is crucial to undertake. These works have to be more than descriptive. For example, there are many works that describe Ibn Khaldun's theory, but there has been a negligible amount of theory building that would result in what we may call neo-Khaldunian social theory, that is, work that goes beyond the mere comparison of some ideas and concepts in Ibn Khaldun with those of Western theorists toward the theoretical integration of his theory into a framework that employs some of the tools of modern social science (Laroui, 1980; Cheddadi, 1980; Gellner, 1981; Michaud, 1981; Lacoste, 1984; Carre, 1988; Alatas, 1993). The stress here should be on drawing upon hitherto marginalized and untapped sources of knowledge.

REVERSING ACADEMIC DEPENDENCY VIA TEACHING IN THE SOCIAL SCIENCES

Essential to counteracting Eurocentric discourse is bringing in non-European ideas into teaching in mainstream social science courses and into mainstream social science textbooks. Due to the relatively greater autonomy that university teachers have, as compared to school teachers, we would be able to inject more non-European content into the courses that we teach. There is no reason why social thinkers such as José Rizal (Philippines, 1861–96), Benoy Kumar Sarkar (India, 1887–1949), and Yanagita Kunio (Japan, 1875–1962) cannot be introduced in syllabi of social thought and theory, for example. This is something that I and a colleague at the National University of Singapore, Vineeta Sinha, have been doing for some years. We departed from the conventional classical sociological theory course that is usually confined to teaching Comte, Marx, Weber, Durkheim, de Tocqueville and other Europeans of the nineteenth and early twentieth century. We introduced Ibn Khaldun, José Rizal, Sarkar and other non-Western social thinkers and teach their ideas systematically. At the same time, we do not neglect Western thinkers. Still, when it comes to Western thinkers such as Marx and Weber, the focus is on those topics generally neglected in similar course taught in Europe and North

America, such as Marx's concept of the Asiatic mode of production, his views on colonialism in India or Weber's work on Islam and Confucianism. The details of how the course was revamped were reported in the journal, *Teaching Sociology* (Alatas and Sinha, 2001).

THE PROSPECTS FOR ACADEMIC DEPENDENCY REVERSAL

As scholars there is much we can do at the individual level in our research and teaching to spread awareness about the problem of academic dependency and go beyond merely talking about the problem to actually practice alternative discourses. Counteracting academic dependency and Eurocentrism in the social sciences also requires our being active in terms of conscientizing students and scholars about the problems of academic dependency and the need for alternative discourses and popularizing non-European ideas by regularly and continuously organizing panels or presenting papers at mainstream social science conferences. This is a matter of organization and funding but also requires a lot of will on our part. Syed Hussein Alatas, in one of his last publications, suggested that the International Sociological Association organize a session at the World Congress of Sociology on the issue of an autonomous sociological tradition in order to 'alert sociologists throughout the world to pool their attention on this extremely vital need for the development of sociology' (Alatas, S.H., 2006: 17).

Indeed, the South is not lacking in creative and original thinkers. Many examples of alternative discourses can be cited from various countries in Asian and Africa. I have documented some of these in my *Alternative Discourses in Asian Social Science*. Of India, Syed Hussein Alatas said:

> A tradition can be expected to emerge. By tradition it is not meant the mere presence of disparate studies of local or regional subjects by indigenous scholars. Apart from the traits we have earlier cited, there

is one significant overriding trait of a tradition, that is, the continuous discussion of a set of major problems and ideas in the course of long duration, decades or centuries, reflecting the cumulative development of knowledge concerning particular subjects. An example is the discussion on the French Revolution or periodization in European history (ibid.: 15).

But, whether such a tradition can emerge in much of the South will depend on our ability to make changes in policy, change the reward systems in institutions of learning, reduce corruption and inefficiency, and remove national and local politics from the centres of learning. In other words, this requires nothing short of the non-interference of the fools in the entire art, science and business of education; but, the fools are dominant.

Alatas, in fact, had also suggested the creation of sessions on a new theme, the sociology of the fools. By this, he meant the sociological fool as opposed to its counterpart, the sociological intellectual. Sociologists should not only be interested in the sociology of the intellectual but also in the sociology of the opposing type, the fool. The concept of the fool is not only an original concept and example of the type of creativity needed for an autonomous social science tradition, it also points to a diagnosis of the problems that alternative discourses face in societies dominated by fools in positions of leadership (ibid.: 17).

Alatas had started discussing the topic of the fool in his book *Intellectuals in Developing Societies* (1977: Chapter 4). Fourteen characteristics for the definition of the sociological concept of the fool and the concrete consequences of power-wielding fools were discussed. Leaders and administrators who are fools stamp their own peculiar foolish imprint on whatever thinking and practices they undertake. For example, in their corrupt practices, 'their corruption bears the imprint of the fool. When they are honest, their honesty can be naïve and immature' (ibid.: 17).

I feel that throughout his intellectual life, my father lived in fear of our society being taken over by fools. Among the traits of fools are (i) the inability to recognize a problem; (ii) the inability to solve a problem if told to him; (iii) the inability to learn what is required; (iv) the inability to learn the art of learning; (v) not admitting that he is a fool (idem., 1977: 45). Furthermore,

> The revolution of the fools which had occurred in many developing societies was to a great extent due to the colonial period. The colonial government did not pay much attention to the creation of high-caliber administrators in the colonies. During that time all the thinking at national levels was done by the colonial government abroad. The commercial and industrial houses were similarly foreign-based. Education in the colonies was mainly geared to provide clerical service or tasks at a subsidiary level. After independence following the Second World War, there was a sudden increase in the volume and intensity of administration and other decision-making centres covering diverse projects which were introduced in increasing number by the newly independent states. During this period there was a shortage of intelligent manpower to deal with the sudden increase of planning and administration, both in the official and in private realms, in the newly independent states. Hence the rise to power of the fools. Once the fools came to power, they perpetuate their own breed. With the fools came nepotism, provincialism, parochial party politics, to condition selection and ascent in the hierarchy of administrative power. Fools cannot cope with a situation where merit and hard-work are the criteria of success, and so corruption is the hallmark of the rise to power of the fools, making a farce of government tenders and leading to bureaucratic intrigues to gain office or promotion. Where fools dominate it is their values which become society's values, their consciousness which becomes society's consciousness. (ibid.: 45–6)

Such is the context within which the critique of academic dependency and the call for alternative discourses is made. Does our society have the leadership of sufficient integrity, resolve, and bravery to combat imitative and cultural slavish ideals that are among the causes of academic dependency to begin with?

NOTES

1. Abd al-Rahman Abu Zayd ibn Muhammad ibn Muhammad ibn Khaldun was born on 1 Ramadan/5 May AH 732/AD 1332. After receiving a customary education in the traditional sciences, Ibn Khaldun held posts in various courts in North Africa and Spain. After a number of unsuccessful stints in office he withdrew into seclusion to write his *Muqaddimah*, a prolegomena to the study of history which was completed in AD 1378 and which introduces his *'ilm al-'umran* (science of civilization).
2. For these exceptions see Gellner (1981: Chapter 1), Michaud (1981), Carre (1988) and Alatas (1993).
3. Smith's source is Spiegel (1881, vol. 1, ll. 17–18, A, l. 25: 50, 54, 246).
4. I consulted both the original Arabic, the *Kitab fi tahqiq ma li al-Hind*, al-Biruni, AH 1377 (*c.* AD 1030) [AD 1958] as well as Sachau's English translation, *Alberuni's India* (Sachau, 1910). Dates in brackets indicate the year in which the work was written. Unless otherwise stated, all quotations in English are taken from Sachau's translation.
5. In fact, a study of Sachau's translation may be more a study of the intellectual Christianization of the religions of India than of al-Biruni's work on India.
6. For more on al-Biruni's method see Jeffery (1951).
7. On al-Biruni's knowledge of Sanskrit, see Chatterji (1951) and Gonda (1951).

REFERENCES

Alatas, Syed Farid and Vineeta Sinha (2001), 'Teaching Classical Sociological Theory in Singapore: The Context of Eurocentrism', *Teaching Sociology* 29 (3): 316–31.

Alatas, Syed Farid (1993), 'A Khaldunian Perspective on the Dynamics of Asiatic Societies', *Comparative Civilizations Review* 29: 29–51.

——— (2003), 'Academic Dependency and the Global Division of Labour in the Social Sciences', *Current Sociology* 51 (6): 599–613.

——— (2006), *Alternative Discourses in Asian Social Science: Responses to Eurocentrism*, New Delhi: Sage.

Alatas, Syed Hussein (1956) 'Some Fundamental Problems of Colonialism', *Eastern World* (London), November.

——— (1969a), 'The Captive Mind and Creative Development', in K.B. Madhava (ed.), *International Development*, New York: Oceania Publications.

——— (1969b), 'Academic Imperialism', Lecture delivered to the History Society, University of Singapore, 26 September 1969.

——— (1972), 'The Captive Mind in Development Studies', *International Social Science Journal* 34, 1: 9–25.

——— (1974), 'The Captive Mind and Creative Development', *International Social Science Journal* 36, 4: 691–9.

——— (1977), *Intellectuals in Developing Societies*, London: Frank Cass.

——— (2000), 'Intellectual Imperialism: Definition, Traits, and Problems', *Southeast Asian Journal of Social Science* 28 (1): 23–45.

——— (2006), 'The Autonomous, the Universal and the Future of Sociology', *Current Sociology* 54 (1): 7–23.

Altbach, Philip G. (1975), 'Literary Colonialism: Books in the Third World', *Harvard Educational Review* 45: 226–36.

——— (1977), 'Servitude of the Mind? Education, Dependency, and Neocolonialism', *Teachers College Record* 79 (2): 187–204.

Becker, Howard and Harry Elmer Barnes (1961), *Social Thought from Lore to Science*, 3 vols., New York: Dover Publications.

al-Biruni, Abu al-Rayhan Muhammad bin Ahmad (1377/1958 [*c.* 1030]), *Kitab al-Biruni fi tahqiq ma li al-Hind min maqbulat fi al-'aql aw mardhulat*, Hyderabad: Majlis Da'irat al-Ma'arif al-Uthmaniyyah.

Carre, Olivier (1988), 'A propos de vues Neo-Khalduniennes sur quelques systemes politiques Arabes actueles', *Arabica* 35 (3): 367–8.

Chatterji, Suniti Kumar (1951), 'Al-Biruni and Sanskrit', in Iran Society, *Al-Biruni Commemoration Volume* A.H. *362*–A.H. *1362*, Calcutta: Iran Society, pp. 83–100.

Chekki, D.A. (1987), *American Sociological Hegemony: Transnational Explorations*, Lanham: University Press of America.

Derret, J.D.M. (1963), *Introduction to Modern Hindu Law*, Oxford: Oxford University Press.

Deshpande, G.P. (1985), 'The Plural Tradition', *Seminar* 313: 23–5.

Dykes, J.W.B. (1853), *Salem: An Indian Collectorate*, Madras: Asylum Press.

Frykenberg, Robert Eric (1989), 'The Emergence of Modern "Hinduism" as a Concept and as an Institution: A Reappraisal with Special Reference to South India', in Gûnther-Dietz Sontheimer and Herman Kulke (1989) (ed.), *Hinduism Reconsidered*, 2nd edn., Delhi: Manohar.

Garreau, Frederick H. (1985), 'The Multinational Version of Social Science with Emphasis Upon the Discipline of Sociology', *Current Sociology* 33 (3): 1–169.

——— (1988), 'Another Type of Third World Dependency: The Social Sciences', *International Sociology* 3 (2): 171–8.

——— (1991), *The Political Economy of the Social Sciences*, New York: Garland Publishing.

Grossman, Lionel (1978), 'History and Literature: Reproduction or Significance', in Robert H. Canary and Henry Kozicki (eds), *The Writing of History: Literary Form and Historical Understanding*, Madison: University of Wisconsin Press, pp. 3–40.

Gellner, Ernest (1981), *Muslim Society*, Cambridge: Cambridge University Press.

Gonda, J. (1951), 'Remarks on Al-Biruni's Quotations from Sanskrit Texts', in *Al-Biruni Commemoration Volume A.H. 362–A.H. 1362*, Calcutta: Iran Society, pp. 111–18.

Klostermaier, Klaus K. (1989), *A Survey of Hinduism*, Delhi: Munshiram Manoharlal.

Kuwayama, T. and J. van Bremen (1997), 'Native Anthropologists: With Special Reference to Japanese Studies Inside and Outside Japan' (Kuwayama–van Bremen Debate: Native Anthropologists), *Japan Anthropology Workshop Newsletter*, 26–7 September 1997, pp. 52–69.

Michaud, Gerard (1981), 'Caste, confession et societe en Syrie: Ibn Khaldoun au chevet du "Progessisme Arabe"', *Peuples Mediterraneens* 16: 119–30.

O'Connell, Joseph T. (1973), 'Gaudiya Vaisnava Symbolism of Deliverance from Evil', *Journal of the American Oriental Society* 93 (3): 340–3.

Sachau, Edward C. (tr.) (1910), *Alberuni's India: An Account of the Religion, Philosophy, Literature, Geography, Chronology,*

Astronomy, Customs, Laws and Astrology of India about A.D. 1030, Delhi: Low Price Publications.

Smith, Wilfred Cantwell (1962), *The Meaning and End of Religion: A Revolutionary Approach to the Great Religious Traditions*, London: SPCK.

Spiegel, Fr. (1881), *Die Altpersischen Keilinschriften, im Grundtext mut Übersetzung, Grammatik und Glossar*, Leipzig.

CHAPTER 3

Defining Archaeology in Ghana: A Historical Interpretation

SAMUEL NILIRMI NKUMBAAN

INTRODUCTION

The discipline of archaeology has been so well established in terms of definition, theory, methodology and practice that it would be repetitive dealing with those issues. It is sufficient to summarize that it is a multi-disciplinary, scientific discipline which studies material remains of past human activities with the objective of reconstructing and re-enacting past life ways. Though this is a generally accepted opinion of the role of archaeology, Trigger (1993: 615) has indicated alternative archaeologies to include the Nationalist, the Colonialist, and the Imperialist. He arrived at this through the realization that 'there is considerable variation from one country or part of the world to another in the kinds of problems that archaeologists think it worth investigating and in what they are predisposed to regard as acceptable interpretations of evidence'. This variation is seen by some scholars including Clarke (1979: 154) as representing the infancy of the discipline, believing that with time, it will be winnowed and consolidated into a single coherent empirical discipline. In fact, the discipline is not that young, and as more evidence is unearthed in different parts of the world, using different or similar techniques, the more it becomes apparent that national variations in archaeology are not disappearing (Trigger, 1993: 615).

The present article only briefly explores the state of Ghanaian archaeology, seeking to chronicle the development of the discipline historically, emphasizing the influence of Western scholars, colonial authority, and the way forward in achieving scientific interpretations or conclusions reflective of real national or indigenous ideas. This is based on the realization that there is a close relationship between the nature of archaeological research and the social milieu in which it is practised (ibid.: 616). More specifically, I seek to suggest that the national or regional approach, involving the use of native scholars be emphasized. The reason being that human developments across the world are influenced by the local, physical or natural, and social environmental conditions. It thus takes the intervention of a person descending from that peculiar region to offer more meaningful interpretations of the developments within the area. This does not, however, suggest that scholars from a certain country cannot research elsewhere and produce good results. Archaeological interpretation relies very much on the context of artefact assemblages to understand past life ways, and such associations may be better understood and explained with the aid of a native scholar with local or indigenous insights into the culture under study. I seek to suggest that the collaboration of expatriate scholars and native scholars in the study of a site may yield more reliable conclusions.

GHANA, THE LANDSCAPE, THE NATURAL AND CULTURAL SETTING

Ghana extends roughly 650 km from the Gulf of Guinea (4° 30'N) to approximately the eleventh parallel, given that it is a land mass of about 238,540 km^2. From the northern margins, the country is characterized by undulating landscape underlaid with sandstone, mudstone and shales of the Voltaian series, principally drained by the river Volta and its two major tributaries: the White and Black Volta, and river Oti. The area is also marked by dramatic escarpments and the Gambaga plateau is an example. The middle belt of the country is generally more forested with lots of relief features. Birimian and Tarkwaian series; comprising quartzites, phyllites, schists, conglomerates, and metamorphosed lavas characterize the region. The mineral wealth of the country in the form of gold, diamond, manganese and bauxite centred in the Birimain and Tarkwaian formations. Further south, towards the coast, Ghana exhibits low undulating plains with a narrow range of mountains northward; the Akwapem-Togo range (Stahl, 1994: 55; Boateng, 1970: 12–21).

Ghana, formerly known as the Gold Coast, was important to the economic fortunes of the Mediterranean world and later Europe. The reason lay in its richness in gold and other resources including ivory. It has been suggested that West African gold reached the Sudanese kings from the second millennium BP (Gerrad, 1982), from where it reached Europe (Wilks, 1982: 333–5). The famous Mansa Musah pilgrimage to Mecca, accompanied by large caravans of gold which caused a depression in the prices of gold in the region around the fourteenth century, sparked the search for Guinea gold (Bovill, 1968: 86–90; Stahl, 1994: 53). In the process, the gold fields of Ghana were located in the middle of the fifteenth century (Wilks, 1982: 335–6). The Portuguese led the way. They landed on the coast of Ghana first in 1471 and established a foothold with the building of a trade fort at Elmina in 1482 (DeCorse, 1992: 164). Intense competition ensued over the next three centuries as rival European powers struggled to control the Gold Coast trade. In line after the Portuguese were the Dutch, the English, the Danes, the Germans, etc. The scramble for trade resources, territory and associated rivalries culminated in the Berlin Conference of 1884/5 which portioned Africa among the European powers. Before then, in 1874, the coastal areas of Ghana had already become colonies to the British through treaties of friendship (Arhin, 1974). By 1902, all of the Gold Coast was a British colony and so it remained until 1957 when she attained her independence and became known as Ghana. It is important to recognize that scientific archaeological inquiry in Ghana was structured during the colonial times (Holl, 1990), and this was likely to influence the development and popularity of the discipline and made it academically dependent on the West for long.

THE BEGINNING OF ARCHAEOLOGY IN GHANA

Most archaeological traditions are probably nationalistic in orientation. For instance, the development of European prehistoric archaeology was greatly encouraged by the post-Napoleonic upsurge of nationalism and romanticism, directed towards strengthening patriotic sentiments (Trigger, 1993: 618). Although Ghana has a great wealth of history regarding human habitation of the region dating back to the Early Stone Age, archaeology was to begin as a scientific discipline only in the 1930s, the colonial era (Anquandah, 1982: 21–9; Kense, 1990). Despite the fact that many of the social science disciplines in Ghana have had their roots from the colonial era, the case of archaeology in this regard seems unique, as it is reflected in the daily thoughts and talks of Ghanaians. It is common among many Ghanaian scholars without a background in archaeology and students of archaeology to refer to the discipline as a 'Colonial subject', a connotation I seek to indicate is the result of its having roots in the colonial period. This may also be the reason for which the discipline has remained embryonic though it has a pretty long history and there is a lot to investigate. It is also not surprising that there is only one Department of Archaeology in Ghana, at the University of Ghana, Legon, the only university founded in the colonial era.

HISTORICAL DEVELOPMENT OF THE DISCIPLINE

The story of the evolution of Archaeology in Ghana may best be classified under four episodes, namely:

1. *The Era of Amateur Explorers, Collectors and Speculators of the Past:* The period could also be termed the epoch of Antiquarianism. It is dated between the 1820s and 1920s in Ghana. In 1822, Monrad, a Danish missionary, collected pre-historic polished stone axes from the area of Osu in Accra and sent them for study, publication and exhibition to the Copenhagen Royal Ethnographic Museum. Some of these collections were deposited at the Dutch Royal Museum at Leyden (Anquandah, 1982: 22).

In 1874, a *London Times* journalist, Winwood Reade, who was in the Gold Coast as a war correspondent for the 1874 British–Asante war amused himself with documenting the art of Fante women hairstyles as well as recording data on polished stone axes collected by Zimmermann, a Basel Missionary from the area of Krobo Odumase (Anquandah, 1982). Early collections were also made by geologists and engineers during road construction and/or geological mapping of the country (Balfour, 1912; Kitson, 1916; Wild, 1927, 1934; Junner, 1935; Braunholtz, 1936; Rattray, 1923, 1927; Stahl, 1994; Anquandah, 1982). The most interesting aspect of all this is the fact that the non-literate indigenous peoples had a native sense for observing and recognizing a 'Cultural Complex' (Anquandah, 1982). Kitson (1916) illustrated this when he said that the Gold Coast indigenes, in narration of oral traditions on ancient settlements, demonstrated awareness that the polished stone axes and cylindrical stone rasps were associated with the pre-historic cultural property collections which were later designated as the Kintampo Culture by Oliver Davies, one of the early Western scholars of archaeology in Ghana.

2. *The Era of Pioneers of Scientific Archaeology (1930s to 1950s):* Three prominent academics from Britain, Thurstan Shaw, Oliver Davies and A.W. Lawrence were the pioneers of scientific archaeology in Ghana. Shaw was appointed in 1937 as curator of the Achimota College Museum of Anthropology and with him began a new era of scientific excavation in Ghana (Anquandah, 1982: 25; Stahl, 1994: 57; Etse, 2003: 8–9). In the 1940s, he excavated an iron smelting site at Achimota, a sixteenth-seventeenth-century midden at Dawu, Akwapem, and a fourth millennium BC Late Stone Age foraging site at Bosumpra Rock Shelter, Abetifi.

Oliver Davies was appointed to the newly established Department of Archaeology at the University College of the Gold Coast, now University of Ghana, in 1952. He emphasized extensive countrywide site surveys or archaeological reconnaissance as against 'sitting down to dig one site' (Davies, 1971: 5). He surveyed and mapped over 2,000 archaeological sites ranging from the Early Stone Age times to the nineteenth century AD from between 1952 and 1966. He also excavated Ntereso, a Kintampo culture site, Limbisi, New Todzi, Legon Botanical Gardens, Christian Village—all Stone Age sites. He further excavated the Akan Mausoleum site of Ahinsan, and Kokobin. His survey work *Ghana Field Notes*, is still a very useful document to contemporary archaeologists for the location of sites (Stahl, 1994: 57; Ozane, 1971: 37). Between 1963 and 1966, he directed the Volta Basin Research Project and surveyed some 450 sites when the Government of Ghana embarked on the Akosombo Hydro Electric Dam project. This was to salvage some cultural property before the flooding of the Volta Basin (Stahl, 1994: 57; Anquandah, 1982: 27).

A.W. Lawrence, the first Professor of Archaeology of the Department used his experience in Classical Architectural History to document in great detail the extant European forts and castles. This work greatly contributes to knowledge in relation to historical archaeology and the subject of the slave trade.

3. *The Era of Absolute or Pure Research (1960s to 1980s)*: This period witnessed a number of developments which launched the episode of pure research. Important among these was the commencement by Peter Shinnie and Merrick Posnansky of graduate and undergraduate teaching at the tertiary level around 1963. The imperative of students' practical field training stepped up, diversified and expanded research. Research became more codified or systematic with the formulation of research proposals, setting out objectives, literature surveys, budgeting and fund-raising, etc. Archaeological research or excavation increasingly assumed large scale dimensions. For instance, researches such as the West African Trade Project excavations at Begho launched in 1970 by Posnansky, the Gonja Archaeology Project (1977–84) headed by Peter Shinnie, who had also initiated a long-term project in Asante directed towards the problem of Asante origins and colonization of the forest (Stahl, 1994: 58). Added to these were a number of small-scale projects, and theses or dissertation projects (Agorsah, 1983; Bellis, 1972; Boachie-Ansah, 1986; Bredwa-Mensah, 1990; Crossland, 1989; DeCorse, 1989; Effah-Gyamfi, 1985; Gavua, 1985; Keteku, 1981; Kiyaga-Mulindwa, 1978; Musonda, 1976; Okoro, 1989; Stahl, 1985), etc. Research from this period also followed specific objectives and thematic patterns. For example, documentation of foraging and farming sites or beginning of food production, urban or commercial sites, art works sites, earth works sites (Birim Valley and Kitare), etc.

4. The last period of the 1990s and the present decade has seen progress in the area of epistemology, method and theory, especially using the multi-disciplinary approach inherited from the preceding era. The period has been marked by the addition of more applied and developmental research, to the previous emphasis of pure research—although the line of separation is quite thin. For instance, the current work of Okoro on water management in the area of Salaga, the research of Gblerkpor and Gavua at the Krobo Mountain site which is culminating

into the development of a major tourism project in the area, and work around the Koma region of northern Ghana by Kankpeyeng and Nkumbaan with the ultimate objective of building a local museum as a way of attracting tourists to the area, reflect developmental issues.

Heritage Management Legislation in Ghana

Legislation in Ghana about heritage is not archaeology-specific, but encompasses the protection or management of all the country's cultural resources, of which archaeological resources are a part. Formal conservation processes in Ghana begun after the Second World War with an Ordinance in 1949, which established the Monuments and Relics Commission of the Gold Coast. This provided legal protection for only the trade forts and castles. In 1951, the Chief Inspector of Ancient Monuments in Britain, B.H. Oneil, was invited to the Gold Coast by the Colonial Government to examine the forts and castles and make recommendations for their restoration and preservation. These recommendations were submitted in October of the same year to Sir Leslie M'Carthy, Governor of the Gold Coast and Chairman of the Monuments and Relics Commission of the Gold Coast. In 1952, the implementation of the recommendations resulted in the consolidation of the 1949 Ordinance with the establishment of a Monuments Division, charged with the sole responsibility of restoring and maintaining the forts and castles.

At independence in 1957 a reorganization culminated in the passing of the Ghana Museums and Monuments Board (GMMB) Ordinance No. 20. It did not, however, define clearly the duties of GMMB. In the 1960s, the scope of the Board was extended to cover other traditional buildings in Asante, the central and northern parts of the country.

Two legislations were passed in 1969, the national Museum Decree (NLCD 387), and the National Museum Regulations (EI 118). These updated the provisions of the 1957 Ordinance on antiquities, National Monuments, and the operations of the GMMB. The duties of the GMMB were codified, and (EI 118), was specifically to regulate the sale and export of antiquities. These regulations were revised in 1973 into the (EI 29), which only revised some of the provisions in the previous one (Etse, 2003). It is worth noting that NLCD 387 and related instruments charged GMMB with protecting the country's cultural heritage, clearly defined antiquity in the context of Ghana, and required of the Board to undertake research and document in detail, Ghana's historic environment, including buildings, archaeological sites, etc. It was also to give permits to both local and foreign researchers and monitor their research and findings. As a result of poor funding and the lack of professionals who understand and appreciate heritage issues, the Board has been reduced to a permit issuing Board without the ability to monitor excavations and other land altering development activities.

LEVEL OF ACADEMIC DEPENDENCY

The background given above shows clearly that archaeology in Ghana has good reason to be dependent on the 'West' for academic research, and funding. The issues of migrated archives, professionals, antique objects, etc., as well as ineffective and non-enforcement of laws add up to the reasons why Ghana is academically dependent.

Academically, the early researches in the country were conducted by expatriate amateurs and professionals who of course had no or little native insight into the traditions and cultures they researched. This is based on the reality that many traditional or indigenous Ghanaian communities will not reveal certain aspects of their culture, particularly those associated with cosmology, religion or sacred places as shrines, to people they see as foreign or alien to their area. It would thus be difficult for expatriates to access certain information without the aid of a native scholar. More so, some

European scholars had attempted attributing developments in Africa that they met to foreign influences, suggesting that Africans could not have achieved such feats. The case of the civilization of Great Zimbabwe is clear. Connah (2001: 223) has indicated that, 'perhaps the most damaging aspect of the whole African colonial experience was the attempted denial to African peoples of their own cultural heritage, of which the attribution of Great Zimbabwe to foreign influence, without a shred of evidence, must be the classic example'.

It will not be far from right to argue that the analysis and interpretations with which the set of models and typologies, which now form reference materials for contemporary researchers in the country might have been flawed. For instance, the work of Oliver Davies on Stone Age chronology, tool identification, and especially his interpretations have been criticized by several archaeologists as inaccurate (Anquandah, 1982: 27). The use of terminologies such as Precambrian, Lupemban, Mesolithic, Olduwan, Sangoan, etc., to describe some of the stone tools from the area of Ghana are some examples. Many of these terms, including his designation of the general beginnings of food production in Ghana as the Kintampo Culture are still popular. Similarly, smoking pipe typologies developed in the 1970s are still the basis for dating many sites by association or cross-dating as well as the identification of types in terms of areas of origin.

In addition, many publications on Ghana's archaeology are from Western scholars who have researched or are researching in Ghana much more, when compared with publications by Ghanaians on their past. The explanation lies in the fact that many Ghanaian archaeologists have no funding to research and publish as quickly as would have been the case with their Western counterparts.

Funding is one major reason why Ghanaian archaeology still remains embryonic and dependent. Archaeologists in the country fund archaeological research from their meagre salaries, either because of the need to acquire a degree or come out with some publications, a requirement for promotion in an academic set up. Research has thus been conducted on a rather small scale in the last few years. The only major archaeological research project in Ghana that got some funding from the state is the Volta Basin Research Project mentioned earlier. Other known major projects have been funded by foreign agencies and have usually involved foreign scholars. For instance, the West African Trade Project directed by Posnansky that excavated Begho, received some funding from the Leverhulme Trust (Anquandah, 1982: 28). Also, Shinnie's involvement in the Gonja Archaeology Project was because he headed a Canadian Project that was interested in it (Stahl, 1994: 58). Those small grants that involve Ghanaian researchers have always come with some form of restriction as 'terms of reference'. Examples may be cited of the researches in Sakpuli, Sankana and Kasana (Okoro, 2002; Nkumbaan, 2002).

Aside from these major archaeological projects in Ghana in recent times, the Kintampo Archaeological Research Project (2000/1) was conducted by doctoral students from the United Kingdom with funding from a foreign agency. The Central Region Archaeological Research Project (2000/3) was directed by a professor from the United States with funding from a US agency. Three major archaeological projects are ongoing in Ghana, two of which are underwater. These are being carried out by scholars or researchers from the United States with huge amounts of funding. In all of these projects, the involvement of Ghanaians has been in the form of two or three weeks' apprenticeship or training for students seeking opportunities to gain more practical experience. Of course, it is the inadequacies in the legislations and national institutions charged with taking care of our heritage that has resulted in this situation.

This situation has been created by the fact that foreign

researchers in Ghana only need to satisfy the condition of applying for permits and pay some fees for it, and once these are granted by GMMB, work commences. Having finished excavations, lists of artefacts are again submitted for permits to take them out of the country for specialist analysis, many of which are yet to be returned and some of which may perhaps never be returned. Funding for archaeological research is so poor that students now pay for their practical training.

In addition to the artefacts taken out, much archival documentation that would have been useful reference materials for scholars within the country found their way out of the country, courtesy colonialism. Similarly, either because of warfare or colonial influence, many state regalia belonging to traditional authorities were sent out of the country. For instance, it is known that during the 1874 British–Asante war, many cultural properties belonging to the Asante kingdom were taken away. The call for their return has so far remained futile. Furthermore, many Ghanaian students are funded by institutions abroad with the objective of them coming back to help the development of institutions in their home country—only to have them recruited onto their staff after they have completed their courses of study.

The inadequacies of the Ghanaian heritage law and the non-enforcement thereof, are a contributory factor. The laws do not provide for a system of raising funds to support the heritage sector. The existing legislation has out-lived its time with regard to the fines and penalties for the destruction of cultural property. It does not require agencies involved in land altering activities such as the construction firms and mining companies as well as individuals to undertake archaeological investigations of sites before they are developed. These are the situations that have rendered archaeologists and archaeological research in Ghana dependent on foreign funding and published materials for academic growth.

OVERCOMING OR COPING WITH ACADEMIC DEPENDENCY

Many changes are required in the Ghanaian national fabric in order to cope with or overcome the problem of academic dependency. There is the need to rekindle in every Ghanaian a sense of nationalism and national pride in relation to our cultural heritage resources. The perception of our cultural and traditional practices as backward, fetishes or evil is profound—these are ideas generally emanating from alien importation of 'foreign' cultural and religious practices and beliefs, and must be changed. For Ghanaian archaeologists to cope with or overcome academic dependency on the West, I suggest the redressing and repackaging of the discipline of archaeology to get rid of the negative connotations of it as a colonial course. The revision of the national legislations on heritage management, with particular reference to the issue of permits to foreign researchers, and funding policies of agencies, are some ways by which academic dependency can be dealt with.

Archaeology is the study of people, societies and their cultures in the past using material remains. These inform about their ways of life, technologies, achievements, failures, etc., which help understand the present socio-economic and political systems, and guide the future. In redressing and repackaging the discipline in Ghana, we may have to modify the name of the Department from Archaeology to a broader name which will attract attention and do away with its linkage with colonialism. This is important with regard to changing the mindset of the people as was the case with the change in the name of the country from Gold Coast to Ghana after independence. Alongside the change of name, we need to revise the course contents of the discipline to reflect the current development needs of the country as well as to make products of archaeology marketable in the job market. For instance, the recognition that the discipline can help law courts in resolving issues of land dispute through the identification of ancestral owners based on artefact assemblage or material remains will not only engender governmental attention but also give the discipline some respect and inform the indigenes of the need to preserve elements of their past. Emphasizing the relevance of the discipline will allow for interest groups to make funds available for research and preservation of the heritage of the nation.

There are cases of archaeological research that are resulting in the development of local areas within which they are being carried out. Mention can be made of the Krobo Mountain Archaeological Project by William Gblerkpor and Kodzo Gavua which in collaboration with the traditional council has culminated in a big tourism attraction of the region. Similarly, the work of Ako Okoro in Salaga is revolutionizing indigenous water management systems as one sure way of sustainable water supply for the water-stressed environment. The ultimate objective of the Komaland Archaeological Research Project is to develop a museum project to house the unique terracotta figurines and other artefacts from the region, and thus open it up as a tourism attraction. The research into the Internal African Diaspora by Kodzo Gavua is uniting families that got separated some time in the past as a result of certain historical developments, including the trade in enslaved people. These forms of research have the potential to rekindle people's interest in their past and engender the preservation thereof, as well as generate funding for their documentation.

The need to revise the legislations on heritage protection is an imperative if we are to mitigate the problem of academic dependency. The current code has not provided for a systematic and sustainable source of funding for the heritage sector. It is also too liberal with the way permits are issued to foreign researchers. The regulations could establish a fund to which all agencies involved in land altering activities pay a percentage of their budgetary allocation for archaeological surveys and preservation of the data. Alternatively, the concept of the 'destroyer pays' as is the case in many developed countries, can be applied where individuals, construction and mining firms, estate agencies, etc., pay for archaeological digs and the preservation of the nation's heritage before they are plundered by 'development'. This will ensure the local availability of funds for research and other preservation needs.

External funding agencies should also be prepared to make resources available to native researchers or archaeologists, based on proposals they have fashioned with specific research questions. In this regard, I vouch for the Danish funding of the archaeological research at the Fredricksgave plantation site and the ultimate reconstruction of the fortress. Also, the GDARCH Project, a DANIDA sponsored collaboration between the Department of Archaeology, University of Ghana and the SAXO Institute, Archaeology Division, University of Copenhagen, provides funding to Ghanaian archaeologists and graduate students to conduct researches based on their own proposals. In addition, the efforts of the British Museum, Institute of Field Archaeology, UK, and the University of East Anglia, etc., are commendable in this regard and I think it is the best way to go forward if we are to overcome academic dependency.

Regarding the issue of permits, the legislation could stipulate that no permit is given to any foreigner for independent research unless he/she is collaborating with a local researcher or institution. Similarly, the funding agencies could make it a policy to provide funding for such researchers only when they show sufficient evidence of collaboration with local counterparts. The gain of policies of this kind is that it lends credibility to archaeological interpretations and minimizes speculative conclusions. It is true that technological, social and ideological developments across the world are relative to local conditions such as the physical and human environment upon which they are built. As a result, it is only advisable to have archaeological interpretations that are influenced by native knowledge.

CONCLUSION

It is certain that the genesis of archaeology in Ghana dates to the colonial era. Pioneering research and the development of paradigms and models for research in the area have antecedents in this era. Many of the researchers of that time were foreigners with either some form of bias about the cultures they studied or lack of indigenous insights and appreciation for the developments of those cultures. Though they may have done a good job, the context of the development of the discipline has influenced the slow pace of its development and appreciation of the relevance of the subject by many ordinary Ghanaians. A revision in the name of the Department of Archaeology, which is seen as 'COLO'—colonial, revision of the courses offered by the department, the revision of the legislations and policies of funding have the potential to let the discipline assume greater levels of recognition and attract meaningful local funding. Education of the traditional authorities, that is, the chiefs, the custodians of the lands that possess the national heritage, and earth priests, on the usefulness of their heritage to them and the nation at large, can help with the protection of sites and monuments. These traditional authorities could even raise funds for their development as is happening in the Techiman and Krobo traditional areas.

REFERENCES

Anquandah, J.R. (1982), *Rediscovering Ghana's Past*, Harlow, Essex and Accra: Sedco and Longman.

Argorsah, E.K. (1983), 'An Ethnarchaeological Study of Settlement and Behaviour Patterns of a West African Traditional Society: The Nchumuru of Banda-Wiae in Ghana', PhD dissertation, University of California, Los Angeles.

Arhin, K. (ed) (1974), 'The Papers of George Ekem Ferguson: A Fanti Official of the Government of the Gold Coast 1890–7', *African*

Social Research Documents, No. 7, Cambridge: African Studies Centre.

Balfour, H. (1912), 'Notes on a Collection of Stone Implements from Ejura, Ashanti', *Journal of African Society* 12: 1–16.

Bellis, J.O. (1972), 'Archaeology and Culture History of the Akan of Ghana: A Case Study', PhD dissertation, Indiana University, Bloomington.

Boachie-Ansah, J. (1986), 'An Archaeological Contribution to the History of Wenchi', *African Occasional Papers 3*, Calgary: University of Calgary Press.

Boateng, E.A. (1970), *A Geography of Ghana*, Cambridge: Cambridge University Press.

Bovill, E.W. (1968), *The Golden Trade of the Moors*, Oxford: Oxford University Press.

Braunholtz, H. J. (1936), 'Archaeology in the Gold Coast', in *Antiquity* 10: 469–74.

Bredwa-mensah, Y. (1990), 'An Archaeological Investigation Conducted at Okai Koi Hill (Ayawaso) and its Significance for Iron Age Archaeology in Ghana', MPhil thesis, University of Ghana.

Clarke, D.L. (1979), *Analytical Archaeologist*, London: Academic Press.

Crossland, L.B. (1989), 'Pottery from the Begho-B2 Site, Ghana', *African Occasional Papers 4*, Calgary: University of Calgary Press.

Connah, G. (2001), *African Civilizations: An Archaeological Perspective,* Cambridge: Cambridge University Press.

Davies, O. (1971), 'The Archaeology of the Flooded Volta Basin', *Occasional Papers in Archaeology*, No. 1, Department of Archaeology, University of Ghana.

DeCorse, C.R. (1992), 'Culture Contact, Continuity and Change on the Gold Coast, AD 1400–1900', in *African Archaeological Review* 10: 163–96.

Effah-Gyimfi, K. (1985), 'Bono Manso: An Archaeological Investigation into Early Akan Urbanism', *African Occasional Papers* 2, Calgary: University of Calgary Press.

Etse, P.Y. (2003), 'The Roles of the Ghana National Museum in the Management of Archaeological and Cultural Resources', unpublished Undergraduate dissertation, University of Ghana.

Gavua, K. (1985), 'Daboya and the Kintampo Culture of Ghana', MPhil thesis, Calgary: University of Calgary.

Gerrad, T.F. (1982), 'Myths and Metrology: The Early Trans-Saharan Gold Trade', *Journal of African History* 23: 443–61.

Holl, A. (1990), 'West African Archaeology: Colonialism and Nationalism', in P. Robertshaw (ed.), *A History of African Archaeology*, London: James Curey.

Junner, N.R. (1935), 'Gold in the Gold Coast', *Geological Survey: Report of the Gold Coast, Mem.*, No. 4, Accra.

Kense, F.J. (1990), 'Archaeology in Anglophone West Africa', in P. Robertshaw (ed.), *A History of African Archaeology*, London: James Curey, pp. 135–72.

Keteku, E.K. (1981), 'Nyanawase: History on the Soil', PhD dissertation, Calgary: University of Calgary.

Kitson, A.E. (1916), 'The Gold Coast: Some Considerations of its Structure, People and Natural History', in *Geographical Journal* 48: 362–92.

Kiyaga-Mulindwa, D. (1978), 'The Earthworks of Birim Valley, Southern Ghana', PhD dissertation, Baltimore: John Hopkins University.

Musonda, F.B. (1976), 'The Later Stone Age in Ghana in Light of Excavation Along the Voltian Scarp', MA thesis, University of Ghana.

Okoro, J.A. (1989), 'Investigation of Iron Smelting Sites in Gambaga and the Implication of Finding of Iron Age Studies in Ghana', MPhil thesis, University of Ghana.

Ozanne, P.C. (1971), 'Ghana', in P.L. Shinnie (ed.), *The Iron Age of Africa*, Oxford: Clarendon Press.

Rattray, R.S. (1923), *Ashanti*, Oxford: Clarendon Press.

——— (1927), *Religion and Art in Ashanti*, Oxford: Clarendon Press.

Stahl, A.B. (1994), 'Innovation, Diffusion, and Culture Contact: The Holocene Archaeology of Ghana', in *Journal of World Prehistory*, 8 (1).

——— (1985), 'The Kintampo Culture: Subsistence and Settlement in Ghana during the Mid-Second Millennium B.C.', PhD Dissertation, Berkeley: University of California.

Trigger, B.G. (1993), 'Alternative Archaeologies: Nationalist, Colonialist, Imperialist', in *A History of Archaeological Thought*, Cambridge: Cambridge University Press.

Wild, R.P. (1934), 'The Inhabitants of the Gold Coast and Ashanti before the Akan Invasion', in *Gold Coast Teacher's Journal*, vols. 6–7.

CHAPTER 4

The Institutions of Higher Education in Burundi and Rwanda: Facing the Challenges of Post-Conflict Societies[1]

THARCISSE NSABIMANA[2]

FROM THE EDITORS

We thought it appropriate to begin this article with parts of the introduction to an article written by a specialist in African Philosophy, Bruce Janz in 2003. Dr Tharcisse Nsabimana refers to this article in his work and it seems that it highly stimulated him to write the paper. The quotation below from Janz, we feel, functions as a perfect backdrop to Nsabimana's contribution:

> The pressure to participate in the global community has as one of its manifestations the requirements of an adequate and even a 'world class' university system. Historically, universities have had more in common with monasteries than with marketplaces. . . . Indeed, the most common critique of the university, and particularly the liberal arts, is that it does not contribute to the real needs or wants of people. Many believe that the governing metaphor should be changed from monastery to marketplace. Needless to say, this change comes with its own set of problems and, for many, a university which is primarily a marketplace is no longer a university. Nevertheless, in the minds of many, tensions between integrity and relevance are the core problems facing the university today. In a country undergoing the stress of war or ethnic strife, this tension between integrity and relevance is all the more acute. In countries such as Rwanda and Burundi, where there is serious ethnic strife, relevance takes on the urgency of a life or death situation. And so, the monastery metaphor becomes all the more

suspect, as the stakes are higher. The answer in many cases has been the marketplace metaphor. If only the university could contribute to the material and economic wealth of the country, if only it could help in raising the general standard of living, the national pressures would dissipate. . . . In both Rwanda and Burundi, issues such as these are of central importance. Both countries have borne great suffering in recent years. The human tragedy of 1994, with body counts as high as 850,000 is Rwanda's recent legacy. In the case of Burundi, there has been long-standing guerilla warfare, particularly since the democratically elected government President Sylvestre Ntibantunganya was overthrown in a *coup d'état* on 25 July 1996, and replaced by the military government of Major Pierre Buyoya. Both countries endure regular ambushes and police actions, and in both countries there are areas which are extremely volatile. Such times raise serious questions for the university. . . . Given that the institution already exists in both Rwanda and Burundi, how might a real university exist in these conditions, and not simply a group of buildings in which some pale simulacrum of a university holds classes and hands out degrees? Answers to these questions will not be found in most writing on the nature of the university. Books and papers on the liberal arts and university affairs in general are overwhelmingly based on North American (and some European) experience, which has a very definite character. . . . These conditions result in certain kinds of Western defences of the university, and of liberal education in particular, which may not be particularly relevant to universities outside of North America, and especially those in situations of national crisis. . . .

I. INSTITUTIONS OF HIGHER LEARNING IN BURUNDI AND RWANDA: SOME FACTS AND FIGURES

The first institutions of higher education in Burundi, created right after the country's independence in 1962, were the University of Burundi (1964) and the Grand Séminaire de Bujumbura (1962), to train the priests of the Catholic Church. The National University of Rwanda was created in 1963. Most of the Burundian private universities and institutions of higher learning were created during the crisis which struck the country from the 1990s onwards, while in Rwanda, it was after the genocide of 1994 that most of private and public universities and institutions of higher education were created. Today, private institutions outnumber the public ones, both in Burundi and in Rwanda.[3]

However, the number of students in private institutions remains lower. The number of students enrolled in public institutions both in Burundi are 39 per cent and Rwanda 45 per cent respectively. Women are less represented in Burundi in private institutions, with 42 per cent of the total number of students and 24 per cent in public ones. In Rwanda, they are better represented with 52 per cent in private institutions and 29 per cent in public ones. The total number of students in Rwanda (31,547) is almost two times higher than in Burundi (18,186).[4]

Concerning the academic staff, the issue is both of quality and number. This can be observed in the entire Great Lakes region, in each country and on institutional levels. Table 4.1 gives some statistics of the academic staff from institutions of higher education in Rwanda and in Burundi.

There are a large numbers of expatriate lecturers in Rwanda coming from Burundi and the DRC. They have contracts especially with public universities such as the National University of Rwanda and Kigali Institute of Education. Some others come from Kenya, India, Tanzania, Uganda and few from as far as the United Kingdom, the USA, etc. While Burundians and the Congolese sign contracts with Rwandan institutions of higher education, their own universities are left with less qualified and less experienced lecturers, although some of them return every year as visiting lecturers. The University of Burundi has been for the last 15 years a provider of lecturers to the whole region. Those who have remained in Burundi are also visiting lecturers in Eastern DRC's universities and other institutions of higher education, in local universities and in Rwanda. This situation has caused a series of problems for the promotion of tertiary education in both Rwanda (the beneficiary) and Burundi (the provider):

Table 4.1: Academic staff from institutions of higher education in Rwanda and in Burundi in 2006[5]

Institutions	Full-time academic staff (senior Lecturers and above)	Full-time academic staff (from Assistants to Lecturers)	Part-time academic staff (senior Lecturers and above)	Full-time academic staff (from TA to Lecturers)
Burundi				
University of Burundi	115	159	–	–
ULT	23	7	93	9
ULBu	4	4	97	13
ENS	1	–	59	3
INSP	1	4	124	4
University of Ngozi	3	10	159	15
University of Mwaro	1	3	44	8
University of Bururi	1	1	7	54
Rwanda				
ULK	–	–	–	174 (2)
UNR	–	97	19	–
UNILAK	–	57	33	60
KIE	–	60	–	–
KH	–	51	–	–

- The students lack supervisors for their research projects. For instance, in Burundi the most qualified for such research work left and those who remained are overloaded with teaching and administrative assignments. In Rwanda, the tertiary education relies on insufficient expatriate staff who are sometimes not even qualified to teach and to carry out research.
- Research does not progress due to lack of research resources (funds, human resources, equipment, etc.). In Rwanda, however, research is much more promoted thanks to multilateral and bilateral cooperation.
- Expatriate lecturers and researchers are not much engaged in long-term research because they have signed short-term

contracts. The Kigali Institute of Education has managed to sign three-year contracts with expatriate lecturers and is starting to get results.

- In Burundi, very few new programmes have been developed since 1990 because of socio-political instability, lack of funds and human resources. The multilateral and bilateral cooperation was suspended in 1996. It is resuming, as signs of peace recovery start to appear.
- Rwanda has, however, embarked on promotion of tertiary education, by reforming its educational system, opening new programmes at NUR, creating new public institutions of higher education (KIST, KIE, KHI, etc.) and encouraging private institutions to invest in education.

Despite these problems, the university and other institutions of higher learning still have to fulfil their classic mission and are assigned new roles especially in post-conflict countries and societies like Rwanda and Burundi.

II. THE ROLE OF THE UNIVERSITIES AND OTHER INSTITUTIONS OF HIGHER EDUCATION

The classic mission of both the University of Burundi and the National University of Rwanda from the early years of their existence was to train civil servants and carry out research in fields where there was a high demand for qualified people: 'The university was to become a centre of higher education which delivers general and technological knowledge, and trains highly qualified civil servants the country needs.[6] This was said by Grégoire Kayibanda, former President of Rwanda, advocating the creation of the National University of Rwanda. It can be extended to the University of Burundi too. Thus, it is clearly indicated that the mission of the university and other institutions of higher learning, whether private or public, is closely linked with the needs for the transformation of the society. Yet the most trenchant critique of universities is that they do not contribute to fulfil the real needs of the people.[7]

In a country which has undergone violent ethnic strife and is still struggling for its economic recovery and social development, the university's concern is to contribute to people's reconciliation, to material and economic wealth, and raising the general standards of life. The pressing task before the country is how to solve the problems which created the crisis and then provide expertise to raise the general standards of living and create jobs.[8] These were the cases of Rwanda and Burundi. The latter had to identify the causes of the crisis, bring the belligerent persons together for negotiations, and find ways for mutual understanding, reconciling people and then reconstruct the country.

Rwanda had gone through the process of negotiation before the genocide. After the genocide, it sought ways of reconciling people and reconstructing the country. It concentrated on solving the problems which caused the genocide to prevent it from happening again and embarked on reconstructing the devastated human resources and the ravaged infrastructures. The economic recovery is an indicator of the growth and the improvement of people's living standards.

Situations like these raise problems for the countries' universities and institutions of higher education. What are their roles in the current situations? Can they deliver high quality knowledge, award diplomas and degrees, and carry out research? While this traditional role has to be fulfilled, today's university has to go beyond as it is seen as a tool for change and transformation of the society. Professor Silas Rwakabamba, Rector of the National University of Rwanda, while talking about the role of the above university, remarked: 'As is readily evident, no country can develop without adequate knowledge, institutions supplying relevant expertise and skills for social and economic transformation. In all winning nations, the role of the university has gone beyond the traditional missions of teaching and research.'[9]

In post-genocide Rwanda, the priority of the national university and other institutions of higher education remains to train teachers, doctors and lawyers, the most needed human resources right after the genocide. However, in Rwanda like in Burundi many other subjects are now taught in the newly, created public and private institutions of higher education including para-medical studies, economics, management, agriculture, veterinary and environmental studies, geography, social sciences, political science, medicine, development studies, technology, computer science, religious studies and philosophy. However, all these subjects are taught in very difficult conditions of dependency.

III. THE NATURE OF DEPENDENCY FACED BY INSTITUTIONS OF HIGHER LEARNING

There are three different types of dependencies faced by scholars in universities in both Rwanda as well as Burundi.

DEPENDENCY ON WESTERN THINKING

The National University of Rwanda and the University of Burundi were created in the colonial context. I already mentioned that their mission was to train people, deliver scientific knowledge and carry out research. However, they were also created to duplicate and to perpetuate Western thought. The concept of 'Western-centrism' is constructed upon three premises:

1. that modern Western civilization, which first centred around Western Europe but has been transplanted to the United States of America and Canada and so on, has reached the most advanced stage of human history;
2. that the historical development of Western civilization is universally valid in all of human history around the world; and
3. that non-Western societies, which still lag behind in historical development can only advance by imitating or adapting the Western developmental model through civilization.[10]

This is particularly true of Rwanda and Burundi, where colonial indoctrination was backed by the powerful Catholic Church. It is the one which initiated education at all levels.[11] 'Westernization' can also be detected through an analysis of the curricula, particularly in the field of history. The most widely read piece on the history of Rwanda and Burundi and taught to school children during the colonial period and even today, teaches that the formation of centralized kingdoms from the Great Lakes Region was not done by [native] Africans because black people were not capable of such great achievements. It is argued that it was rather the work of migrants of Euro–Asian people, the hamites and the said ancestors of the Tutsis. The latter were considered as invaders, conquerors and foreigners. This is the historical reason given for the present-day ethnic conflict in the two countries. Implementing the colonial principle of 'divide and rule' Rwandans and Burundians were divided into distinct groups and opposed to each other, termed as different races, in spite of the fact that they speak the same language, share the same beliefs and culture and occupy the same territory.

This way of thinking was perpetuated uncritically due to the fact that most of the students went to Europe for tertiary studies until the national universities developed academic programmes up to the Bachelor level in the 1970s. Besides this, the Western model of thinking is still propagated in the universities in the two countries as teaching and learning materials were and are still Western oriented: The textbooks were and still are not adapted to local cultures and the social and economic environment. Teaching history for instance was to disseminate the history of Europe in Rwanda and in Burundi. History of Africa or 'national history' (i.e. history as seen by the Africans and not through European eyes) was absent from the curriculum until the Departments of History were opened and the first PhD graduates returned home and reviewed the curricula.

Yet, there is no doubt that scholars from Rwanda and Burundi still depend academically on Western-centrism thinking, and it will last as long as 'they have internalized the belief that the Western world-view, values, institutions, and practices are superior and universal and have assimilated them'.[12] The question is how to overcome this self-negation and self-marginalization?

Economic Dependency

From the beginning, higher education in Burundi relied on multilateral and bilateral cooperation. It was suspended in 1996 following the embargo imposed on the country and due to the war. Today the Belgian and the French governments are resuming it. International organizations such as the University Agency of French Speaking Association and UNESCO have also started to support the University of Burundi for research, distance training, publications and exchange of researchers and lecturers. In Rwanda, after the genocide, international and bilateral donors have financially supported the country to rebuild its educational system. Table 4.2 indicates the origin of financial support to Rwandan public institutions of higher education.[13]

Some of the private institutions get also support from religious organizations, but their main source of funding is the tuition fees paid by the parents, the students themselves or their sponsors.

These funds, whether from bilateral, multilateral cooperation or from parents, students and their sponsors are used to pay salaries, to create and maintain infrastructure, to equip laboratories, to buy library material and consumables, etc. However, in spite of it these institutions still remain ill-equipped, especially the private ones. Moreover, relying on external support attests to great dependency on the donors who can impose on the beneficiaries their views and their policies.

Table 4.2: Origin of Financial Support to Rwandan Public Institutions of Higher Education from 1999 onwards

Institutions	Origin*
Kigali Institute of Education (KIE)	World Bank African Development Bank DFID (UK)
National University of Rwanda	USAID Belgian Cooperation Swedish Government Canada Government of Rwanda UNDP McArthur Foundation Rhenamie Palatinat (Germany) Danish Government French Cooperation European Union The Netherlands
Institute of Agriculture and Animal Husbandry (ISAE)	Dutch NGOs/Government ITA St. Hyacinthe (Canada) ADB Belgian NGOs/Government World Bank
Kigali Institute of Sciences and Technology (KIST)	UNDP ADB World Bank Swedish Bank for International Development UNIFEM Japanese Government The Netherlands Government (GTZ) Germany (UK) DFID (USAID)

*This list of donors is not exhaustive.

MOBILITY OF ACADEMIC STAFF: SOURCE OF REGIONAL (INTER-)DEPENDENCY

As mentioned before, lecturers move from one institution to another, but there generally is not much benefit from it as the movement is from one poorly equipped institution to another. These teachers cannot update their knowledge through this mobility. They rely on what they once learned and on the material they acquired when they were still university students. Nevertheless, such human resource exchange could be the key to development as well. This mobility also is most likely the reason why some of these institutions of higher education have managed to survive despite the problems they encountered. The mobility has indeed become a strategy for the survival of some of the institutions of higher education.[14] Yet, it also caused regional (inter-)dependency and (therefore) competition among the universities in the two countries.

IV. COPING WITH DEPENDENCY

COPING WITH DEPENDENCY ON 'WESTERN-CENTRISM THINKING'

The scholars from the Great Lakes Region are aware of their dependency on 'Western-centrism thinking'. They try to free their minds by all means, but have not been very successful so far. Ways by which they tried to become less dependent were the organization of conferences and seminars where issues of identity and rehabilitation of culture were discussed. Scientific contributions were also published.[15] During 'the crisis', some scholars contributed towards finding solutions to it by delivering lectures, issuing declarations, by the creation of associations to advocate peace and reconciliation, etc. However, many others failed to fulfil their mission and to play their new roles. In fact, I feel that in this way the University has played at least an indirect role in the genocide.

It failed to address the issue of ethnicity and exclusion.[16] Professor Laurent Nkusi from the National University of Rwanda also pointed to the Rwandan scholars' devastating role in the 1994 genocide. To quote from him in French:

'*Nous savons que des intellectuels rwandais ont délibérément choisi de se détourner de la vérité dans leur lecture de l'histoire et de la sociologie de notre pays. . . . Ce sont des professeurs de l'Université qui ont propagé l'idéologie génocidaire*' (We know well that Rwandan scholars have willingly chosen to distance themselves from the truth, while reading the history and the sociology of our country. . . . The university professors are the ones who have disseminated the ideology of genocide).[17]

In Burundi, in order to rehabilitate the country's values and culture, an academy of Kirundi language was created and headed by a professor of the university. History and African Languages and Literature Departments were created at the University of Burundi. History and the culture of Burundi has a big share in the curricula of these departments. Textbooks on the history of Burundi were published. Colonial writings on Burundi were also revised.[18] However, changes in ways of thinking are slow and will take a long time. We still fall short to overcome Western influence in our minds. In Rwanda, before the genocide, many scholars had opted for distortion of truths. They are now, however, revisiting the old literature in history and the culture of Rwanda to reform minds.

The most encouraging outcome of all these efforts is that whether in Rwanda or in Burundi, scholars are now aware of the negative impact of a Western model of thinking. They are working to find alternative approaches and initiating research projects towards this goal. This self-assessment is vital to rebuild a cultural identity wherein everyone recognizes him or herself.

Coping with Economic Dependency

We figured out that the institutions of higher education in the region are in general ill-equipped. Scholarship dependency is linked to the economic conditions of a country. One of the means of improving the working conditions had been to secure aid from international donors and partner-governments. Yet now, most of the institutions no longer get it or have ever got this kind of aid. Moreover, those which obtain it are at risk of being dictated by the donors of what to do and not to do and may not enjoy the academic freedom cherished by academicians.

To overcome this material dependency many institutions have initiated income generating activities, such as production, consultancies, offering short courses in computer skills and language proficiency. However, this does not fully alleviate the material needs of these institutions. Many of them, especially the private ones also do not deliver high quality knowledge because they cannot recruit highly qualified lecturers as they are not supported by the government. This may result in the closure of many of these institutions which of course impacts academic mobility. The disappearance of these institutions will reduce the capacity of the countries to offer tertiary education to the citizens. This indicates the importance of private institutions of education. Therefore, they deserve support from governments and international donors.

Alternatives to Academic Mobility

Academic mobility can be fruitful. No one can deny this. It can promote exchange of views and allow access to learning and teaching material not available in one's own institution. However, in the Great Lakes Region the physical mobility of the academic staff has been one caused by shortages and the need for highly qualified and competent academic staff remains high. Though this mobility needs to be reinforced, at the same time, laboratories and other equipments and consumables are to be provided as well as updated library material. Besides, MA and PhD programmes are to be developed; lecturers need continuing education to update their knowledge and the alternative to the shortage of teaching and learning material is the development of the Technologies of Information and Communication. 'It was urgent for us to benefit from new technologies', said Juma Shabani, a principal specialist at the UNESCO for Education in Africa. He added: 'The development of telecommunications, in particular, can enable us to connect to international research networks and thus make use of publications and other available documents.'[19] While different institutions continue to hire external scholars, other means are indeed sought to reduce this dependency on the physical presence of scholars. But, one can ask: How developed are these technologies in the Great Lakes Region?

In Rwanda, the development of Information and Communication Technology (ICT) indeed is a government priority. The institutions of higher education all have internet connections. This allows distance training as in the Kigali Institute of Education for instance. The University Agency of French Speaking Association is helping to install a digital campus at the National University of Rwanda and at the Independent University of Kigali. It will allow researchers and lecturers to access scientific information electronically.

In Burundi, the University of Burundi and the Light University of Bujumbura are developing their own websites. E-mails are widely used by researchers and lecturers. A dynamic digital campus has been opened in Bujumbura, funded by the University Agency of French-speaking Association in close collaboration with different universities, particularly the University of Burundi which is hosting it. However, the Eastern DRC institutions of higher education are less advanced in ICT matters. There are only few computers for teaching computer skills and for use by the administrative staff.[20] In each of these countries, there is still a lot to be done, but it is important that academic staff, lecturers and students are aware of these shortcomings and are committed to update themselves.

CONCLUSION

Traditional and old universities did not fulfil their mission. Today they are aware that they should be more involved in transforming their societies and they are trying their best. However, they encounter serious problems which make them academically dependent. These problems are economic, insufficient infrastructures, shortage of human resources (academic staff), lack of teaching and learning material, etc. The wars, genocide and political instability have destabilized the whole educational system in these three African regions, like they have impacted other sectors in society. It is true that tertiary education has been the most affected by the loss of students, academic and administrative staff, by the suspension of the international cooperation and the destruction of infrastructures. Yet, the demand for tertiary education has continuously increased. As a result, private institutions have mushroomed and have increased pressure on the academic staff at the expense of quality. ICT seems to be a miraculous solution, but it is not yet much available. Moreover, the outcome of all this is that the institutions of higher education in the Great Lakes Region are heavily dependent on each other and on international donors. This surely has lead to academic dependency. Scholars have, however, tried as much as they could to cope with it in different ways, but the threat is still there.

During a conference held in Bujumbura-Burundi in September 2008 organized by the University of Burundi on 'Reconstruction Challenges in the Great Lakes Region of East Africa', scholars emphasized the need for the universities to bring their expertize together to solve the problems of development; for the regional organizations to include research programmes on these issues in their programmes; for the universities to reform their programmes and methodologies to adapt them to the needs of the society; to update their research facilities, to publish, to promote research and teaching careers and to link-up with other African universities as well as with those from the North and international organizations. In this way, universities all over the world will collaborate with, instead of depending on each other.

NOTES

1. This paper owes much to a study carried out in 2006 by Professor Gilbert Midende of the University of Burundi and Alain Massiéra, Director of the Representative Office of the University Agency of the French-speaking Association in the Great Lakes region in Bujumbura. This study explores the situation of tertiary education in the Great Lakes region. I am thankful to the authors who allowed me access and use of their data.
2. This paper was once revised by Dr. Tharcisse Nsabimana himself after presenting it at the workshop in Patna. The second revision was, however, done by the editors of this volume due to Nsabimana's sudden demise in August 2009.
3. G. Midende, and A. Massiéra (2006), *Etat des lieux de l'enseignement supérieur in Afrique des Grands Lacs, Burundi, Kivu (DRC), Rwanda* (Report), p. 21, table 2.
4. Ibid., pp. 28–33.
5. Ibid., pp. 42–4.
6. B. Kanyehera (2006), 'L'évolution historique de l'Université Nationale du Rwanda (UNR) de 1963 à 2000', *Research Project Paper*, Kigali: Kigali Institute of Education, p. 28.
7. B. Janz (2003), 'Universities in Times of National Crisis: The Cases of Rwanda and Burundi', in Malinda Smith (ed.), *Globalizing Africa*, Trenton, New Jersey: Africa World Press, pp. 465–82.
8. Ibid.
9. S. Rwakabamba, 'Towards a Knowledge Institution to Support

Development in Rwanda: The Role of the National University of Rwanda', available at the website of the National University of Rwanda, consulted on 5 October 2007.

10. Kang, Jung In (2006), 'Academic Dependency: Western-centrism in Korean Political Science', in *Korea Journal,* Winter, p. 118.
11. The two universities were founded respectively by the Dominican and the Jesuit fathers who were renowned for their expertise in education.
12. Kang, op. cit., p. 119.
13. Midende and Massiéra, op. cit., pp. 46–8.
14. This theme was also discussed during an international conference on 'Scholars and Universities in the Great Lakes Region of East Africa' organized by the French Institute for Research in Africa (IFRA Nairobi) and the University of Pau (UPPA, France), held at the Makerere University, Kampala from 4 to 6 June 2007.
15. For instance: J. Gahama (ed.), 'Démocratie, Bonne Gouvernance et Développement dans la Région des Grands Lacs', Université du Burundi, Université Catholique de Bukavu, Université Libre des Pays des Grands Lacs, Université Nationale du Rwanda, Bujumbura-Burundi. These are the proceedings of a conference organized from 18 to 22 May 1998. Participants came from different universities of the Great Lakes region.
16. See also Janz, op. cit., p. 6 (internet version).
17. L. Nkusi, 'Le rôle des universités dans la promotion d'une culture de la paix: le cas de la région des Grands Lacs', in Gahama, op. cit., p. 366.
18. For instance: T. Nsabimana, 'Relecture des Ecrits sur le Burundi, Nouvelles Perspectives de Recherches, Mélanges Offerts à Jean Baptiste Ntahokaja', Université du Burundi, Bujumbura, Juin 1994.
19. M. Amat, 'Overcrowding, Low Funding Plague African Universities' (available on the internet, last downloaded on 1 October 2007).
20. Midende and Massiéra, op. cit., p. 45.

CHAPTER 5

Malaise in Indian Academia

HETUKAR JHA

INTRODUCTION

Practising sociology today is different from the past. The traditional focus was on issues such as class, the economy, the state, etc. Yet now, post-modern sociology has taken in other issues such as identity formation, the role of mass media, cultural code, etc. What is more, these latter issues are sometimes considered more important than the former. This post-modern situation allows for sociology to be qualitative, ethnographic and interpretive. Besides, voices are also being raised for sociology to metamorphose into public philosophy (Seidman, 1996: 283–309). It now has 'broad ambitions and the legitimate ways of practising it are extremely varied' (Bourdieu, 1990: 34). Under these circumstances, it does not seem out of place to discuss the future of sociology in India. However, before taking up this question, it is necessary to examine the socio-political and historical factors that affect the practice of sociology in the Indian context and what the consequences are thereof. In the present paper, an attempt has been made to discuss these factors with a view to understanding how and why the pursuit of sociology in India is coming under examination. An important question that subsequently arises, concerns the actions that should be undertaken by the discipline's practitioners. The pursuit of sociology in India has become a very complex issue and requires serious thought as to what its desirable future should be. This paper will also attempt to give brief suggestions in this regard.

HIERARCHIZATION OF UNIVERSITIES

Before 1947 when India became independent, there were only few colleges and universities in the country. The number of colleges was less than 600 and that of universities only 27 until 1950–5 (Tilak, 2007: 36). Colleges were of two kinds; there were constituent colleges under the control of the education department of the state (provincial) government and there were private colleges that were affiliated to universities. The former were very few in number. They had relatively adequate infrastructure, library facilities, assured financial support from the government, etc. Besides, teachers and principals of such colleges enjoyed great prestige in society, since government jobs were (and still are) highly valued in India. Therefore, these colleges attracted students of the best quality as well as highly qualified teaching staff. The private colleges, however, did not have such facilities, quality of students and teaching staff. So for practical purposes, an intra-university hierarchy of colleges emerged. This trend of the 'hierarchization' of institutions of higher education gained further ground after Independence.

The universe of higher education in the country began to expand rapidly after 1950/1. By 1963/4, the number of universities increased from 27 to 55 and by 1973/4 to 95, while the number of colleges increased from about 600 in 1950/1 to 2,122 by 1963/4 and to 2,197 by 1973/4 (University Grants Commission [UGC], 1978: 3). At present, the educational sector (including primary and secondary levels) of India is supposed to be the second largest in the world; there are about 17,000 colleges and 329 universities (Tilak, 2007: 36). However, along with this phenomenal increase in the number of institutions, the course of higher education was affected by an important policy decision of the Government of India. Before Independence, the British government had 'washed their hands off any educational policy by devolving (it) . . . to the provincial ministries . . . following the Government of India Act of 1919' (Hagen, 1981: 342). This led to education being taken over by the provincial governments after 1921. Since then, universities continued to remain under the control of state (provincial) governments. However, after Independence, the central government decided to establish and maintain universities and institutions of advanced research and training on its own, and simultaneously, to continue the old policy that had subjected the educational sector to the control of the state governments. Thus the large numbers of universities created after Independence in different Indian states are known as state universities, while a few universities and institutions such as Jawaharlal Nehru University, IITs, etc., established by the central government came to be known as central universities and institutes. Consequently, a two-tiered hierarchy of universities emerged in India.

The first tier consists of those few universities and institutes where facilities and resources for teaching and research are plentiful, in comparison with those of the state universities. As a result, the best students and teachers/researchers from different states make all possible efforts to join the central universities. This allows them opportunities to build their careers at the international level. Though there are also problems in universities of this tier—which will be discussed later—in comparison, the situation in state universities appears to be alarming.

POLITICIZATION OF EDUCATION

Socio-political and economic conditions vary significantly from one Indian state to another. An overwhelming number of state universities are thus vulnerable to the pressures of different local political interests and activities. Only a few decades after Independence, colleges and universities of different states began to show signs of being afflicted with politicization, which 'involves the appropriation of educational structures and resources and the displacement of educational goals by organized political and community (religious, caste, locality) interests' (Rudolph and Rudolph, 1972: 8). In this regard, Harold Gould (1972: 94) took note of the following observation of J.P. Naik:

> In Uttar Pradesh, they have a phrase, 'The Congress has abolished the zamindari in land and has created a zamindari in education.' Such zamindars . . . are managers of colleges, who are well fed, well clothed . . . all on the profits from the institutions which they run. It is now recognized that running an educational institution can be an important means of economic and political power.

Harold Gould (1972: 103) who researched the working of colleges in the district of Faizabad (where a university is now established) in U.P. observed the growing politicization of campuses and warned of the following consequences:

> The politicization of educational institutions makes the maintenance of academic standards and promotions based on merit very difficult. . . . The real costs . . . are the sacrifice of academic standards and the violence and chaos sometimes produced by attempts to discipline student bodies, or, notably in Uttar Pradesh and Bihar, to compel honesty in examinations. Why should a student who is conditioned to believe that the political services he renders are his most important academic contribution, accept the verdict of such a non-political criterion of performance as marks?

Problems of increasing politicization, loss of discipline, growing bureaucratization and state control, lack of commitment to research and teaching, increase in favouritism due to considerations of caste/political connections, bribery, etc., both in the examination of students and the recruitment of teachers, are commonplace in a state such as Bihar. Educationists and journalists have often voiced their anxiety in this context (see, for example, John, 1976; Sawney, 1984;

Abraham, 1984; Kumar, 1985; Guha, 2009, etc.). Inevitably, a trend is being seen within state (second tier) universities, which indicates that a positive correlation between merit and examination results on the one hand and merit and faculty recruitment on the other hand, is no longer true. In the present scenario, a student who is academically meritorious may not get a good degree, and at the same time scholarly aptitude and merit is not essential for becoming a teacher in a college/ university. The system has thus become a source of frustration for meritorious students and teachers, and it is feared that it is also becoming a breeding ground for inauthentic learning. The case of sociology is discussed here as an example.

PREFERENCE FOR HINDI/VERNACULARS

It has been discussed elsewhere that in state universities the medium of teaching and research is generally Hindi or regional languages, whereas in the central universities and institutes the medium of teaching and research continues to be English (Jha, 2005: 398). As a result of the dependence on Hindi/vernaculars for teaching and research, social sciences in regional (state) universities seem to have suffered a great deal. For example, one may look into reports on the status of sociology and social anthropology teaching in the different states of India by M.S.A. Rao, K.L. Sharma, Indra Deva, Hetukar Jha, Dhirendra Narain and C. Rajagopalan (UGC, 1979). These reports indicate in clear terms that the inappropriate translation of sociology books into vernaculars/Hindi, the problem of student numbers, lack of infrastructural facilities, inadequate syllabus, etc., have all contributed to the dilution of the normative standard in this regard. Writing on the teaching of sociology in a regional university, at the end of the last century, Kushal Deb (1998: 242) expressed,

> a sense of unease arising from one's endeavour to maintain certain academic standards, the earnest wish to engage in certain creative

> efforts at reading and writing, efforts at making the students feel passionately for the subject. . . . The authority structure of regional universities . . . works against the interests of the . . . discipline.

In this regard Jayaram (1998: 240–1) contends that,

> the problem of teaching sociology in the Indian languages to students who have scant proficiency in English is a . . . challenge . . . [which] is compounded by the nominal presence or even the total absence of qualitative components in sociology courses, which by default has given a spurious qualitative orientation to the subject. The lamentable decline in the standards of doctoral theses and MPhil dissertations is admitted everywhere.

One may thus infer from these observations and experiences of sociologists, that teaching and research in sociology through vernaculars in state universities is feared to be transmitting more or less spurious or inauthentic knowledge. For this kind of sociology, the term 'vernacular sociology' has been used elsewhere (Jha, 2005: 398).

One may assume on the basis of all that has happened to sociology (as described previously), that other social sciences such as Political Science, Psychology, Economics, etc., might have also been affected in varying degrees by a somewhat similar trend. It may be mentioned here that in the context of vernacular sociology, generally only textbooks aimed at examination purposes are used by the majority of students. New findings and reports of serious research in sociology seldom appear in any vernacular/Hindi publication. Under the circumstances, students' knowledge in the field of sociology remains more or less confined to what they learn from their textbooks containing 'spurious' versions of original concepts, analyses, methodology, etc. Thus, as a result of the impact of regional/local forces on most of the state universities, the sociology taught at both undergraduate and postgraduate levels appears to be questionable.

DEPENDENCE ON WESTERN APPROACHES

In the universities of the first tier, however, sociology (along with other social sciences) is flourishing exclusively through the medium of English. Since English as the medium of communication has had an elitist image for a long time, the term 'elitist sociology' has been used for sociology as a subject of teaching and research in central universities (Jha, 2005: 400). This kind of sociology receives acknowledgement at the international level. The report prepared by Ramkrishna Mukherjee in 1977, the reports brought out by the Indian Council of Social Science Research from time to time, books and monographs published by leading publishing houses like Sage India, Oxford University Press, etc., all indicate clearly that sociological studies in India (pursued through the medium of English) have attained impressive intellectual sophistication, matching that of Western standards (ibid.: 401).

However, right from the 1960s, it has been pointed out that Indian sociologists have been borrowing from or imitating the ideas, concepts, perspectives, etc., of American/European sociology. For example, Ram Ahuja (1967: 118–19) wrote that 'It is indeed regrettable that even though Sociology is now being taught . . . in our country for the last forty to forty-five years, yet it continues to be on the American pattern.' Later, Andre Beteille (1974: 7) observed that '. . . The kinds of concerns which Indian sociologists brought to their study were largely a reflection of the concerns of sociologists and social anthropologists from the more advanced Western countries.' K.N. Sharma (2000: 94) bemoaned the fact that 'We academicians have been victims of academic globalization since long. It is extremely difficult to shed Western perspectives'. Ramkrishna Mukherjee (1977: 51, 71), while analysing the trends in Indian sociology since its beginning (in the second decade of the last century) also took note of the dominance of Western approaches, particularly after Independence. These comments and remarks reveal that the approach of Indian sociologists to the social reality of their country has been coloured by a Western perspective.

PROBABLE CAUSES OF DEPENDENCE

Why is this trend prevailing? In this context, one may consider the nature and consequences of the project of modernity. Lucius Outlaw (1994: 23) contends in reference to it, that 'it was a decidedly political project in the widest and most substantive senses whose essence was supposed to be carried in the historical realization of Enlightenment'. However, during the eighteenth century, liberalism emerged as the vehicle for this project, having such elements (of the project of modernity) as individualism, universalism, egalitarianism and meliorism (Outlaw, 1994: 1, 24). According to John Gray (1986: 82, 21), liberalism virtually became 'the political theory of modernity', and the upholders of Enlightenment liberalism asserted 'human imperfectability'. Outlaw (1994: 25) writes in this connection that Enlightenment thinkers were particularly aware of the 'realities of human diversities and of their possible social and political consequences. . . . The egalitarian and universalist elements of liberalism had to be tempered . . . by the need to put into play . . . the meliorist element of liberal conviction. These were the grounds on which a . . . dominated world was created.' Thus, 'Liberalism was reason—prepared, by both classical and modern Enlightenments, to handle diversity through a reason-privileged hierarchy that restricted egalitarianism to equality among equals' (Outlaw, 1994: 27).

This 'reason-privileged hierarchy' of the superior/dominant/colonizers and the subordinated/dominated/colonized was then not only created but institutionalized quite vigorously. Harry Redner (1982: 13) writes in this context that

> . . . we Europeans launched ourselves an unparalleled drive for power, which we called progress. . . . All other societies and cultures were . . . forced to engage with us in our race of progress . . . All the

natural and human resources were put at our disposal to be transformed in accordance with our sovereign will. . . .

The said 'race of progress' was carried out through science that had become the 'authority figure of modern reason' which was used by 'the executors of the project of modernity . . . to erect . . . a reason-certified hierarchy . . .' (Outlaw, 1994: 28). It seems that the notion of the 'white man's burden' was projected and exercised to such an extent that those placed in the lower level of the said hierarchy, that is, the colonized and the dominated people were compelled by the force of their circumstances to consider the superiority of those dominating them as almost natural. This hierarchical relation, perhaps contributed to the emergence of the belief in the superiority of the latter, and consequently, any thing/idea branded Western, began to be valued. For example, getting a degree of PhD from a 'foreign' (Western) university is more valued in our society. So, the ideas, concepts, etc., used in the social sciences in the universities of Europe and America are perhaps, considered more scientific and therefore worth imitating.

Besides, along with the political evolution of the said hierarchy, the discourse of Orientalism was also created and institutionalized. Edward Said (1979: 3) contends in this context that,

Orientalism can be discussed . . . as the corporate institution for dealing with the Orient—dealing with it by making statements about it, authorizing views of it, describing it, by teaching it, settling it, ruling over it: in short, Orientalism as a Western style for dominating, restructuring and having authority over the orient.

He (1979: 3) further writes that

. . . so authoritative a position did Orientalism have that I believe no one writing, thinking, or acting on the Orient could do so without taking account of the limitations on thought and action imposed by Orientalism . . . because of Orientalism the Orient was not (and is not) a free subject of thought or action.

It seems that the legacy of Orientalism is still prevailing. It influences us implicitly or explicitly to consider Western perspectives, ideas, theoretical approaches, etc., to be more authentic.

It may also be mentioned here, that since the eighteenth century, the value of scientific knowledge began to be 'passionately asserted' (Bershady, 1992: 37–8). Modern sciences gave rise to scientific and industrial technology. This helped European nations in consolidating their rule in the colonized world of Asia and Africa. The intellectuals of the colonized countries, experiencing the performativity of Western scientific industrial technology, also gave primacy to science education. For example, in 1823, when colonial policy regarding education in India had not been finalized, Raja Rammohun Roy wrote a long letter denouncing the traditional system of education and demanding the introduction of Western sciences in Indian education (Sharp, 1920: 99–101). Gradually, as colleges and universities were established under the aegis of colonial power, science education spread and became quite valued. It is not necessary here, to discuss how each of the subjects of study known as the social sciences, came to be recognized as science. What is important to note is that sociology, psychology, etc., all having acquired the image and status of science in the academic centres of the West, also began to be taught and studied in our universities and colleges from the colonial period onwards. Science was (and is still) characterized by generality or universality, that is, its methods, concepts, models, etc., are taken to be universally valid and applicable. So the concepts, perspectives, methodology, etc., of social sciences, developed by and adopted from Western social scientists, are supposed to be quite authentic and scientifically appropriate, and therefore perhaps, Indian sociologists depend on them in order to secure some space for themselves in the mainstream of international (Western) social sciences.

There is another trend that seems to have emerged in the

institutions of the first tier in the recent past. International agencies have begun the practice of providing finance to social scientists and institutions for conducting their (action, evaluation, etc.) projects. Generally, such projects are financially very alluring and therefore it is feared that most of the research time of such social scientists would be spent on those projects. Consequently, conceptual or theoretical research in India is bound to suffer. Social sciences in first tier institutions thus seem to be drifting towards a deep crisis. Besides imitating or borrowing Western ideas and approaches, social scientists, now also tend to depend on Western (international or multinational) agencies (such as the World Bank, Ford Foundation, etc.) for the selection of research issues and areas, guided by the attractive monetary benefits they offer.

SUGGESTIONS

Improvement of the academic milieu of regional/state universities depends largely on how the gap between the two hierarchized university tiers is reduced. This hierarchy emerged as a result of government policy (discussed earlier). So, unless determined political will is applied in this context, and policy makers and educationists make a concerted effort, the environment of the academic universe of regional universities will remain captive to the different kinds of local political interests, machinations and forces. Academic considerations would continue to have a slim chance of getting priority in affairs of higher education. This may be taken to be a pessimistic view. However, drawing on the experience of teaching sociology and doing research for more than three decades in the state of Bihar, the author only contends what is quite obvious.

When it comes to reducing dependence on Western concepts, models and paradigms, the situation is perhaps not quite so desperate. Conceptualization regarding the indigenization of social sciences is coming into the picture. This does not intend to plead for parochialization. Rather, it involves generating knowledge while drawing on the concepts and perspectives of a particular socio-cultural order which can also claim to have universal/general relevance (Mukherji, 2005: 319–20). It may be mentioned that a somewhat similar approach is being considered in the field of Indian history as well (Bhattacharya, 2002: 81–90). Indian sociologists have been discussing the desirable or necessary conditions for the indigenizing of Indian sociology (Mukherji, 2005: 313–20). It may be mentioned here that it is not at all undesirable to use the concepts, approaches, etc., of Western social sciences. It is rather the dependence, or complete dependence on them, that tends to beg the question of the efficacy of the concepts, approaches, etc., developed in the advanced sector of the globe, for understanding and explaining the social reality of a region that is more or less an entirely different socio-cultural universe. Indian society has had a long and different historical experience. It has various culturally distinct zones having different kinds of traditions. So for generating valid sociological knowledge of the Indian social reality, the consideration of Indian standpoints and perspectives in what is known as 'sociological' study, would hopefully contribute, one way or another, to the growth of this discipline at both national and international levels. However, an important question that arises in this context is how to decide what is the appropriate Indian standpoint or perspective.

Taking the example of an individual research initiative, doing fieldwork in both history and philosophy in the beginning, may be considered important. Knowledge of the historical conditions of the region, in the context of the topic of research, in fact, contributes to it. Durkheim held the view that history should be used as a microscope of sociology 'by which structures are discovered, invisible to the unaided eye' (Collins, 1999: 1). Such a history, one may suppose, is field-view history that reveals variations in the conditions of life lived by people, the way(s) in which traditions work, and ideas about the world-views which prevailed in different periods. Besides written records, oral traditions, proverbs, folk tales, etc., should be used in this connection. The importance of the historical perspective for sociological studies had been aptly considered by the pioneers of Indian sociology such as A. Coomaraswamy, B.N. Seal, B.K. Sarkar, G.S. Ghurye, Radha Kamal Mukherjee, D.P. Mukherji, and others (Mukherjee, 1977: 41–2). D.P. Mukherji made a significantly bold appeal for the study of social traditions. Considering the historicity of traditions, he said

> Sociologists should take courage in both hands and openly say that the study of the Indian social system . . . requires a different approach to sociology because of its special traditions, its special symbols, and its special patterns of culture. . . . (Mukherji, 1955: 15)

The historical approach helps in getting a comprehensive understanding of the situation—an understanding of the totality of the variations in space and time.

Besides, fieldwork in Indian philosophical schools is perhaps also required in the context of indigenization. The era of the virtual monopoly of empiricism in the field of sociological research, according to which 'the original source of all our information about the world is sense' (Wright, 1965: 140), seems to have undergone a transition to a phase when the value of diverse epistemological positions is well recognized. One finds today, that along with the practice of quantitative research (depending chiefly on a positivist/empiricist epistemological position), the prevalence of qualitative research, which draws on diverse epistemological bases such as those of the hermeneutic tradition, ethno-methodology, critical school, etc. (Hesse-Biber and Leavy, 2004: 4–5). Under the circumstances, it is not out of place to consider the question of the relevance of Indian theories of knowledge to sociological research.

In an epistemological tradition, its core relates to the theory or theories of 'evidence, justification, or truth determination'

(Goldman, 1999: 41). The theory of 'evidence, justification, or truth determination' varies from one epistemological tradition to another. Indian theories of knowledge also deal with such issues and are found to be centred around *pramana* (evidence), the means of knowledge (Perrett, 2001: XIII). For example, the Charvaka school admitted only 'perception' as a valid means of knowledge; Vaisheshika philosophy and Buddhists admitted 'perception' and 'inference' as *pramanas*; in Nyaya philosophy, 'perception', 'inference', 'analogy' and 'testimony' are considered valid means of knowledge; Sankhya Darshan recognizes only 'perception', 'inference' and 'testimony' in this context. It is not possible to describe the epistemology of each of the philosophical schools of India. However, the relevance of Sankhya epistemology to the methodology of empirical research (in sociology) has been discussed elsewhere by the present author (Jha, 2008: 73–80). The contribution of ancient Indian philosophies to knowledge in the areas of grammar, phonology, psychology, anthropology, etc., is widely recognized (Larson, 2000: 223). Considering perhaps this background of Indian philosophies, and on the basis of his own studies of Western and Indian philosophical theories, Roy W. Perrett (2001: XIII) holds the view that Western epistemology and Indian *pramana* theory have enough in common to warrant communication between them. So *pramana* theories deserve to be examined in terms of the feasibility of the incorporation of their points of view in the methodology of sociological research. Indigenization of sociology in this context would probably contribute to its universality as well.

REFERENCES

Abraham, A.S. (1984), 'Chancellor as Supremo, Maharashtra University in Peril', in *The Times of India* (New Delhi edition), 28 September.

Ahuja, R. (1967), 'Problems of Teaching Sociology with Special Reference to Rajasthan', in T.K.N. Unnithan et al. (eds.), *Sociology for India*, New Delhi: Prentice-Hall.

Bershady, H.J. (ed.) (1992), *Max Scheler: On Feeling, Knowing and Valuing*, Chicago: The University of Chicago Press.

Beteille, A. (1974), *Studies in Agrarian Social Structure*, New Delhi: Oxford University Press.

Bhattacharya, S. (2001), 'Reflections on the Concept of Regional History' in H. Jha (ed.), *Perspectives on Indian Society and History: A Critique*, New Delhi: Manohar.

Bourdieu, P. (1990), *In Other Words: Essays Toward a Reflective Sociology* (English translation by Mathew Adamson), Palo Alto: Stanford University Press.

Collins, R. (1999), *Macrohistory*, Palo Alto: Stanford University Press.

Deb, K. (1998), 'Teaching Sociology in a Regional University', in *Sociological Bulletin*, 47 (2).

Goldman, A.I. (1999), *Knowledge in a Social World*, Oxford: Clarendon Press.

Gould, H. (1972), 'Educational Structures and Political Processes in Faizabad District, Uttar Pradesh', in S.H. Rudolph and L.I. Rudolph (eds.), *Education and Politics in India*, New Delhi: Oxford University Press.

Gray, J. (1986), *Liberalism*, Minneapolis: University of Minnesota Press.

Guha, R.C. (2009), '*Jaat Na Poochho Kulapati Ki*' (in Hindi), in *Hindustan* (Patna edition), 4 September.

Hagen, J.R. (1981), 'Indigenous Society: The Political Economy and Colonial Education in Patna District: A History of Social Change from 1811 to 1951 in Gangetic North India', Virginia: University-Microfilms International.

Hesse-Biber, S.N. and P. Leavy (eds.) (2004), 'Introduction', *Approaches to Qualitative Research*, New York: Oxford University Press.

Jayaram, N. (1998), 'Challenges to Indian Sociology', in *Sociological Bulletin*, 47 (2).

Jha, H. (2005), 'Indian Sociology in Crisis: The Need for Regional Orientation', in *Sociological Bulletin*, 54 (3).

——— (2008), 'Sankhya Philosophy and Empirical Research', in Anirudha Prasad et al. (eds.), *Social Research Methodologies in Action*, Ranchi: Xavier Institute of Social Service.

John, V.V. (1976), 'Too Many Colleges: A Way to Waste Public Funds', in *The Times of India* (New Delhi edition), 21 September.

Kumar, K. (1985), 'Little Research in Universities', in *The Times of India* (New Delhi edition), 25 February.

Larson, G.J. (2000), 'An Eccentric Ghost in the Machine: Formal and Quantitative aspects of the Sankhya-Yoga Dualism', in R.W. Perrett (ed.), *Metaphysics*, New York: Garland Publishing Inc.

Mukherji, D.P. (1955), 'Indian Traditions and Social Change', in T.K. Oommen and P.N. Mukherji (eds.) (1986), *Indian Sociology: Reflections and Introspections*, Bombay: Popular Prakashan.

Mukherji, P.N. (2005), 'Sociology in South Asia: Indigenisation as Universalising Social Science', in *Sociological Bulletin*, 54 (3).

Mukherjee, R. (1977), 'Trends in Indian Sociology', in *Current Sociology*, 25 (3).

Outlaw, L. (1994), 'Lifeworlds, Modernity, and Philosophical Praxis: Race, Ethnicity and Critical Social Theory', in E. Deutsch (ed.), *Culture and Modernity: East-West Philosophic Perspectives*, Delhi: Motilal Banarsidass.

Perrett, R.W. (ed.) (2001), 'Introduction', *Indian Philosophy, Epistemology*, New York and London: Garland Publishing Inc.

Redner, H. (1982), *In the Beginning Was the Deed: Reflections on the Passage of Faust*, Berkeley: University of California Press, quoted in Z. Bauman (1992), *Intimations of Postmodernity*, London: Routledge: XXVI–XXVII.

Report (1985), 'Exams in Bihar Merely a Farce', in *The Times of India* (New Delhi edition), 21 April.

Rudolph, S.H. and L.I. Rudolph (eds.) (1972), *Education and Politics in India*, New Delhi: Oxford University Press.

Said, E.W. (1979), *Orientalism*, New York: Vintage Books.

Sawney, I. (1984), 'Inroads into Academe', in *The Times of India* (New Delhi edition), 24 July.

Sharma, K.N. (2000), 'Comments on Viewpoints', *Sociological Bulletin*, 49 (1).

Sharp, H. (ed.) (1920), *Selections from Educational Records*, Part 1, Calcutta: Government Printing Press.

Seidman, S. (1996), *Contested Knowledge: Social Theory in the Postmodern Era*, Cambridge and Massachusetts: Blackwell Publishers Inc.

Tilak, J.B.G. (2007), 'Education: A Saga of Spectacular Achievements and Conspicuous Failures', *India: Social Development Report*, New Delhi: Oxford University Press.

University Grants Commission (UGC) (1978), *Third All-India Educational Survey, Higher Education*, New Delhi.

——— (1979), *Report on the Status of Teaching of Sociology and Social Anthropology*, New Delhi.

Wright, W.K. (1965), *A History of Modern Philosophy*, New York: The Macmillan Company.

CHAPTER 6

Academic Dependency and Sociological Theorizing in the Third World: The Case of Akiwowo's *Asuwada* Theory of Sociation[1]

AYOKUNLE OLUMUYIWA OMOBOWALE

INTRODUCTION

Theorizing is a vital part of Sociology as an academic discipline. Just like most other professions taught in Nigerian universities, Sociology has its roots in Western civilization, even though its theories and empirical findings have implication for societies across the globe. The main focus of sociology is the empirical study of group behaviour and culture by understanding the norms, values and expectations which determine and guide intra- and inter-group interactions. Just like the natural sciences, Sociology has theories, which guide researchers in data collection and empirical explanation of findings (some of these theories are discussed later in this introductory section). Most of these theories are, however, Western-oriented and may not be able to adequately capture and understand the African ways of life; often described as primitive in Western scholarship. The focus of this paper in general is the fate of social theories Third World scholars have attempted to propound into global scholarship; with a special case study of Akiwowo's *Asuwada* Theory of Sociation.

Professor Akiwowo propounded the *Asuwada* Theory of

Sociation in the early 1980s, with the aim of providing a relevant indigenous/African sociological explanation for the African ways of life often described as primitive and/or substandard in Western scholarship. The theory is based on indigenous Yoruba social thought that captures the normative essence/expectations in social interactions, especially among the Yoruba and other so-called traditional societies in Africa. In spite of its intellectual worth, it is not popular in Nigerian universities. Also, Nigerian scholars hardly ever propound alternative theories. This is an indication of academic dependency which somewhat subordinates African scholarship not only in the international realm but even locally in Africa, as Western ideologies are prioritized and clothed with superiority, preventing the propounding of an alternative irrespective of their shortcomings. Rather, any alternative that may be acceptable as scholarly must necessarily originate outside the continent and preferably from the northern hemisphere or 'the West'.

Indeed, academic dependency describes a disadvantaged placement in the global scholarly community. More often than not, this disadvantage is usually associated with Third World countries of the southern hemisphere whose contemporary civilization(s) have been influenced by developed (Western) countries, most especially since colonization. Nonetheless, it is important to note that formalized academic endeavours did not originate solely from the West. Records show that formalized training/academic endeavours were commonplace in Asia (especially in China, India, Japan and Arab nations) (Numata, 2003; Rao, 2001; and Hu, 1984) and Africa (for example in Egypt, Timbuktu in present-day Mali) (Wikipedia, 2007; Timbuktu Educational Foundation, 2002; Bentley, 1996; Cummings, 1986; Brenner and Robinson, 1980; Kinsey, 1971) and to some extent among Ifa priests and trainees amongst the Yoruba of present-day South-Western Nigeria, prior to colonization. Western-oriented academe has, however, become the standard in most of the Third World, especially in contemporary times.

In Nigeria, the advent of colonialism also advanced the exposure of Nigerians to academic activities—initially at the primary and secondary levels through the activities of Western missionaries. It reached a peak with the establishment of the University College, Ibadan[2] in 1948, as an affiliate of the University of London. The teaching of Sociology as a distinct discipline consequently commenced in Nigeria (at the University College, Ibadan) in the 1950s and thenceforth assumed a departmental status in the 1960s through the contributions of Western and Nigerian scholars trained in Western citadels of learning. Some of these scholars include Professors Peter Lloyd, Francis Olu Okediji, Albert Imohiosen, Ulf Himmelstrand and Ruth Murray (Rotimi, 2006; Faculty of the Social Sciences, 2005–6; Ekpo, 1995).

Sociology emerged in the nineteenth century through the contributions of August Comte who sought to understand social disorder brought about by the French Revolution. He is credited as the one who gave the discipline its name; first as social physics and later sociology (Pickering, 1993, 1989). Sociology has subsequently advanced and developed through the theoretical postulations and contributions of scholars such as Durkheim, Marx, Weber, Parsons, Merton and Garfinkel among other Western sociological theorists.

It is important to note that the basic fulcrum in the works of these sociologists is their theoretical postulations, which seek to explain, account for and give meaning to social relations. This is a tradition that has been borrowed from the natural sciences, with standardized theories for the explanation of natural phenomena. Thus, in seeking to utilize the positivistic methodology of the natural sciences, sociology as a discipline too, has adopted theories aimed at explaining human/social behaviour. Unlike the natural sciences, however, it is inundated with many theories which seek to explain from different and sometimes divergent/conflicting perspectives.

Sociological theories could be broadly divided into two, viz., the macro/structural theories and micro/social action theories. Structural theories attempt to explain social behaviour by viewing society as a whole. Structural theories include functionalism and conflict perspectives. Functionalism views society as a complex whole, whose different parts have to work together for the normal functioning of the whole. Theorists with such postulations include Durkheim and Parsons among others (Wagenaar, 2004; Trevino, 2003; Black, 2000; Charmaz, 2000; Turner, 1998). On the other hand, conflict perspective is mostly associated with the writings of Karl Marx who posited that society is dialectically separated between the owners (bourgeois) and non-owners (proletariat) of the means of production. The non-owners sell their labour to the owners who exploit them through the appropriation of the surplus value produced by the proletariat. This situation is thought normal as the proletariat remains in a state of false consciousness due to the socialization process and the workings of the ideological apparatuses of the bourgeois class, which present exploitative tendencies as normal. For Marx, the exploitation will subsist unless the proletariat class gains consciousness and engages the bourgeois class in a revolution that will change the *status quo* (Ritzer, 1996; Giddens, 1971).

Social action theories base their explanations on the individual. They are more concerned with the meanings individuals attach to social phenomenon. It is from such meanings that social/individual actions could be interpreted and/or explained. Examples of such theories include Weber's Social Action Theory, Symbolic Interactionism, Phenomenology and Ethno-methodology (Ritzer, 1996; Giddens, 1971).

Indeed, the study of sociology is not complete without introducing and actually teaching students these theories. Inasmuch as they have their roots in Western societies, they take central positions in academic sociological thought; hence making the Third World/Nigerian sociological curriculum dependent on the Western syllabus. This is in spite of their seeming inadequacies, especially in terms of explaining contextual social phenomenon in non-Western societies. As stated earlier, Professor Akiwowo attempted to address this anomaly through his *Asuwada* Theory of Sociation. As much as the theory remains extant, it is hardly taught by scholars in institutions of higher learning in Nigeria. This study, therefore examines, academic dependency and sociological theorizing in Nigeria with a view of probing its possible impact on the acceptance of the *Asuwada* Theory of Sociation.

Both secondary and primary data were collected for the study, from Nigerian universities located in the Yoruba dominated South-Western Geo-Political Zone. Universities in the South-Western Geo-Political Zone were purposely selected because the *Asuwada* Theory is a derivative of indigenous Yoruba social thought directed at explaining social relations among the Yoruba. Hence, since Nigerian universities are divided into three main categories, viz., the federal, state, and privately owned, at least two universities were selected from each category. However, Obafemi Awolowo University, Ile-Ife (OAU) (federal) was purposely chosen because it was the base of Professor Akiwowo. Other universities were randomly selected using the ballot technique. The other universities selected were the University of Ibadan, Ibadan (UI) (federal), Olabisi Onabanjo University, Ago-Iwoye (OOU) (state) and Lagos State University, Ojo (LASU) (state). Likewise, two private universities including Redeemers' University, Mowe (RU) and Bowen University, Iwo (BU) were also selected randomly. In the universities selected, secondary data was collected through the assessment of the sociological theory curriculum and course outline, while primary data was collected in the form of oral interviews with lecturers teaching sociological theory in the selected universities. Likewise, oral interviews were conducted with final year and postgraduate students of the universities. In addition, an interview was also conducted with Professor Onoge,[3] a renowned Nigerian sociologist of international repute, during a chance meeting at the National Conference of the Nigerian Anthropological and Sociological Association (NASA), held on 26 and 27 September 2007. A total of 14 interviews were conducted with the aid of a specially designed interview guide and finally the data was subjected to content analysis.

ACADEMIC DEPENDENCY AND SOCIOLOGICAL THEORIZING IN NIGERIA

Admittedly, the discipline of sociology as it is in contemporary times emerged from Europe. This is not to say, however, that particular individuals had not been theorizing about their societies prior to the evolvement of sociology as a distinct discipline. Exemplary instances include the pioneering works of Ibn Khaldun who theorized about his Arabian/North African society in the fifteenth century (Hamdani, 2000; Weiss, 1995; Otite and Ogionwo 1979). Likewise, reliving his experience as a graduate student in the United States of America in 1970, Professor Onoge stated:

> As a graduate student at Harvard University, we had a seminar where Sorokin[4] was asked to speak. For about 90 per cent of the period, he referred to Asian sociologists. It was only at the tail end he spoke about the Europeans. This is just to say there are others. . . . People had always been talking about their societies even before European sociologists emerged. I hold the view that all humans theorize about their societies. . . .
>
> Oral interview with Professor Onoge (27 September 2007)

Nevertheless, since Sociology got its contemporary nomenclature, form and standardization from Europe, emphasis has often been laid on the study and teaching of Western theories[5] in academic institutions in Nigeria. Indeed, Sociology has developed within the last two centuries through the works of Western scholars who have not only standardized its theoretical and methodological applications, but have also popularized and exported it to other non-Western nations (both colonized and un-colonized) in Africa, Asia and Latin America (Alatas and Sinha, 2001). Thus, their efforts at giving theoretical postulations about the internal workings of societies deserve commendation. It has come to a point where sociology would be understood to lose its fineness and currency if the contributions of these scholars were to be ignored. Hence, the sociological curriculum and scholars remain dependent on theories which emanated from the West. This is against Dennis (Dennis, 1974: 83) submission and recommendation made as far back as 1974:

> Sociological theories are constructed in an attempt to understand society. The development of sociology in nineteenth-century Europe is explicable in terms of the disruption of the social order of Europe as a consequence of industrialization. It was therefore an attempt to do systematically what people in general and sociology students in particular wish to do—to make sense of their own society. But the nineteenth-century sociologists were trying to understand industrial capitalist society. The history of sociological thought must examine the work of these theorists within this context. It is necessary to do this in order to analyse the relevance of these theories, or their non-relevance for the post-colonial or neo-colonial world. This world, which includes Nigeria, was transformed by the impact of industrial capitalism. It transformed the social structure and the whole system of values of these societies. But to try to understand post-colonial societies through the perspective of nineteenth-century European or twentieth-century American social theory is, as it were, to look at them down the wrong end of a telescope. If theories were studied in order to apply them to Nigerian society, there would be little point in studying theorists who were concerned to explain a very different kind of society. But they can be extremely useful if one studies them in order, by critical analysis, to determine what ought to be the elements of an adequate explanation of society, which is the first step towards the construction of a theoretical explanation of one's own.

This position was first presented by Dennis in 1971 at the maiden session of the NASA Conference held at Ahmadu Bello University, Zaria, Nigeria, where Akinsola Akiwowo as president indicated the need for NASA '. . . to consider the direction we as social scientists are going in Nigeria, to review our course offerings, and to assess the relevance or irrelevance of their content to a deep understanding of our society' (Akiwowo, 1974: 4). More than three decades after the clamour for a contextual sociological theoretical postulation was made, data show little has been achieved in this respect. Thus in the words of a respondent:

> The truth of the matter is this, when you consider the theories taught and used, you will discover they are Western theories. We cannot claim these theories came from Nigeria or Africa and neither can we claim they are irrelevant, though they may be inadequate; due to cultural differences. However, there is no way we can isolate ourselves from Western sociological theories because the discipline of sociology came from there.
>
> Oral interview with Lecturer of a State University (26 September 2007)

Yet, another informant stated:

> The theories that are taught are largely those that came from outside. They seem to have preconceived ideas about what is happening locally. Many times they may not be valid. However, very little comes locally in terms of sociological theory development.
>
> Oral interview with Lecturer of a Private University (15 September 2007)

Still another interviewee stated that

> . . . we depend on Western scholars because we do not have enough indigenous scholars publishing even in Nigeria. . . . This is just because we depend on foreign ideas. In our libraries, all you will see are foreign books.
>
> Oral interview with a Lecturer of a State University (18 September 2007)

As for Professor Onoge:

> Of necessity, since they were the first to write, they were the classical founders, we use their languages; we cannot refuse the contributions of those people. For example, I was influenced by Karl Marx and Max Weber, but when people like Frantz Fanon came out, their thoughts were incorporated in my teachings. Likewise I incorporated

the works of Soyinka and Claude Ake and other African writers. I even started a course; sociology of literature in Ibadan.[6] . . . You cannot limit yourself to sociological texts alone. There are others which are also about sociology and society.

Oral interview with Professor Onoge
(27 September 2007)

The interviewees above buttressed the indispensability of Western sociological theories in sociological scholarship and discourse in Nigeria. They have given the discipline its direction ever since its introduction into the global academy and both scholars and students in Nigeria are more familiar with them. Inasmuch as many of the respondents indicated the contextual inadequacies of these theories in appositely explaining local social relations, they are still forced to use them in the seeming absence of indigenous alternatives. Indeed whereas Professor Onoge[7] indicated that he taught aspects of African sociological thought by incorporating the ideas of African scholars such as Wole Soyinka and Claude Ake while Dr. Alliyu[8] of Olabisi Onabanjo University likewise stated that he had continually taught the social thoughts of the Late Fela Anikulapo Kuti in his sociological theory class, the ideas of these individuals who may be taken as social thinkers are yet to be consciously developed into standardized theoretical postulations to be accepted by the Nigerian sociological community and universally incorporated into the Nigerian sociological curriculum. The inability and/or failure to standardize indigenous social thoughts into theoretical postulation for the explanation of contextual social relations in Nigeria, may not be unconnected with the dependent nature of the scholarship in Nigeria, which looks up to Western 'assessors' for the acceptance of its scholarship. Hence a respondent stated:

There is no gainsaying the fact that academic dependency is, perhaps, an expected phenomenon in a dependent nation. School curricula, therefore, would almost always, reflect the national situation. Indeed, I would say there has not been any sociological theorizing in Nigeria, not just because of this dependency syndrome but also because of lack of curricula synergy amongst academics and neither have there been enough conferences where ideas are shared or disseminated. . . .

Oral interview with Lecturer of Federal University (11 September 2007)

The interviewee's expression above succinctly presents the state of contextualized sociological theorizing in Nigeria. The dependent nature of the curricula has stifled attempts made at indigenous theoretical postulations, such that Western sociological theories retain the pride of place in the often disadvantaged assessment of African societies. This, Ake (1979) subsumed within the labyrinth of imperialism in a classic book he titled *Social Science as Imperialism*. . . . For Ake, '. . . sociology scholarship on Third World countries . . .' is imperialistic because it relegates Third World values as substandard and thus inferior to Western values, with the expectation that Third World societies have to adopt Western values in order to attain development. In an attempt to channel a course for a better understanding of social relations in Africa in general and amongst the Yoruba of South-Western Nigeria in particular, Akiwowo propounded the *Asuwada* Theory of Sociation in the early 1980s. This we now turn to.

ACADEMIC DEPENDENCY AND AKIWOWO'S *ASUWADA* THEORY OF SOCIATION

As earlier stated, Akiwowo's attempt was an effort directed at correcting the seeming inadequacies of Western theories by propounding a theory based on Yoruba social thought. His *Asuwada* postulations were derived from *Ifa* epistemology. According to Akiwowo, the *Asuwada* oratory was usually chanted among the Yoruba when a new settlement was to be established. It is basically on the importance of sociation/association of human existence and development (Akiwowo, 1986a and b). Broadly, Akiwowo (1986a: 353) described his preposition using nine postulations including:

1. The unity of social life is the individual's life, being, existence, or character.
2. Although each human being is metaphysically a unique emanation of a Divine Being, yet each individual's life, as a corporeal self, needs the fellowship of other corporeal selves to feel whole and be complete.
3. The corporeal individual essentially, cannot continue-in-being without a community.
4. Since the social life of a group of individual beings is sustained by a spirit of solidarity, any form of self-alienation for the purely selfish aim is, morally speaking, an error or sin.
5. A good society, in an axiological sense, is one which recognizes the uniqueness of each life's authentic nature and its right to self-expression and self-actualization.
6. A genuine social being is one who works daily, and sacrifices willingly, in varying ways, his or her cherished freedom and material acquisitions for self-improvement as well as for the common good. For without one, the other cannot be achieved.
7. Every individual, as may be observed within the diverse contexts of social life in Africa, is capable of being an initiator or a recipient of true (good) or erroneous (bad) conduct.
8. The social worth of an individual within his or her community can be measured by the qualitative value of the differential between types of conduct he or she has initiated or received.
9. A social scientist in the Nigerian universities who studies with a view to acquiring an understanding of people and society in Africa and to planning effectively to develop the quality of life in both Westernized and traditional communities may find that he or she needs to work with this derived conceptual scheme of *iwa*, *ihuwasi*, *isesi* and *ajumose* as these apply to a single actor or to a plurality of actors in the community's social life.

Hence, embedded in Akiwowo's theoretical postulation are notions of the recognized individuality of a person or being whose existence only becomes meaningful through association and working for common or social good through his conduct (this is obviously somewhat repeatedly reflected in postulations one to eight). Thus, every individual is an *asuwa* (physiological being) who has the capability of becoming an *asuwada* (social being), as any individual who refuses to associate/sociate becomes an *aisuwa* (self-alienation/deviant) which may possibly wreck the individual and/or the society (Lawuyi and Taiwo, 1990; Makinde, 1988).

Of course, Akiwowo's attempt at an emic sociological paradigm (Payne, 1992) could be described as a noble pioneering effort from an indigenous scholar. Nevertheless, his theoretical construction within the precincts of spiritism/spirituality creates inhibiting barriers against its use for scholarly/empirical research. Indeed, the spiritist construction of *Asuwada* principle/oration among the indigenous/aboriginal people may have been due to the need to create notions of sacredness around social values intended for social survival (cf. Durkheim, 1976). It is, however, the responsibility of the scholar to appositely decipher indigenous social thoughts and bring out the meanings which can be subjected to empirical scrutiny. Thus, beyond the spiritualist claims of the *Asuwada* postulation, more emphasis should be put on its potential as an 'epistemic opening' in the world of sociological imagination/theorizing (Adesina, 2002), for the purpose of understanding African indigenous culture/social relations which is often described as primitive in Western scholarship and theoretical postulations (cf. Welz, 2009; Connell, 2006).

From here on we focus on the concepts of *iwa*, *ihuwasi*, *isesi* and *ajumose*, which Akiwowo posits should be the focus of social researchers in Africa; but to which he did not provide further elaboration in consulted texts. For the Yoruba, the biological and social construction of *iwa* is a prime factor in social relations, harmony and development. *Iwa* is therefore viewed from two focal points. There is *iwa* (being/existence) and *iwa* (character). Inasmuch as a person has to exist (*iwa*) in order to actively engage in social relations, he would be able to do so normatively, only if he has socially acceptable character (*iwa*). Hence, this term with two mutually engaging conceptual meanings goes a long way in defining and determining a person's place within the Yoruba social structure. Thus, at the birth of an individual, the social environment (including significant others, i.e. parents and all others who may responsibly socialize the child), strives to socially construct/ socialize the individual into an *Omoluabi*. The meaning of *Omoluabi* is a responsible person with a socially acceptable character (Akinyemi, 2003; Makinde, 1988; Awoniyi, 1975). A person considered to be an *Omoluabi* is someone who has *iwa rere* (good character) while a social deviant is one who has not internalized socially acceptable norms and values, fails to *suwada* (appropriately sociate) and thus is said to be an *Omoburuku* (a deviant) because of his *iwa buruku* (bad character). Thus, even though the construction of a person's being may predate the formation of his character, which (i.e. character) inevitably lasts a lifetime, the latter, however (i.e. *iwa*-character), informs the social perception of being/existence as an *Omoluabi* (good personality) or *Omoburuku* (bad personality). Hence a Yoruba proverb says *iwa ni yoo fi on'iwa han*, meaning; a person's character will reveal him (Omobowale, 2008).

Closely associated with the concept of *iwa* are *ihuwasi* and *isesi*. Whereas *ihuwasi* refers to acts of expression of character, *isesi* refers to habitual expressions of character. Thus, since the indigenous communal culture favours mutual association for social survival, the appropriate internalization of values associated with *iwa, ihuwasi* and *isesi* will bring out individuals who will be ready to work in unison (*ajumose*) for social survival.

It is the position of this paper that an empirical utilization of this theory may explain elements of the indigenous social structure favouring communalism and kin dependence for example; which has somewhat survived from pre-colonial times to the contemporary era. The question which deserves an answer, however, is its relevance for Nigeria's sociological/ academic community. A respondent posited that:

> *Asuwada* theory is very relevant in sociological discourse, but not relevant in Departments of Sociology in Nigeria. Lecturers hardly know about Akiwowo, not to talk about his theory. If we pick Akiwowo's work and build it beyond its originality, we might actually get to a stage where we will build his theory to the level of empirical practicality, just as it was done for sociologists such as Weber and Marx. This is because it explains particular African situations that European theories cannot explain. . . . However, I do not teach Akiwowo's theory. It is not in my curriculum. . . .
>
> Oral interview with Lecturer of a State University (18 September 2007)

Yet another respondent stated:

> Concerning its relevance, I would say no idea is irrelevant. Nonetheless, my view concerning his theory is its high level of abstraction with direct application for human societies. In other words, even though the *Asuwada* principle may be said to have been abstracted from Yoruba ethnology, there are, to me, better African, perhaps, sociological theories of sociation-found in proverbs—that are more applicable both to African and world societies. The *Ifa* oracle [i.e. the introduction of *ifa* epistemology to academic discourse]—a product of the Obafemi Awolowo University, Ile-Ife axis of Yoruba studies, to me, should be seen as only a mere representation of the understanding of Nigerian sociation. What may have been added to knowledge is the 'grounding' of myths often attached to indigenous religion but such myths are, themselves, representations, or if you like, 'images' of socio-economic circumstances of the Nigerian society which, as you know, has undergone fundamental changes. Thus, we need to know how the sociation theory has been affected by this change. . . . Specifically I do not teach it because of the above reasons, but, more importantly because I think it is limited or without sounding condescending, myopic.
>
> Oral interview with Lecturer of a Federal University (11 September 2007)

Still another respondent stated:

> It is very relevant. However, the way it is now, it has to be taught with other things like sociological concepts in Africa. It cannot be taught in isolation. If we do that, some of the concepts like *iwa* and *omoluabi* among others may be further developed into theories. . . . No, we do not teach *Asuwada* theory in my University. This is because it was not developed beyond Akiwowo. That is why it is not taught anywhere. Right now, I teach symbolic interactionism, conflict theory, etc. These are all European theories. None is Nigerian. Theorizing has become a luxury in Nigeria. It is when you do not have to worry about how to buy a car, build a house . . . , or work on two or three jobs, as an academic, that you can sit down to theorize. And not when you are struggling to survive and feed your family. As you know, academics are poorly paid in Nigeria. So it is easy to pick up my book and teach theories therein instead of theorizing. The deplorable socio-economic environment has robbed us of intellectual engagements.
>
> Oral interview with Lecturer of a Federal University (8 October 2007)

The responses of students interviewed simply confirmed what the lecturers had said that Akiwowo's theory is not taught. Accordingly a postgraduate student stated:

> We were taught many Western sociological theories such as Marxism, functionalism, social action, etc. We were not taught any African sociological theory however. I heard about Akiwowo's theory during a personal discussion with a colleague in Anthropology and not in a class session.
>
> Oral interview with postgraduate student of a Federal University (19 September 2007)

Still, another student stated:

> We were principally taught Western sociological theories. The lecturer only mentioned Akiwowo in passing when out of curiosity we asked him whether those Western theories he taught us were universally applicable to local situations; giving the differing socio-cultural environments. It was then that he mentioned Akiwowo as someone

who has tried to propound an African sociological theory. He did not teach it.

Oral interview with postgraduate student of a Federal University (13 October 2007)

From the responses of these interviewees, it appears that there is a general acceptance of the relevance of Akiwowo's theory in sociological postulation in Nigeria. It remains largely obscured, however, because attempts are not being made to further develop and standardize it for empirical utilization and verification. Moreover, academics who claim the theory is very much relevant also maintained that they leave it out of the curriculum while Western sociological theories are taught. This is at variance with the pioneering Indian experience where attempts at indigenization of sociology started as far back as 1917 (Patel, 2008). The challenge the phenomenal Indian attempt has, however, been facing is particularly associated with disparity in central and regional universities. Whereas the central universities have access to better finance and resources, utilize English as medium of classroom communication and teach more of Western theories, regional universities are short of resources, utilize regional languages and teach more local examples. The regional universities are unfortunately, placed at a disadvantage in institutional hierarchy, which favours the Western-oriented central universities (Welz, 2009; Patel, 2002). Whereas Welz justifies the lower prestige accorded to the regional universities due to the quality of academic resources they have access to and produce, it is important to note, however, that their ability to reduce foreign scholarly and theoretical orientations to vernacular interpretations is itself an astounding scholarly achievement, which must be overtly acknowledged and applauded. The disadvantaged positions they occupy should not be seen as merely a reflection of their standards. Rather just as in other colonized territories where indigenous knowledge is reduced to inferiority, Indian regional universities attract the conceptions of the inferior even when they strive to contribute to knowledge utilizing the resources they have access to, because of the conception of superiority attached to Western ideas and establishments. Nonetheless, rather than seeing regional universities as inferior, it is necessary for regulatory agencies to provide the necessary wherewithal and institutionalize standards that will appositely accommodate both central and regional universities with a view to ensuring a basic standard for quality control in knowledge production and dissemination. And thus, the Indian sociology project will be achievable not only in India but it will be transmitted to other parts of the world, just as the case of Indian Engineering and Economics, whose books and other publications are getting increasingly popular among scholars and students in Nigeria as against Western texts, which hitherto held exclusive sway in both fields. That Indian tertiary educational institutions are able to indigenize, i.e. translating scholarly concepts, ideas and theories to local languages, is a phenomenal achievement that is worthy of emulation by African institutions of higher learning.

In the case of Nigeria, English is the language of classroom communication in all institutions of higher learning. This is a direct result of the nation's experience with colonialism. After independence, Nigeria has found it difficult to introduce any of the indigenous languages as *lingua franca*. This is because of the deep ethnic schism, which dates back to the colonial period. Thus, an attempt to adopt one language as a *lingua franca* will be considered an attempt at domination by other ethnic groups. This reflection of the ethnic divide that was the bedrock of colonial administration in Nigeria has thus outlived colonialism such that English remains the main official language of communication at the national level, in formal institutions and amongst individuals of different ethnic groups (who do not understand each other or one another's languages) in Nigeria. This partly further explains the non-inclusion of Akiwowo's theory in sociology curriculum and unpopularity among scholars who are supposed to further verify or falsify it through empirical research. Akiwowo's theory has intricate vernacular concepts with a strong leaning on Yoruba tradition and custom. Thus, teaching Akiwowo would mean exploring the theory's vernacular concepts for a deep and elaborate explanation in the English language, for a non-Yoruba audience. As much as such an attempt will be credible, the deplorable Nigerian socio-economic context, ethnic schism and even loss of touch with the local vernacular by scholars who are trained in the English language do not readily encourage such unfinanced ground breaking and elaborate research by poorly paid academic professionals.

Besides, Nigerian scholars hardly publish texts on sociological theory. And so, most sociology lecturers and students are exposed to foreign texts that emphasize only Western theories. Hence, since lecturers depend on foreign texts, they continually teach only foreign theories without giving relevant consideration to Akiwowo or attempting to provide alternatives. This is because, what is taken as the primary objective of teaching sociological theory, is exposing students to pioneering sociological theorists and the advances that have been made thenceforth by Western theorists still involved in the development of the discipline. Thus whereas recent Western sociological theories such as Anthony Giddens' Structuration theory, Habermas' Conflict theory and Ritzer's theory of MacDonaldization are read in Western texts and taught, exploring and teaching Akiwowo's theory is an enterprise of secondary importance because it is demeaned or considered inferior because of its dependence on vernacular concepts, which are yet to be internationalized unlike the theories which have been written in the language of the colonial masters and transmitted round the world as authenticated (universal) theoretical paradigms. Of course, what is vernacular to local Western audiences transforms into internationality and general acceptance among scholars in colonized territories; Nigeria inclusive.

This explains the primacy of Western theories even when they are found to be inadequate in local situations. Thus, any attempt to develop and/or apply Akiwowo's theory in sociological discourse and/or research in Nigeria is portrayed as having little value at present, keeping in mind the plethora of already supposedly standardized Western theories that can be easily found in sociological texts. Since Akiwowo's theory is not subjected to further development and empirical validation, it is viewed as abstract in spite of its relevance. Thus, Akiwowo's *Asuwada* Theory of Sociation remains in the doldrums in Nigeria's academic/sociological circles; while Western theories take the centrestage. The acceptance, development and spread of the theory may have of course, been adversely affected by its location since it emerged from the Third World and in this case Nigeria, which is still academically dependent on the West for the evaluation and standardization of its academy. For as long as this unequal relationship persists, Akiwowo's theory may remain in the doldrums with a possibility of an eventual recession into total irrelevance and obscurity—even in Nigeria—as the generation of academics with relative knowledge of it, gradually passes away. This is because irrespective of the perceived or actual relevance and/or potentials of a viable knowledge, if it is not transmitted via teaching, it may die out one day. Such was and is the case of undocumented African herbal/pharmaceutical knowledge which is continually and increasingly dying out with herbal practitioners who are in a sense Africa's encyclopaedia of herbs.

CONCLUSION

Conclusively, inasmuch as Akiwowo attempted providing an African sociological-theoretical perspective to the understanding of contextual social relations in Africa, his theory has remained largely obscured in Nigeria's academic environment. This is not unconnected to the preference for Western sociological theories even among scholars who accept the relevance of Akiwowo's theory to sociological applications in Nigeria. This is a classic evidence of the disadvantaged position of African scholarship *vis-à-vis* Western scholarship, not only in the perspective of Westerners, but even among indigenous scholars in Nigerian universities. For as long as this persists, it may be difficult for Africa to channel an independent course to development from its local experience, as it remains dependent on the West in an ever increasingly globalizing World, where the West has remained dominant at the expense of Third World nations.

NOTES

1. An earlier version of this paper was presented at the 'Coping with Academic Dependency: How?' Workshop, Patna, India, 4–7 February 2008. The author appreciates all who made comments, which have further improved the quality of the paper. Special thanks to Professor Onoge and other academicians who were interviewed. Without their cooperative efforts and the interviews they granted, this study might have been unachievable. I also appreciate all the students who willingly consented to be interviewed and the organizers of the 'Coping with Academic Dependency: How?' Workshop, i.e. the South-South Exchange Programme for Research on the History of Development (SEPHIS) and the Asian Development Research Institute (ADRI)); their initiative engendered the impetus to carry out this study. Finally, I appreciate Professor Oyekanmi for her support and suggestions, which improved the overall quality of this work.
2. The University College, Ibadan was later renamed the University of Ibadan in 1963 after it was granted autonomy from the University of London through an Act of the Nigerian Parliament.
3. Professor Onoge died on 12 July 2009 in India. He was trained at the prestigious Harvard University in the USA. He contributed immensely to Nigeria's sociology and attempts towards its development and indigenization. He was a role-model in Nigeria's sociological circles. In spite of persecutions from Nigeria's military

regimes in the late 1970s, Prof. Onoge remained committed to academic development in Nigeria and was at the forefront of the development of sociology in the country. Though he was forced out of the University of Ibadan by the military rulers in the late 1970s, Prof. Onoge subsequently transferred his services to the younger University of Jos in the 1980s. I personally respected and revered him because he refused to leave Nigeria in spite of the challenges he faced from the military regimes. As an international scholar, Prof. Onoge could have opted out of Nigeria's then turbulent academic environment where university lecturers were hunted and hounded by the military regimes' secret police. But he stayed back to give his service to Nigerian sociologists, other academics and students in particular and the nation in general. He was a sociologist and scholar *par excellence*. May his soul rest in perfect peace.

4. Sorokin was a renowned sociologist of Russian origin who was exiled to the USA in 1922. He later became a Professor of Sociology at Harvard University. Professor Onoge noted that Talcott Parsons was a student of Sorokin.
5. Western theories as used in this paper include all sociological theoretical postulations which emerged from Europe and later, the USA, including socialist oriented Marxian and neo-Marxian theories.
6. Reference to Ibadan here means the University of Ibadan, where he started his teaching career in Nigeria in the 1970s before moving to the University of Jos where he retired.
7. Coincidentally, Professor Onoge played an active role in the 1971 NASA Conference where the need for African sociological theoretical postulation was canvassed.
8. Dr Alliyu teaches Sociological Theory at the Olabisi Onabanjo University. He indicated he teaches Fela's thoughts in his theory class in an interview conducted with him on 18 September 2007.

REFERENCES

Adesina, J.O. (2002), 'Sociology and Yoruba Studies: Epistemic Intervention or Doing Sociology in the Vernacular', in *African Sociological Review* 6 (1).

Ake, C. (1979), *Social Science as Imperialism: The Theory of Political Development*, Ibadan: Ibadan University Press.

Akinyemi, A. (2003), 'Yoruba Oral Literature: A Source of Indigenous Education for Children', in *Journal of African Cultural Studies* 16 (2): 161–79.

Akiwowo, A. (1974), 'Presidential Address: Association for What?', in *The Nigerian Journal of Sociology and Anthropology* 1 (1): 3–6.

——— (1986a), 'Contributions to the Sociology of Knowledge from an Oral Poetry', in *International Sociology* 1 (4): 343–58.

——— (1986b), 'Asuwada-Eniya', in *Ife: Annals of the Institute of Cultural Studies* 1: 113–23.

Alatas, S.F. and V. Sinha (2001), 'Teaching Classical Sociological Theory in Singapore: The Context of Eurocentrism', in *Teaching Sociology* 29 (3): 316–31.

Awoniyi, T.A. (1975), '*Omoluabi*: The Fundamental Basis of Yoruba Education', in W. Abimbola (ed.), *Yoruba Oral Tradition*, Department of African Languages and Literature, University of Ife, pp. 357–88.

Bentley, J. H. (1996), 'Cross-Cultural Interaction and Periodization in World History', in *American Historical Review* 101 (3): 1–26.

———, 'Cross-Cultural Interaction and Periodization in World History', in *American Historical Review,* 101 (3): 749–70.

Black, D. (2000), 'The Purification of Sociology', in *Contemporary Sociology* 29 (5): 704–9.

Brenner, L. and D. Robinson (1980), 'Project for the Conservation of Malian Arabic Manuscripts', in *History in Africa* 7: 329–32.

Charmaz, K. (2000), 'Looking Backward, Moving Forward: Expanding Sociological Horizons in the Twenty-First Century: 2000 Presidential Address to the Pacific Sociological Association', in *Sociological Perspectives* 43 (4): 529–47.

Connell, R. (2006), 'Conocimiento Indigena y Ponder Global: Lecciones de los debates Africanos', in *Nomadas*, 25: 86–97.

Cummings, R.J. (1986), 'Africa Between the Ages', in *African Studies Review* 29 (3): 1–26.

Dennis, C. (1974), 'Sociological Theory in Nigeria: What For?', in *The Nigerian Journal of Sociology and Anthropology* 1 (1): 79–86.

Durkheim, E. (1976), *The Elementary Forms of the Religious Life*, London: George Allen & Unwin Ltd.

Ekpo, M. (1985), 'Two Decades of Sociology in Nigeria, 1960-1980: A Developmental Overview', in *International Journal of Contemporary Sociology* 22 (1&2): 81–111.

Faculty of the Social Sciences (2005–6), *Prospectus Faculty of the Social Sciences, University of Ibadan, Ibadan, Nigeria*, Ibadan: Faculty of the Social Sciences, University of Ibadan.

Giddens, A. (1971), *Capitalism and Modern Social Theory: An Analysis of the Writings of Marx, Durkheim and Max Weber*, Cambridge: Cambridge University Press.

Hamdani, S. (2000), 'The Dialectic of Power: Sunni-Shi'i Debates in Tenth Century North Africa', in *Studia Islamica* 90: 5–21.

Hu, C.T. (1984), 'The Historical Background: Examinations and Control in Pre-Modern China', in *Comparative Education* 20 (1): 7–26.

Kinsey, D.C. (1971), 'Efforts for Educational Synthesis under Colonial Rule: Egypt and Tunisia', in *Comparative Education Review* 15 (2): 172–87.

Lawuyi, O.B. and O. Taiwo (1990), 'Towards an African Sociological Tradition: A Rejoinder to Akiwowo and Makinde', in *International Sociology*, 5 (1): 57–73.

Makinde, M.A. (1988), '*Asuwada* Principle: An Analysis of Akiwowo's Contributions to the Sociology of Knowledge from and African Perspective', in *International Sociology* 3 (1): 61–76.

Numata, H. (2003), 'What Children Have Lost by the Modernization of Education: A Comparison of Experiences in Western Europe and Eastern Asia', in *International Review of Education* 49 (1/2): 241–64.

Omobowale, A.O. (2008), 'Clientelism and Social Structure: An Analysis of Patronage in Yoruba Social Thought', in *African Spectrum*, 43 (2): 203–24.

Otite, O and W. Ogionwo (1979), *An Introduction to Sociological Studies*, Ibadan: Heinemann Educational Books (Nig.) Limited.

Patel, S. (2002), 'The Profession and Its Association: Five Decades of Indian Sociological Society', in *International Sociology*, 17 (2): 269–84.

——— (2008), Unpublished Comments on the paper presented by A.O. Omobowale at the workshop on 'Coping with Academic Dependency: How?', Patna, 4–7 February.

Payne, M.W. (1992), 'Akiwowo, Orature and Divination: Approaches to the Construction of an Emic Sociological Paradigm of Society', in *Sociological Analysis* 53 (2): 175–87.

Pickering, M. (1989), 'New Evidence of the Link between Comte and German Philosophy', in *Journal of the History of Ideas* 50 (3): 443–63.

Pickering, M. (1993), 'August Comte and the Saint-Simonians', in *French Historical Studies* 18 (1): 211–36.

Rao, S.B. (2001), 'The "Modern" in Modern Indian History', in *Social Scientist* 29 (5/6): 3–39.

Ritzer, G. (1996), *Sociological Theory*, New York: The McGraw Hill Companies, Inc.

Rotimi, W. (2006), 'The Development of Sociology as a Field of Discipline in Nigeria', in K.A. Ogunbameru and W.R. Rotimi (eds.), *Man and his Social Environment*, Ibadan: Spectrum Books Limited.

Timbuktu Educational Foundation (2002), *University of Timbuktu* Retrieved on 7 September 2007 from http://www.timbuktu foundation.org/university.html

Trevino, A.J. (2003), 'Sociological Theory at the Crossroads', in *Contemporary Sociology* 32 (3): 282–8.

Turner, J.H. (1998), *Structure of Sociological Theory*, Belmont: Wadsworth Publishing Company.

Wagenaar, T.C. (2004), 'Assessing Sociological Knowledge: A First Try', in *Teaching Sociology* 32 (2): 232–8.

Weiss, D. (1995), 'Ibn Khaldun on Economic Transformation', in *International Journal of Middle East Studies* 27 (1): 29–37.

Welz, F. (2009), '100 Years of Indian Sociology: From Social Anthropology to Decentring Global Sociology', in *International Sociology*, 24 (5): 635–55.

Wikipedia (2007), *Dar al-Ulum*, Retrieved on 7 October 2007 from www. en.wikipedia.org/wiki/Dar_al-Ulum.

II. MOUNTING CHALLENGES TO ACADEMIC DEPENDENCY

CHAPTER 7

Local Scholars, Global Academy

ANJAN GHOSH

INTRODUCTION

In a globalized world where knowledge is becoming the principal currency of accumulation beyond the boundaries of the local, how are the scholars from the global South placed in the great chain of being? Are they still caught up in dependency to their colonial mentors? Or are they able to exert their intellectual autonomy through a critical decolonization of the social sciences? The passage from decolonization to post-colonial identity has remained a fraught journey. In this paper I seek to trace a part of this course with special reference to sociology and the social sciences in India. While charting this course I will pay attention to the negotiations between the demands of indigenization and identity and reconstruction and autonomy that has manifested itself in the social sciences.

Academic dependency is the effect of academic imperialism. The exercise of direct control over educational institutions, universities, publishing houses by the colonial powers created the structures of academic colonialism. After Independence the grip was loosened but not absent. It became more indirect and covert. Explaining the concept in the contemporary situation Alatas writes, 'Academic dependency may therefore be defined as a condition in which the social sciences of certain countries are dependent on the development and growth of the social sciences in those countries to which the former countries are subjected' (Alatas 2006: 63).

Issues of academic dependency have emerged in the wake of unravelling academic imperialism at the time of the anti-Vietnam war protests in the US universities after the mid-1960s. The indictment of the involvement of some social scientists in counter-insurgency research not only evoked critical introspection among disciplines like sociology and social anthropology but also attuned it towards greater reflexivity in research outlook. Since the mid-1960s were proximate to the withdrawal of European colonizers from a number of Afro-Asian countries, the emergent new nations rode the crest of nationalist assertions against imperial machinations.

LINEAGES OF *SWARAJ*

India along with some of its subcontinental neighbours had attained political independence from British rule nearly two decades earlier. Its struggle against colonialism through the national movement not only prepared the ground for political sovereignty but also created a space for intellectual awakening among the public intellectuals. This awareness was represented in the idea of *swaraj* or self-rule first advocated by the nationalist leader Gopal Krishna Gokhale and then substantively elaborated upon by Gandhi in his prescient treatise *Hind Swaraj* (1938/82). Gandhi's exposition of self-rule or home rule was not simply a political demand but called for eschewing the world-view of Western civilization and the pursuance of ethical living (Prasad, 1985: 15). As Gandhi explained, 'My conviction is deeper today than ever. I feel that if India will discard "modern civilization", she can only gain by doing so' (Gandhi, 1938/82: 17).

For Gandhi ethics was inextricably related to politics. Political emancipation could hardly come about without the ethical imperatives being put in place and the practices being instituted. In a prefatory word of explanation to *Hind Swaraj*, Gandhi states:

But I would warn the reader against thinking that I am today aiming at the Swaraj described therein. But today my corporate activity is undoubtedly devoted to the attainment of Parliamentary Swaraj in accordance with the wishes of the people of India. (Gandhi, 1910/82: 17)

In keeping with the ethical consciousness achieved by the Indians, Gandhi says that, 'I am not aiming at destroying railways or hospitals, though I would certainly welcome their natural destruction' (Gandhi, 1910/82: 17). Further Gandhi did not consider *swaraj* as the political withdrawal of the British. In response to a query he puts forward his views:

Editor: . . . Do you think that it is necessary to drive away the English, if we get all we want?

Reader: I should ask of them only one thing, that is: 'Please leave our country'. If, after they have complied with this request, their withdrawal from India means that they are still in India, I should have no objection. Then we would understand that, in their language, the word 'gone' is equivalent to 'remained'. (Gandhi 1910/82: 28)

Gandhi clearly understands that the eviction of the British from India would not necessarily lead to the rejection of the values and institutions of Western civilization. It is against this that he wants to exert his moral force. Subsequently the notion of *swaraj* would be deployed by Indian philosophers and social scientists to mark their distance from the West.

The Indian philosopher Krishna Chandra Bhattacharya in a lecture to his students at the Hooghly College during 1928–30, spoke of 'Swaraj in Ideas'. The lecture recovered from his unpublished writings was published in *Viswa Bharati Quarterly* in 1964. In the essay, Bhattacharya, distinguishing between cultural subjection and cultural assimilation considers the latter to be 'healthy' and does not 'mean a lapse of freedom' (Bhattacharya, 1977: 13). On the other hand, cultural subjection implies slavery and as Bhattacharya says, 'slavery begins when one ceases to feel the evil and it deepens when the evil is accepted as a good' (ibid.). He thereby well presages the contemporary ideas of 'normalization' and 'subjection' by about four decades. Clarifying his notion of 'swaraj in ideas' Bhattacharya states,

> There is cultural subjection only when one's traditional cast of ideas and sentiments is superseded without comparison or competition by a new cast representing an alien culture which possesses one like a ghost. This subjection is slavery of the spirit: when a person can shake himself free from it, he feels as though the scales fell from his eyes. He experiences a rebirth and that is what I call Swaraj in Ideas.
> (Bhattacharya, 1977: 13)

Bhattacharya's idea of *swaraj* calls for a critical engagement with the dominant culture in order to exorcise it. He is not in favour of rejection but critical distancing from the dominant frameworks of thinking that would allow the subjugated to form their concepts and analytical frameworks. Bhattacharya's notion of *swaraj* is in keeping with the Gandhian tradition of autonomous thought.

The journey of the idea of *swaraj* continued into the post-Independence era. In 1968 J.P.S. Uberoi wrote a brief note on 'Science and Swaraj' for a conference on urgent research in social anthropology at the Indian Institute of Advanced Study, Shimla. Its publication in the *Contributions to Indian Sociology* (New Series) soon after as an early piece for the discussion forum on 'For a Sociology of India', triggered a debate which has continued itinerantly till today. In his essay, Uberoi (1968: 119) argued that, 'I believe that the advancement of science in India cannot be separated from the advancement of independence'. Characterizing 'scientific internationalism' as a 'bridge of illusion, a cloak of comfort across the chasm' (Uberoi, 1968: 120), he goes on to add,

> The existing system of foreign aid in science, to which the internationalist notions of collaboration lends credence, in truth upholds the system of foreign dominance in all matters of scientific and professional life and organization. It is nothing but the satellite system, with an added subsidy. It subordinates the national science of the poor to the national and international science of the rich. It confirms our dependence and helplessness and will not end them. The reason

for these efforts is simple and fundamental: the national and the international systems inherently are opposites for the poor.

Uberoi upholds the national endeavour in science as a means of developing autonomous knowledge pertaining to local needs. Its autonomy lies in the recognition of national relevance as distinct from the requirements of universal significance. This calls for different levels of generalization and a capacity to develop frameworks to engage with conceptual heterogeneity rather than homogeneity. Singh (1970: 142) remarks in continuing the debate that 'sociology is a system of conceptual operations and also a form of consciousness which accentuates societal self-awareness'. How this consciousness mutates through its relation with international social science is the subject of academic colonialism and will be discussed later.

In an insightful analysis of colonialism, Nandy (1983: 2) defines colonialism 'as a shared culture which may not always begin with the establishment of alien rule in a society and end with the departure of the alien rulers from the colony'. Colonialism enjoins certain internal displacements through the shared codes of the rulers and the ruled. As Nandy (1983: 2) maintains,

> The main function of these codes is to alter the original cultural priorities on both sides and bring to the centre of the colonial culture subcultures previously recessive or subordinate in the two confronting cultures. Concurrently, the codes remove from the centre of each of the cultures subcultures previously salient in them.

Further, Nandy argues that the culture of colonialism has a manner of containing dissent. As he puts it, 'It creates a culture in which the ruled are constantly tempted to fight their rulers within the psychological limits set by the latter' (Nandy 1983: 3).

This confines the ruled to the ruler's discourse thereby drowning their voice. Any uncovering of muteness calls for a critical engagement with the dominant discourse to reconstruct and free the colonized self. The process of recovery entails first the creation of an identity and then an attempt at autonomous articulation, coinciding initially with the phase of decolonization and later with that of post-colonial intervention.

DECOLONIZATION AND INDIGENIZATION

The process of decolonization is not only a process of dismantling the edifice of colonial rule but also a means of distancing from the rulers. This distancing is a reversal of the imposed constraints on the self. Thus decolonization has been defined as,

> (T)he process of revealing and dismantling colonialist power in all its forms. This includes dismantling the hidden aspects of those institutional and cultural forces that had maintained the colonialist power and that remain even after political independence is achieved. (Aschcroft, Griffiths and Tiffin, 2004: 63)

Decolonization signified not only a distantiation from the colonial modes of knowledge production but also the projection of a distinct identity for the social sciences. The latter had been implicated in colonial governance and continued to be harnessed by the national government when it came to power. But were the embedded assumptions and frameworks substantially altered with the change of government? The focus on science and technology overshadowed the presence of social sciences in the new states. Moreover, for the social sciences, it was the task of social engineering which was accorded priority. The facilitation of 'development' became the prime objective of the social sciences with the analytics developed during the colonial era. An interregional conference on social sciences organized by UNESCO in 1976, found that 90 per cent of the social scientists of the world came from the developed countries. The meeting reported not only disparity in numbers but also in terms of intellectual relationship between peripheral and metropolitan social scientists:

It is not merely the fact of a linkage that is noteworthy, but more so the fact that in the case of the developing regions, it is a relationship of dependency to put it in other words (repeatedly used at the meeting), it is a 'vertical' relationship between the donors and recipients, between patrons and clients. . . . Though practically all the Third World Countries are now politically independent, 'self-rule' in the field of social sciences remains still to be achieved. . . . [The] numbers of indigenous social scientists have undoubtedly increased but they are more in contact with their Western colleagues than with their counterparts in the Third World or, for that matter, even within their own region, the question these social scientists ask, the paradigms and research techniques are for the most part imported from the West, or at best adapted from the work of Western thinkers including social scientists. No wonder then, that social sciences in the Third World are often judged to be irrelevant and the social scientists accused of being alienated from their societies. (quoted in Atal 1981/2004: 200)

Clearly political independence from colonial powers did not entail academic autonomy, as scholars in the developing world were located in a subordinate position in the international division of intellectual labour. Four years earlier Syed Hussain Alatas in his celebrated essay on 'The Captive Mind in Development Studies' wrote,

A captive mind is the product of higher institutions of learning, either at home or abroad, whose way of thinking is dominated by Western thought in an imitative and uncritical manner. A captive mind is uncreative and incapable of raising original problems. It is incapable of devising an analytical method independent of current stereotypes. (Alatas 2004: 83)

In other words, there was a continuation of academic dependency and enthrallment with Western thought. As the newly independent countries of the developing world struggled to define themselves, their social scientists were prey to imitative and uncritical practices. The dominance of the West was far too proximate for the social thinkers to distance themselves, and as Bhattacharya mentioned above, to assimilate their ideas into their analysis. The call for indigenization which persisted among sociologists in the 1960s and 1970s was more of an effort to create a distinct identity for the social sciences in India. Yet this was no '*swaraj* in ideas' but an 'orientalism' in reverse (Dube, 1982), which drew upon upper caste traditions of knowledge as the primary source of social conduct. The conflation of upper caste prescriptions as Indian tradition not only marked the quest for identity as a Brahminical predilection but later would also generate a politics of 'elite revolts' and Hindu revivalism (Corbridge and Harriss, 2001).

That this privileged understanding of indigenization was not only specific to India but pervaded social science trends in many of the new nations is borne out by Chun and Shamsul's (2001) comments on Asian social sciences. While tracing the alterity of cultural studies and critical science tradition in Asia, they are mindful to point out the 'special challenges' faced by the Asian scholars and the pulls of 'local scholarly discourses that not only have their own intellectual lineages but also are, in effect, products of an intertwined collusion between state and academia' (Chun and Shamsul, 2001: 171). Arguing that indigenization tendencies in Asia tend to develop involutionary outlooks, they state unequivocally,

> Because indigenization movements in contemporary Asia militate against hybridity and multiculturalism, they tend to be inward looking. Instead of being imposed from the outside, any local theory of critical knowledge must be able to engage directly nativist fundamentalisms within the same framework of cultural meanings and differences, even while embracing cosmopolitan social values. The search for cultural authenticity is thus less of a relevant concern in this regard than the need to articulate in cultural terms the values of justice and morality. (Chun and Shamsul, 2001: 171–2)

Indigenization of social thought accompanied the consolidation of the nation state after colonialism. Privileging the national identity obscured the internal displacements that the elites effected in the process of nation-building. Indigenous identity of the national subject was normatively tilted towards elite perceptions. It would require substantive research into the steep inequalities, disparities, fragmentations and dispersions spawned by post-colonial developments, before the trajectory of national development could be interrogated. As modernity in terms of the institutional framework of the state and development of manufacturing industries accompanied the making of the nation, it became metonymic of the latter. With the national becoming commensurate with the modern, challenges to the former became relegated to the fold of tradition and the past. Hence non-elite or popular intervention was an impediment to the sequence of progress and to be viewed as sectional and divisive. However, the invocation of tradition as part of indigenous theorizing, allowed for the recuperation of the concept as interrogative of the national-modern.

Academic dependency corresponded to economic dependence and created a multilayered structure of dependence which stymied the independence of social scientists in the developing countries. Alatas (2006: 63) uncovers the pattern of dependence,

> The relations of interdependence between two or more social science communities and between these and global transactions in the social sciences, assumes the form of dependency when some social science communities (those located in the social science powers) can expand according to certain criteria of development and progress, while other social science communities (those in the Third World, for example) can only do this as a reflection of that expansion, which can have mixed effects (positive and negative) on their development according to the same criteria. There is a psychological dimension to this dependency whereby the dependent scholar is a passive recipient of research agenda, methods and ideas from the social science powers.

Alatas proposes a linear pattern of dependence between institutional locations and the transmission of their ideas in the Third World. He allows for little discursive autonomy of the receiving subject, as he enumerates the various dependences:

1. Dependence on ideas.
2. Dependence on the media of ideas.
3. Dependence on the technology of education.
4. Dependence on aid for research as well as teaching.
5. Dependence on investment in education.
6. Dependence of Third World social scientists on the Western demand for their skills.

(Alatas 2006: 64)

The powerful economies not only create the infrastructure of scientific knowledge but also shape the production of knowledge in the global South. Here decolonization of the knowledge complex remains formal but not substantive.

Contrasted to this, Assayeg and Benei (2003: 13) herald the decolonizing of the imagination of the social sciences. Taking account of the spatio-temporal reconfigurations under globalization, they argue,

> Today, not only have 'other' cultures ceased to be confined to other parts of the world with the overcoming of spatial and temporal distances inherent in technological globalization, but human diversity and cultural differences have taken on new significance. Historians, whether Euro-Americans or others, are studying regional interconnectedness within the same world history. In other words, social scientists now put themselves in the same frame of reference as their objects of study.

Does this mean that parity in communication has been established between the ethnographer and their object of research? Has the presence of the 'periphery' in the metropolitan centres and vice versa in the Southern countries brought about an interconnectedness within a common frame of reference of neo-liberal globalization? Primarily considering the diasporic South Asian scholars can provide a skewed perspective on the circulation of knowledge in the subcontinent.

In a recent essay, Chakrabarty (2009) has traced the discursive passages from decolonization to post-colonial scholarship. This is discussed in terms of a 'pedagogical style of developmental politics' to a 'dialogical' form of exchange. Distinguishing between decolonization and post-coloniality, Chakrabarty (2009: 264) remarks,

> The urge to decolonize, to be rid of the colonizer in every possible way was internal to all anti-colonial criticism after the end of the First World War. Post-colonial critics of our times, on the other hand, have emphasized how the colonial situation produced forms of hybridity or mimicry that necessarily escaped the Manichean logic of the colonial encounter.
>
> After all, the demand for political and intellectual decolonization arose mainly in the colonized countries among the intellectuals of anti-colonial movements.
>
> Postcolonial writing and criticism on the other hand were born in the West. They were influenced by anti-colonial criticism but their audiences were in the West at the beginning itself, for these writings have been an essential part of the struggle to make the liberal-capitalist (and, initially, mainly Anglo-American) Western democracies more democratic with respect to their immigrant minority and indigenous groups.

Taking our cue from Chakrabarty it is possible to designate indigenization as the problematic of decolonization while difference, dialogue and the constitution of the subaltern comprises the problematic of post-coloniality. While Chakrabarty accords subjecthood to the immigrants and indigenous minorities in the West, it is the subalterns in all their diversities, whose constitution marks the advent of the post-colonial in the periphery.

POST-COLONIAL DEPARTURES

If the construction of a separate identity convergent with indigenization was the principal object of social science research in the phase of decolonization, the split in the political domain between elite and subaltern nationalism and the uncovering of rebel consciousness constituted the post-colonial movement. The fracture in the unitary domain of the national showed up the fault lines of power which prevailed in civil society. And it was the consciousness of the peasant rebel which exemplified the autonomy of the subaltern. Writing about the post-colonial discursivity of *Subaltern Studies*, Said remarked in his 'Foreword' to *Selected Subaltern Studies*,

> It's rather sharply contestatory attempt to wrest control of the Indian past from its scribes and curators in the present, since as we shall see much of the past continues into the present. And if there can be no actual taking of power in the writing of history, there can at least be a demystifying exposure. (Said, 1988: vii)

The post-colonial shift did not celebrate the national structure of power but was equally critical of the national elites as that of the imperial ones. But the recovery of the rebel subject from the historical archives, created and maintained for the dominant classes through 'reading against the grain', created an impression of the subaltern as the protagonist of history. This was critiqued by deconstructionist analysts like Gayatri Chakravorty Spivak who maintained that as the subaltern historian was only representing the subaltern voice, it was necessary to make explicit the technologies of representation through which the fragments of subaltern consciousness could be apprehended. Chatterjee, in his *Subaltern Studies*, recapitulates Spivak's criticism which changed the direction of subaltern studies scholars:

> The historian of the subaltern classes had already successfully demonstrated that the entity called 'man' or 'citizen' who was the sovereign subject of bourgeois history-writing was in truth only the elite. Why had it become necessary to clothe the subaltern in the costume of the sovereign subject and put him on stage as the maker of history? As a matter of fact, what subaltern historiography had challenged was the very idea that there had to be a sovereign subject of history possessing an integral consciousness. Why were they trying to bring back that same idea into their history of the subaltern classes? It was only a myth that the subaltern would directly speak

through the writings of the historian. At best, that was merely an expression of the historian's good intentions. In fact, the historian was merely representing the subaltern on the pages of history. (Chatterjee, 1998: 25)

It was this criticism which prompted the move from the search for the sovereign rebel subject to the 'defense of the fragment' (Pandey, 1992) and the positioning of subaltern studies historians as the composers of oppositional histories. The abdication from a transformative role was not taken kindly to by the radical critics of *Subaltern Studies* but they glossed the long-term methodological implication of the project. Recounting the shift in emphasis, Chatterjee (1998: 19–20) writes,

> The task of subalternist history-writing was to criticize dominant historiographical practices. The history of the subaltern classes would therefore always be an oppositional history. Subalternist historians could not offer a fully fledged programme for an alternative historiography. . . .
>
> Oppositional and critical history-writing: that was the agenda of *Subaltern Studies*. It assumed that there would always be a dominant historiography, just as there would always be the dominance of the elite. In any case, history-writing would never bring about the end of this dominance. What could the historian of the subaltern classes do? He or she could write oppositional histories where the subalterns could be given the space to deny the dominance of the elite, to talk about their own historical initiatives, to present themselves as active historical agents. These historical accounts could never attain the fullness of national histories. The subaltern could never speak on behalf of society as a whole. The history of the subaltern classes would therefore always remain fragmentary, partial and perhaps even to a certain extent incoherent.

This less than apocalyptic vision of subaltern dissonance revealed the enduring role of critique as a mode of clearing the space for dissent and opposition. But there was little scope of the absolution of sovereign rebel power, for countervailing forces were constantly necessary to constrain absolute power.

The democratic framework had to be sustained for active intervention and dialogic possibilities of the subalterns and minorities.

Here lies the departure from literary post-colonialism which also spoke of the 'effects of colonial representation' in order to identify the 'resistances to that force [colonialism] wherever they may be' (Ashcroft, Griffiths and Tiffin, 2004: 189). Defining the 'post-colonial' they wrote, 'The term "post-colonial" *per se* was first used to refer to cultural interactions within colonial societies in literary circles' (ibid.: 186).

Circumventing the celebration of resistance, the post-colonial intervention as proposed by Chakrabarty (2009) calls for a dialogical cosmopolitanism in a globalized world. The methodological cues provided by the latter day subalternist scholars do not restrict its deployment to the Western democracies as mentioned by Chakrabarty. Global networks of dominance call for global strategies of resistance and a polyphonic response from within the space of the nation.

SOCIAL SCIENCES AS INSTRUMENTALITIES

The social sciences expanded rapidly during the 1970s and 1980s. For instance, departments of sociology proliferated all over India. In an overview of the scenario in sociology, Rao (1982: 26) reported that of the 16 new universities established in the 1970s, 10 had sociology departments. Sociology which was a latter day addition to the stable of social sciences, is indicative of the expansion of the social sciences in India. As faith in social engineering through planning and development persisted with the advent of the 'Green Revolution', the government's role in development underwrote the growth of the social sciences. But by the mid-1980s when state regulation over trade and industries were sought to be loosened and neo-liberal policies fostered the market impulse, a 'growing amnesia' (Kothari, 1994) gripped the middle-class imagination about poverty, deprivation, environmental degradation and the vulnerabilities of rural social life. As steep social inequalities continued between the country and the city and also within them, the radiating effects of the urban centres overshadowed the rural areas. The electronic mass media transmitted urban aspirations of consumption and career development into the impoverished rural hinterlands thereby creating a discrepancy of development. The logic of the market which had been constrained by the state's participation in industries and services began to shed its fetters and corrode the basis of the state's redistributive functions. Increasingly the public sector enterprises which were a source of social mobility for sections of the underprivileged became choked in order to compete with the private sector. The demand for specialized skills increased in the private service sector. But the poor access to secondary and higher education meant that the private sector employment precluded the lower castes and underclasses. In this scenario the critical and ethical skills of the social scientist largely went by default. There was a burgeoning demand for professional and 'soft' skills which were the prerogative of the middle classes.

Students who had economic and cultural capital made a beeline for professional rather than general education. On the other hand, the children of the better-off peasantry seeking lateral linkages with the urban modes of power, found their passages into professional education blocked owing to their scarce cultural capital. Hence they sought to enter into the social sciences in order to improve their mobility prospects. The composition of the social science classrooms underwent a change in the 1980s and early 1990s when students from the backward classes and *dalit* sections began to enter the institutions of higher education in larger numbers. The anti-reservation students stir provoked by the implementation of the Mandal Commission Report by the V.P. Singh government in 1990, bears testimony to their presence. Their search for social mobility through education resulted in their entering the middle brow sciences like social sciences. For many of these students who brought their experiences of social deprivation and exploitation from their life-worlds into the classroom, it enabled an interrogation of their curriculum from their own vantage point. Reading about caste, class, village, kinship and the family system represented by upper caste sociologists generally, they found a discrepancy between their experiences and the way these institutions had been written about. This mismatch led to the emergence of different perspectives like *dalit* sociology (Mahapatra, 2006). Intervening in the debate on the crisis in Indian sociology initiated by Veena Das (1993) which bemoaned the quality of research and teaching of sociology in the country, Bairy articulated a different view of the crisis. From his impressions of sociology students in Hyderabad and Bangalore, Bairy located the crisis in the discipline's unwillingness to become 'a craft, a specialisation, a skill, a profession and thus a livelihood' (Bairy, 2001: 14). If sociology was to nurture its application orientation and improve the employability of its practitioners, then sociology would be more highly valued by its students and perhaps could secure greater commitment from them to overcome their academic ennui.

The demand for instrumental knowledge converges with the demands of neo-liberal globalization and the emergence of a global academy. Nayyar, as the erstwhile Vice-Chancellor of University of Delhi, spells out some of the implications of globalization on higher education,

> In the world of higher education, markets and globalization are beginning to influence universities and shape education not only in terms of what is taught but also in terms of what is researched. In the sphere of teaching, there is discernible departure from the liberal intellectual tradition where education was about learning across the entire spectrum of disciplines. Choices of students were shaped by their interests. [. . .] Even so, universities endeavoured to strike a balance across disciplines, whether literature, philosophy, languages, economics, mathematics, physics or life sciences. But this is changing, as students and parents display strong revealed preferences to

demand higher education that makes young people employable. The popularity and availability of courses are thus being shaped by markets. . . .

It is also inducing universities to introduce new courses, for which there is a demand in the market, because these translate into lucrative fees as an important source of income. Similarly, markets are beginning to exercise an influence on the research agenda of universities as resources for research in life sciences, medicine, engineering or economics are abundant while resources for research in philosophy, linguistics, history or literature are scarce. There is a premium on applied research and a discount on theoretical research. (Nayyar, 2007: 32)

In his paper Nayyar goes on to elucidate the asymmetry that prevails in the field of professional education. He says,

The professionals, at the top of the ladder of skills, are almost as mobile as capital. Indeed we can think of them as globalised people who are employable almost anywhere in the world. . . . In a sense it is a part of the secession of the successful [. . .] it is globalisation of higher education that has made it possible. But there is a crucial asymmetry. The investment is made by the home countries. The returns accrue to the host countries. This process is associated with a privatisation of benefits and a socialisation of costs.

The globalisation of higher education is also changing the nature of higher education in the developing world. Its links with and relevance to the society in which the higher education is provided is somewhat tenuous, because the content and scope is determined in industrial societies. What is more, there is a clear and present danger that an internationalised higher education system may stifle rather than develop domestic capabilities in the higher education system of the developed world, particularly in the least developed countries.

(Nayyar, 2007: 35)

This indeed is happening on a wide scale. Institutions of higher learning in developing countries like India are primarily engaged in teaching. Original research based on primary data collection is little encouraged and scarcely conducted in the local universities which are usually sponsored by the state governments. This means that local research hardly feeds into the instructional loop and teaching is conducted through textbooks which are composed either by foreign authors or by scholars at the national level. However, even in the textbooks composed by Indian authors there is reproduction of mainstream Euro–American theories, frameworks and models with little efforts at adaptation. Hamstrung by their teaching, administrative and evaluative loads, as well as by the paucity of resources for research, teachers of state universities hardly have an opportunity to engage in meaningful research. Lack of research means, that received frameworks of knowledge or theories go uninterrogated in terms of their relevance and appropriateness for Indian conditions. This of course is not an Indian problem but widespread in the developing nations.

In spite of severe constraints, some state universities are able to demonstrate their research excellence in the social sciences in exceptional cases. Here the roles of visionary individual scholars who are able to overcome resource scarcity by developing collegial networks of mutual support have to be taken into account. However, in general, the lack of a research derived critical apparatus leads to the dependence on mainstream theories.

THE TECHNOLOGY OF 'WESTOXICATION'[1]

In a prescient essay on Western-centrism in Korean political science, Kang (2006) analyses the way in which Western-centrism or more precisely US-centrism has displaced the specificity of Korean politics into a universal mould. He elaborates on the notion of 'Western-centrism',

> The concept of 'Western-centrism' is constructed upon three premises: that modern Western civilization, which first centered on Western Europe but has been transplanted by the United States and Canada and so on, has reached the most advanced stage of human history; that the historical development of Western civilization is universally valid in all of human history around the world; and that non-Western

societies, which still lag far behind in historical development can only advance by imitating or adapting the Western developmental model through either civilization (colonial/imperial period) or modernization (post-colonial period). (Kang, 2006: 118)

Using the leverage of Western-centrism Kang then goes on to examine the gamut of Korean political science literature to find how Korean critical thinking has been overpowered by Westernization. Also how Korean realities have been viewed through the Western theoretical prism and how it has resulted in the marginalization of Korean experience and indigenous categories. Explaining why Western-centrism must be overcome Kang states,

[I]t legitimizes Western cultural domination by indoctrinating non-Western societies into accepting the superiority and universality of Western civilization. Non-Western people have internalized the belief that the Western world-view, values, institutions, and practices are superior and universal and have assimilated them. This has driven them to self-marginalization, self-abasement and self-negation. In this state they have not been able to form independent world-views, a fact that eventually rendered them as self-alienated. (Kang 2006: 119)

Kang's notion of self-negation and self-alienation resonates well with Nandy's idea of colonialism as the 'intimate enemy'. However, Kang continues to analyse particular Korean texts to highlight their misplaced borrowings from American liberal political theory. He goes on to also illustrate the irrelevance of neo-Marxist and post-modern theoretical tendencies which scarcely engage with Korean realities. He explores the Korean literature on democratization to show how specific Korean characteristics are assimilated into a universal Western theory. Finally he points out how instead of the Korean notions of power derived from Confucius, Prof. Lee, a well-known political scientist, in his textbook has abjured the Confucian categories of power for universal categories. Academic dependency persists through the emulation of the West.

Even the integrative technology of the Internet as represented in the World Wide Web has remained elusive for users in the developing world. As Mathew and Parikh (1996) point out through their analysis of different search engines, they find a pattern of streamlining and standardizing of categories which obscures their specificity. Thus different kinds of violations like caste, communalism, and gender related violence are docketed under human rights issues and drained of their particularities.

CONCLUSION

If dependency was the paradigm of decolonization, asymmetric interdependence appears to be the form of interrelationship that post-colonial globalization induces. The way this plays out for the social sciences is not only through the internalization of metropolitan frameworks by scholars in the developing world or the objectification of the knowledge produced in the periphery. It often plays out through the displacement of the object of knowledge and its constitution by default at the grassroots levels. There the transnational transmission of knowledge seeps in through received paradigms of instruction and becomes a part of the knowledge of the self. The impositions are either obliterated or celebrated as the conduit of global knowledge. The international division of academic labour now includes the diasporic scholars who often mediate the theory absorption capacity in the Indian situation. The continuum of 'non-Western scholars living and working in non-Western contexts and Western scholars living and working in Western contexts on others', as pointed out by Deshpande (2003: 268) now has to incorporate non-Western scholars living and working in the Western academy on their 'home' situations.

The advantages that accrue to the non-Western scholars in specific disciplines like anthropology are enumerated by Deshpande,

Given its dependence on detailed access to the everyday life in which culture or society is embedded and manifested the relationship between the Western and non-Western academic is somewhat different when it comes to anthropology. In a certain sense scholars who happen to be natives of non-Western societies can claim privileged access to the raw materials out of which anthropological knowledge is fashioned. (Deshpande, 2003: 268)

This 'privileged access', is not available to the local scholars who have to unlearn the received knowledge before engaging in a reconstruction of the dialogic self. That is the promise of post-colonial scholarship in the periphery.

NOTE

1. 'Westoxication' is a concept introduced by the Iranian thinker Jalal Al-e Ahmad in his book *Gharbzadegi* (Weststruckness or Plagued by the West), translated from the Persian by Paul Sprachman, Delmor, NY: Center for Iranian Studies, Columbia University, 1982.

REFERENCES

Alatas, Syed Farid (2006), 'The Structure of Academic Dependency and the Global Division of Labour in the Social Sciences', in Syed Farid Alatas, *Alternative Discourses in Asian Social Science, Responses to Eurocentrism*, New Delhi: Sage, pp. 57–79.

Alatas, Syed Hussein (1974/2004), 'The Captive Mind and Creative Development', in Partha Nath Mukherji and Chandan Sengupta (eds.), *Indigeneity and Universality in Social Science: A South Asian Response*, New Delhi: Sage, pp. 83–98.

Assayag, J. and V. Benei (eds.) (2004), *At Home in the Diaspora* Delhi: Permanent Black.

Ashcroft, Bill, Gareth Griffiths and Helen Tiffin (2004), *Key Concepts in Post-Colonial Studies,* London: Routledge.

Atal, Yogesh (1981/2004), 'The Call for Indigenisation', in Partha Nath Mukherji and Chandan Sengupta (eds.), *Indigeneity and Universality in Social Science: A South Asian Response*, New Delhi: Sage, pp. 99–113.

Bairy, Ramesh (2001), 'Rethinking the Debate on the "Crisis" in Sociology', paper presented at the All India Conference of the Indian Sociological Society, Amritsar, unpublished, pp. 1–21.

Bhattacharya, Krishna Chandra (1977), 'Swaraj in Ideas', in Sisir Kumar Ghose (ed.), *Four Indian Critical Essays*, Calcutta: Jijnasa, pp. 13–22.

Chakrabarty, Dipesh (2009), 'Legacies of Bandung: Decolonization and the Politics of Culture', in Saurabh Dube (ed.), *Enchantments of Modernity: Empire, Nation, Globalization*, New Delhi: Routledge, pp. 264–90.

Chatterjee, Partha (1998), 'A Brief History of Subaltern Studies', paper presented to the VI Subaltern Studies Conference on 'Fractured Societies, Fractured Histories', at Giri Institute of Development Studies, Lucknow, January, unpublished, pp. 1–31.

Chun, Allen and A.B. Shamsul (2001), 'Other "routes": The Critical Challenge for Asian Academia', in *Inter-Asia Cultural Studies*, 2 (2): 167–76.

Corbridge, Stuart and John Harriss (2001), *Reinventing India: Liberalization, Hindu Nationalism and Popular Democracy*, New Delhi: Oxford University Press.

Das, Veena (1993), 'Sociological Research in India: The State of Crisis', in *Economic and Political Weekly*, June 5: 1159–61.

Deshpande, Satish (2003), *Contemporary India: Sociological Perspectives*, New Delhi: Penguin Books.

Dube, Leela (1982), 'The Challenge of Indigenisation', paper presented at the 10th World Congress of Sociology, Mexico City (Topic B: Theme 3: *Universalism versus Indigenisation in Sociological Theory*), unpublished.

Gandhi, M.K. (1938/82), *Hind Swaraj or Indian Home Rule*, Ahmedabad: Navajivan Publishing House.

Guha, Ranajit (1982), 'On Some Aspects of the Historiography of Colonial India', in Ranajit Guha (ed.), *Subaltern Studies – I*, New Delhi: Oxford University Press, pp. 1–8.

Kang, Jung In (2006), 'Academic Dependency: Western-centrism in Korean Political Science', in *Korea Journal*, Winter: 115–35.

Kothari, Rajni (1994), *Growing Amnesia*, New Delhi: Viking.

Mahapatra, Samir Kumar (2006), 'Dalit Sociology: Making a Case for it', in *Journal of Indian Education*, 31 (4), February: 1–13.

Mathew, Biju and J. Parikh (1996), 'The Web as a Marginalizing Technology', in *Bulletin of Concerned Asian Scholars*, 28: 3–4.

Mills, C. Wright (1963), *Power, Politics and People*, New Jersey: Transaction Books.

Nandy, Ashis (1983), *The Intimate Enemy: Loss and Recovery of Self under Colonialism*, New Delhi: Oxford University Press.

Nayyar, Deepak (2007), 'Globalisation: What Does it Mean for Higher Education', in *Economic and Political Weekly*, 15 December: 30–5.

Pandey, Gyanendra (1992), 'In Defense of the Fragment', in *Representation*, no. 37, Winter.

Prasad, Nageshwar (ed.) (1985), *Hind Swaraj: A Fresh Look*, New Delhi: Gandhi Peace Foundation.

Rao, M.S.A. (1982), 'Sociology in the 1980s: Retrospect and Prospect', in P.K.B. Nayar (ed.), *Sociology in India*, Delhi: B.R. Publishing, pp. 15–43.

Said, Edward (1988), 'Foreword', in Ranajit Guha and Gayatri Chakravorty Spivak (eds.), *Selected Subaltern Studies*, New York: Oxford University Press, pp. v-x.

Singh, Yogendra (1970), 'For a Sociology of India', in *Contributions to Indian Sociology* (N.S.), no. IV, pp. 140–4.

Uberoi, J.P.S. (1968), 'Science and Swaraj', in *Contributions to Indian Sociology* (N.S.), no. II, pp. 119–23.

CHAPTER 8

Social Sciences in Chile (1957–1973): A Laboratory for an Autonomous Process of Academia-building

FERNANDA BEIGEL[1]

INTRODUCTION

The internationalization of social sciences in Mexico and Brazil during the 1950s and 1960s has been recently revised; particularly the role played by the United Nations Education Science and Culture Organization (Maio, 2007; Reyna, 2005; Trindade, 2005a; Miceli, 2001). Chile has received less attention, although it became a regional platform for the cooperation system. It was in Santiago where the Economic Commission for Latin America (ECLA) was established, along with the regional offices of UNESCO, FAO, and the so-called Small Vatican. This country attracted funds from public agencies (US-AID, Fulbright Commission) and private resources (American and German Foundations). It played a leading role in the 'Alliance for Progress' and other major international projects, like the Charity Collections of the Catholic Church, lead by Misereor and Adveniat.

Recent studies (Devés Valdés, 2004; Garretón, 2005) have found that the exceptional stability of Chile's political system favoured its international openness and the emergence of this country as an intellectual cosmopolis, all of which was stimulated by the growth of an important reformist movement during the Presidency of Eduardo Frei Montalva (1964–70). But a comparison with Buenos Aires, São Paulo or Mexico

City shows that these metropolises had much higher cultural indicators than Santiago. While the former had a very well-developed publishing market, the latter only had an incipient graphic industry. Besides, foreign scholars who lived in Santiago at the time describe it as a small, 'provincial' city, with poor cultural life. Therefore, it still hasn't been answered how Chile became the axis of a regional academic circuit and the laboratory for an endogenous process of knowledge production. I will attempt to provide data related to the constant stimulus received by the higher education system and the role played by the Chilean diplomacy in the capture of international resources available in the cooperation system.

In the brief years that go from 1963 until 1970, the political atmosphere in Chile changed substantially: the leftist Popular Unity increased its popular support and a process of radicalization occurred within the Christian Democratic Party, in power since 1964. Numerous groups of exiled intellectuals arrived after the military coups in Brazil and Argentina. In 1970, Salvador Allende won the Presidential election and implemented a democratic socialism, an experience that rapidly gained international recognition. This passage in Chile became an important factor for the emergence of new knowledge, such as the Structuralist School of Thought (*Estructuralismo cepalino*[2]), Dependency Analysis, Marginality Studies—and for the international recognition of a new group of Latin American scientists. Accordingly, this country can be considered a 'peripheral centre', with a dominant position in the region, although a marginal space in the international academic system.

Dependentists were aware of the dominance of Eurocentric patterns and of the necessity to think autonomously with respect to Northern social sciences. They enriched the structuralist method of historical diagnosis of the region and contributed to the re-thinking of the concept of underdevelopment. In order to do so, they critically articulated a set of

European and Latin American theories. In another work I discussed the intellectual traditions convergent in Dependency Analysis, focusing on the bridling between *Estructuralismo Cepalino,* critical Marxism and Colonial Studies. I analysed to what extent these foci were really autonomous from theoretical or methodological hierarchies imposed by the 'international academic system', considering also the fact that these critical trends emerged within research centres supported by foreign aid (Beigel, 2009).

All this raises multiple aspects of academic dependence and the existence of different notions of autonomy/heteronomy that must be distinguished: (1) 'intellectual autonomy' independent from foreign traditions or conceptual models), (2) 'institutional autonomy' (independent from the universities in relation to the State), and (3) 'academic dependence' (on foreign aid). In this paper, I will focus on the two latter, in order to describe the particular environment in which those social knowledges emerged and the role played by the increasing political engagement of the faculty. I will address the issue of academic dependence in relation to the intervention of the Chilean State, demonstrating that during this period, many international flows were 'nationalized' by a set of public agencies that served as 'filters' for foreign aid, preserving, however, the institutional autonomy of the universities.

THE PROFESSIONALIZATION AND INTERNATIONALIZATION OF LATIN AMERICAN SOCIAL SCIENCES

Latin American contributions to social knowledge have not received much attention in Northern studies of Social Sciences. As a matter of fact, they had a minuscule place in the list of 'advances in social science from 1900 to 1965' published by *Science* magazine, in February 1971. According to Daniel Bell, the list implied the acceptance of the fact that there *are* such things as 'social science achievements' and that these 'have commonly been the result of conscious and systematic research and development efforts by individuals or teams working on particular problems in a small number of interdisciplinary centres' (1985: 12). Only Raúl Prebisch and J.B. Souto were included in a list of more than one hundred social scientists. The city of Santiago de Chile was mentioned once, among hundreds of contributions located in Europe, the United States and the former Soviet Union.

However, by the date this list was built, the development of Latin American social sciences showed an important level of institutionalization. Considered historically, a comparison of the cases of Argentina, Brazil, Chile, Uruguay and Mexico shows significant similarities in the trends of internationalization and professionalization of the social sciences. Several studies (Garretón et al., 2005; Devés Valdés, 2003) have shown that these disciplines were born in the first half of the twentieth century, in diverse spaces: (1) the university domain: chairs of social sciences, first research schools and institutes; (2) journalism and literary criticism; and (3) in the state domain: research work related to the implementation of public policies, particularly in the field of Economics. During the second half of the century, matriculation in national universities grew consistently in a modern direction—favouring social sciences and education in detriment to traditional graduate programmes in Law and Medicine. At a regional level, higher education lecturers, whose number was 68,000 in 1960, reached in 1976 the number of 371,000, with an accumulative annual growth rate of 8.9 per cent between 1960 and 1970; and of 15.0 per cent between 1970 and 1976 (UNESCO–UNDP, vol. 3, 1981: VIII–92).

Two international organizations played a central role in this process: the United Nations Educational, Scientific and Cultural Organization (UNESCO) and the Organization for American States (OAS). The latter created the Inter-American

Statistics Institute and the Pan-American Educational Institute. The same year of its constitution (1948), its Cultural Council opened a 'Social Science Division' to help the development of social sciences in Latin America. UNESCO certainly played a dominant role in promoting research and the teaching of the social sciences in our region. During the Secretariat of the Mexican Jaime Torres Bodet, the 'Department of Social Sciences' was created, under the direction of the Brazilian anthropologist Arturo Ramos. This Department had a particular vitality and relevance in the first years of the Organization, because it triggered the famous debate on the concept of race. There were two divisions in this Department which shows the importance given by the organization to the international dimension of the social sciences: the 'Division of Applied Social Sciences' and the 'Division of International Development of the Social Sciences'. By 1949, Latin American delegations had an important presence within UNESCO: 14/47, this is, 31 per cent of the total state-members (Chor Maio, 2007: 188, 193). Besides, UNESCO's international legitimacy was built on the basis of an equal representation of its state-members. It was the unique specialized agency of the UN which developed a network of national commissions (Casula, 2007: 97). The Chilean National Commission was exemplary, with a network of provincial sub-commissions and a decisive role in UNESCO's Aid Program for state-members.[3]

As far as development organizations are concerned, we can mention the United States Agency for International Development (US-AID), the International Cooperation Administration (ICA), as well as the Fulbright Program; from Europe: International Development Research Cooperation (IDRC, Canada), Swedish Agency for Research Cooperation (SAREC, Sweden), NOVIB-CEBEMO (The Netherlands) and CNRS-CCFD (France). This foreign aid favoured particularly the circulation of Latin American students in the North American and European postgraduate systems (Garcia, 2006; Picó,

1996; Trindade, 2005; Ansaldi and Calderón, 1989). Regarding private foundations, the relevance acquired by North American foundations, such as Ford and Rockefeller, as well as from the German foundations Misereor, Adveniat and Konrad Adenauer is well known. An important part of the subsidies granted by these foundations was allocated to 'university development' in Latin America. The annual reports of Ford Foundation show that Chile's part of the total donations worldwide grew from 0.31 per cent in 1960 to 1.74 per cent in 1968 (Szymanski, 1973: 813).

During the 1950s, the Catholic Church underwent a worldwide renewal process that lead to the institutional and intellectual changes forged in the Second Vatican Concilium (Krebs, 1993; Fleet and Smith, 1997; Lowy, 2000; Zanca, 2006). An increasing interest in social sciences emerged and numerous Centres of Research and Social Action (CIAS) were created in Latin American cities. The Society of Jesus played an active role in promoting socio-religious studies and they were entrusted with the administration of a great part of the Catholic Universities. More than thirty of these were created in Latin America between 1940 and 1960, mostly dedicated to graduate programmes in social sciences (Zapiola, 2006: 209–10). Active academic exchanges existed between the Catholic Institute (Paris), the University of Louvain (Belgium) and the Gregorian University (Rome: Vatican). In Latin America, Jesuits promoted another international academic network that took off from Santiago de Chile; this time open to the Americas. Its launch was made in the Seminar 'University Triangle' (1965) and its main vertexes were the University of Louvain (Belgium), The University of Notre Dame (USA) and the Catholic University of Chile.

Another flow of internationalization came from 'scientific missions', coming mainly from French and American universities. Recent studies show that these missions had an important role in the institutionalization of social sciences in

Brazil, but also that the Latin American experience was key to the itinerary of many French sociologists and anthropologists, such as Claude Lévi-Strauss and Roger Bastide (Peixoto, 2001). What started as an inter-personal exchange was replaced by inter-institutional cooperation based on the recognition of mutual academic traditions (Trindade, 2005b).

The creation of Economic Commission for Latin America= ECLA (CEPAL) (1948) in Santiago constituted a fundamental turn in the development of economic knowledge in the region. Statistical information accumulated in public dependencies during previous decades was systematized, studies at the national and regional level were carried out, and technical training for public officials of the treasury and planning departments was encouraged. CEPAL was a conduit for a network of economic and social research agents and institutions, which began to develop since its very creation, thanks to the driving force of Raúl Prebisch, Celso Furtado, Aníbal Pinto, Jorge Ahumada, among others. From 1952, CEPAL selected students who would be awarded scholarships to travel to Santiago and participate in the 'Basic Course on Economic Development Problems'. CEPAL's courses became an training alternative for contesting scholarships abroad offered by foundations, other international organizations, and universities from United Kingdom and the United States, especially Cambridge, Oxford and Chicago. It is not sufficiently known that CEPAL's constitution within UN was conflictive: it didn't receive support from the United States delegation and a parallel commission was founded at the Organization for American States (OAS).[4] This situation experienced an important shift with the John F. Kennedy presidency, because CEPAL was one of the main threads for the constitution of the Alliance for Progress—in fact, Raúl Prebisch headed its Board of Experts (Comité de los Nueve Sabios).

By the beginning of the 1960s, the institutionalization of

social sciences had reached an important level in the major Latin American cities. Schools of Sociology were founded and, some time later, degree courses in Political Science, Social Psychology, Anthropology, Social Work and Journalism were extended. The creation of the Latin American Faculty of Social Sciences (FLACSO = Facultad Latinoamericana de Ciencias Sociales), at Santiago de Chile, in 1957, contributed significantly in this respect. Fostered by UNESCO and the Chilean state, it had a strong impact on the specialization dynamics of the region, mainly through the formation of social science graduates and the recruitment of lecturers and specialists coming from most Latin American countries. Until 1973, FLACSO had an office in Santiago and received important support from the Chilean state. In 1967, the Latin American Council of Social Sciences was created, with headquarters in Buenos Aires. Research and educational institutions were increasingly connected through informal networks, regional professional associations (ALAS = Asociación Latinoamericana de Sociologia), conferences, scientific publications and specialized publishing houses.

THE CHILEAN HIGHER EDUCATION SYSTEM

The Chilean state had gradually acquired a more predominant role in the direction of the economic, social and cultural development of the country. With the creation of the University of the North (1956) a system of eight universities in total was completed, holding all the functions of higher education in Chile until 1980 (Krebs, 1979). The University of Chile, created in 1842, exercised a significant influence on governmental policies and played a significant role in the formation of public officers; majority of the elected presidents were its graduates (Gazmuri, 1999).

The consolidation of an academic field in Chile is in great deal due to the modernizing role played by a triple set of public organizations since the passage of Law No. 11575, in 1954: (1) the Bureau of Higher Education, which supervised the sustained policy of increasing public expenses on higher education through direct and indirect expenditures established in Laws No. 11575 and 13964, (2) the Board of Chancellors, in charge of supervising the accreditation system and scientific research projects related to national development, and (3) the University of Chile, which presided over the Board and became the herald of the professionalization of the system. The Chancellor of the University of Chile, Juan Gómez Millas seemed to corporatize this public policy based on a triple institutional articulation. History professor and dean of the Philosophy and Education Faculty (El Pedagógico) between 1946 and 1953, he had conducted its structural adjustment to the massive enrolment and the institutionalization of social sciences in Chile. His chancellorship at the University of Chile (1953–63), his presidency of the Board and Ministry of Education, placed him at the summit of the process of the modernization of the system.

The higher education public policy implemented since 1954 exhibited its results after a decade. By the mid-1960s, Chile had the highest comparative rate of public expenditure at the third level (28.0 per cent), triplicating France (8.0 per cent) and Noruega (8.7 per cent) (Schiefelbein, 1968: 62).[5] At the same time, 64.3 per cent of the university enrolment belonged to public universities, and 50 per cent of the total student body was enrolled at the University of Chile (Bases, 1966: 21, 31). Public expenditures assigned to higher education increased in a sustained way from the second half of 1950s, and they were more than doubled, between 1960 and 1972. After the military coup, in 1973, the higher education system changed completely and public expenditure on higher education experienced a sustained decreasing tendency, reaching 2.20 per cent by 1988 (Arriagada, 1989: 28). (See Figure 8.1).

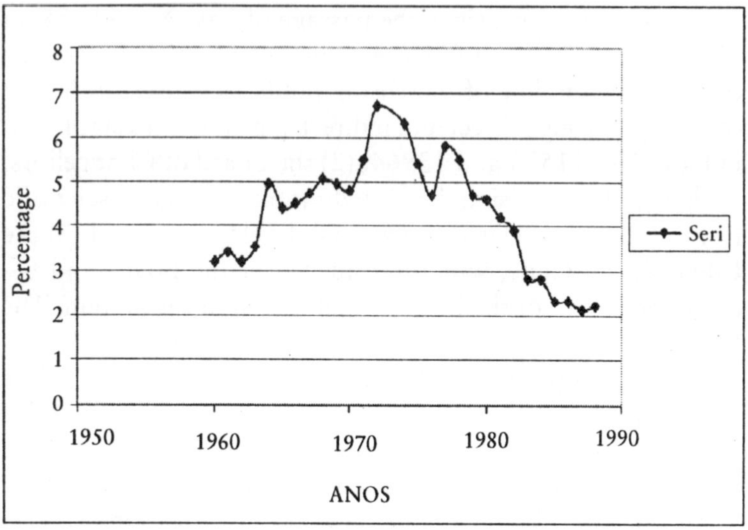

Source: Compiled by author on the basis of: *Arriagada, P. Financiamiento de la educacion superior en chile 1960–88*, Santiago: FLACSO: 28.

Figure 8.1: Fiscal Expenditure on Higher Education as a Percentage of Total Fiscal Expenditure.

UNIVERSITY MODERNIZATION AND ACADEMIC PROFESSIONALIZATION (1950–1964)

Between 1950 and 1964, two major academic networks functioned in the Chilean territory—linked, in different ways, to the international cooperation system. The first one was articulated by the University of Chile, the oldest, biggest and strongest university in the country. Very influential in the Bureau of Higher Education and the Chilean diplomacy, this university led a sustained policy of professionalization and development of scientific research. Occupying the presidency of the rector's council, it favoured the institutionalization of education and social sciences and it played a major role in the creation of research centres. By the mid-1950s, schools of sociology and political science were created in the University of Chile, not only in Santiago but in provincial headquarters also. In 1956 was created the first postgraduate school in social sciences: the Latin American School of Economics (ESCOLATINA = Escuela de Estudios Económicos Latinamericanos) sustained by a Rockefeller Foundation grant and installed in the Faculty of Economics.

This network was linked to an international academic space located in Santiago, mainly built around regional centres and international organizations such as Food and Agriculture Organization of the United Nations (FAO, UN) and OAS. With the support of the University of Chile, the Inter-American Training Centre for Economic and Financial Statistics (CIEF) was created in 1952. A few years later, the Latin American Centre of Demography (CELADE) was installed and also the regional office of FAO, which conducted studies on land reform. In the domain of Sociology and Political Science, the FLACSO was created by 1957, an inter-governmental organization sponsored by UNESCO and the Chilean government. Finally, in 1962 the Latin American Institute for Social Planning (ILPES = Instituto Latinamericano y del Caribe de Planificación Económica y Social) was created within the orbit of CEPAL. This network was stimulated in the domain of economics through CEPAL's training courses, which were articulated with the chair of Economic History at the University of Chile, headed by Jorge Ahumada and Osvaldo Sunkel.

The second academic network was clearly separated from the first one, at least until 1967, as we will see below. It was organized around the Pontifical Catholic University (PUC = Pontificia Universidad Católica de Chile) and the Chilean Province of the Society of Jesus. Chile had a strong Church and a great majority of its population was Catholic (Lehmann, 2001: 2). The Society of Jesus had a great bearing on the institutionalization of the University and particularly in social sciences, given that its members had been trained in Sociology, Economics and Psychology. The PUC was created in 1888 and acknowledged by the state in 1928, but it had been maintained under the supervision of the University of Chile until

1953, when its diplomas gained direct official recognition. In 1956, a regional 'think tank' of the Company of Jesus was founded in Santiago: 'the Bellarmino Centre'. As a priestly residence, it quartered the Jesuits that had obtained their doctoral degrees abroad and functioned as a cultural centre; favouring the reception of new trends in education, psychology, sociology and economics. It was the result of the fusion of the initiatives that father Alberto Hurtado had promoted a few years before his death: the Centre of Social Research and Action (CIAS, 1956) and the *Mensaje* magazine (1951-open publication).

A key role performed by a Belgian sociologist expanded this academic network beyond pastoral action: He was Roger Vekemans, who was transferred to Santiago in 1956. Indeed, by 1959, he created the School of Sociology at the Catholic University, and invited several Jesuits and laic scholars to Chile, sponsored by Rockefeller fellowships. From 1961 onwards, Vekemans left the Catholic University and created an independent centre of social research. The 'Centre for Latin American Social and Economic Development' (DESAL = Centro para el Desarrollo Económico y Social de América Latina) was modelled on CEPAL. In 1966, a new institute was created under the orbit of the Bellarmino: 'the Latin American Institute for Social Development (ILADES = Instituto Latinamericano de Doctrina y Estudios Sociales), under the direction of French Jesuit Pierre Bigó. DESAL and ILADES constituted the most sophisticated academic projects started by the Society of Jesus in Chile (Beigel, 2008).

The two academic networks were dynamic and highly internationalized. The University of Chile's was linked to regional centres in the orbits of United Nations or OAS. The Catholic network was linked to the international projects of the Society of Jesus and the American and European Catholic Universities. The University of Chile had a dominating role in the creation of international academic centres such as FLACSO and officials from CEPAL, ILPES and CELADE taught at the University of Chile and participated in research centres. The Catholic University, on its side, brought many foreign experts for its Faculty and scholars had a regular contact with other universities linked to the Society. At the local level, however, these networks had a diverse influence. The University of Chile played the role of kingpin to the whole university system and concentrated 50 per cent of total university enrolment. By the mid-1950s it had an impressive presence in the territory: 10 centres distributed in major provinces from South to North. Meanwhile, the Catholic University recruited 15 per cent of total matriculations and had only two centres (Santiago and Concepción)—its national cultural influence was concentrated in the secondary education level, particularly the sixteen Catholic colleges (Bases, 1966: 31–4). During this period, circulation in-between both academic networks was almost non-existent. Only informal links occurred between scholars graduating in the two major universities and theoretical orientations were substantially different.

In spite of these differences, and the fact that the University of Chile was the indisputable herald of modernization, general data shows that at this stage all universities underwent a geometric expansion, an intense internationalization process and a gradual professionalization of the Faculty (see Table 8.1). Chilean university enrolment had an early modern distribution of specializations—concentrating in education and social sciences at the expense of Law, Medicine and other scientific graduate programmes. The share of the social sciences in the Chilean enrolment rates showed a sustained increase, from 10.4 per cent in 1957, up to a stable rate of 15 per cent, between 1967 and 1973. Law programmes virtually lost their predominance in the enrolment rates, descending from 15.5 per cent in 1957 to 2.4 per cent in 1973. The area of education, which had already experienced an increase before 1957, registered high sustained values: 27.8 per cent in 1957 and 27.4 per cent in 1973 (Brunner, 1986: 35).

Faced with this expansion, since the late 1950s, the Uni-

Table 8.1: Teaching Positions: University of Chile and Catholic University, 1965–6

Type of position	University of Chile, 1966 (%)	Catholic University, 1965 (%)
Full-time lecturers (36 hrs/week)	32	13.5
Half-time lecturers (18 hrs/week)	17	–
Part-time lecturers	51	86.5
Total	100	100.0

Sources: Compiled by author on the basis of: Bases, 1966: 72; Krebs, 1988: 805; Guía Informativa de las Universida des Chilenas, 1965: 226.

versity of Chile headed a general process of the professionalization of the faculty: New teaching positions were created for new graduate and postgraduate programmes, innovative regulations for academic careers were established along with a substantial increase of full-time positions. By 1966, the results of this policy were evident. Some units, such as *El pedagógico*, had established a statute with modern procedures for an ascending academic career. It had distinguished standards for administrative/professional/hierarchic positions.

Scientific research was strongly encouraged at the University of Chile, not only as an activity complementary to lecturing, but also as a full-time practice, supported with material resources for the development of empirical research. This policy became evident in the quality/numbers of research positions and in the distribution by functions of the university's budget. The number of research projects rose rapidly, from 382 in 1964 to 914 in 1966, and to 1,300 in 1967 (Schiefelbein, 1968: 47). Of a total of 14,180 positions within the University of Chile, those assigned exclusively for research represented 17.45 per cent (2,474) and the positions for teaching and teaching associates (agregados a la docencia) 70.46 per cent (9,991). 85 per cent of the research positions were full-time (Bases, 1966: 72). The distribution of the budget changed according to the type of scientific area and the modernization process of each academic unit. Physics and Mathematics spent 78.9 per cent in research and 19.7 per cent in teaching, while the distribution in the Law School was precisely the opposite (11.4 per cent for research and 85.5 per cent for teaching). Economics used 35.9 per cent for teaching and 60.9 per cent for research, while distribution in Philosophy and Education (including Humanities and Social Sciences) was 69.7 per cent for teaching and 22.5 per cent for research (Bases, 1966: 83). Table 8.2 compares the distribution of annual expenses by functions in the two major Chilean universities.

In this period, Chile was a major recipient of foreign aid and received substantial funding from public and private sources (Puryear, 1994). It was one of the countries most favoured by the US Alliance for Progress as well as European

Table 8.2: Distribution of Annual Expenditure Universidad De Chile-Universidad Católica

Function	Universidad De Chile, 1965 (%)	Universidad Católica, 1966* (%)
Teaching	51.7	60
Research	28.8	15
Extension	8.3	10
Administration	11.2	15
Total	100.0	100

Sources: Compiled by author on the basis of: Data of the Catholic University collected from Superior Council's records 29 March 1966 (folios 344–60) and data of the University of Chile in Bases, 1966: 83.

Note: *I aggregated expenditures that were divided into 10 items in the original budget.

funds. American governmental programmes such as US-AID and the Point IV Program as well as the private foundations like Ford, Carnegie and Rockfeller played an important role in the funding of both academic networks. German foundations such as Konrad Adenauer, Misereor collaborated primarily with the Catholic University. With the installation of the Ford Foundation's regional office in Santiago, by 1963, Chile's share in its subsidies was strengthened. However, it is relevant to say that, in all cases, academic institutions relied on substantial and increasing fiscal resources, as is shown in Figure 8.1, including the private universities and the regional centres dependent on international organizations, such as FLACSO.

By 1964, Christian Democracy's candidate was elected for presidency and Juan Gómez Millas, former Chancellor of the University of Chile was assigned as minister of education. He was aware that serious reforms were indispensable to fulfilling the process of modernization. Accordingly, reformist trends were stimulated in the system. The new chancellor of the University of Chile, Eugenio González Rojas, formed a commission that was given the task of analysing the general situation of the university after the modernization and expansion that was held during the 1950s. The diagnosis was that the accelerated growth had outgrown the university structures: fundamental reforms were necessary to assess curricular duplications, atomization of economic resources and lack of articulation.[6] Besides, the intense growth of matriculation had not been complemented by good rates of retention and graduation. Professional formation was a historic trend at the University of Chile, while scientific research was a new practice, developed within a great deal of isolation[7] (Bases, 1966: 50–4). The commission's report formulated a plan for new infrastructure, decentralization in provincial centres, a dialogue between research and teaching by reforming academic programmes, and the establishing of a general admission exam.

But the University of Chile and the rest of the Chilean universities started to feel the radicalization process that undertook society and the tremors of the student movement, which would soon involve the academic field.

EXILE, UNIVERSITY REFORM AND RADICALIZATION (1964–70)

The government of Eduardo Frei Montalva (1964–70) was characterized by a radicalization of the national and international political scenario. US President's Kennedy's murder, the weakening of the Alliance for Progress, the Vietnam war and guerrilla movements in Latin America seemed to build a revolutionary tunnel, even though its end was not clearly illuminated. Economic progress through social reforms, that had reached the top of the academic agenda by 1960 was now seen as unviable without structural transformations. Brazil's military *coup d'etat* had a direct impact on CEPAL's economic thought and Chile became the territory for exiled scholars that were soon recruited within research institutes and regional centres located in the orbit of the University of Chile.

In 1965, Chilean academics massively refused to participate in the 'Camelot Project', an initiative of the Special Operations Research Office = SORO (American University) aimed at searching for social conflict in Latin America. Increasingly, Chileans had started to become aware of the role that social sciences were playing within the struggles of the Cold War and by the middle of 1965, a general scandal took place. The denunciation of 'Plan Camelot' was exploited by the Chilean press and a massive cover of suspicion was thrown over American science. The Catholic University's administrative files show evidence of governmental requests for information on 'American scientific research in Chile' revealing a general assumption of the existence of some kind of espionage behind sociological projects originating in the United States.

The academic network that became most fragmented during this period was of the Catholic Universities. The 2nd Vatican Concilium (1962–5) and the radicalization of Catholic priests had a profound impact on the cultural institutions created around the Bellarmino Centre. The Jesuit sociologist Roger Vekemans had already dissociated himself from the Catholic University in 1962, when he created DESAL. From the mid-1960s he clashed with Marxist trends and became involved in numerous controversies. Finally, Vekemans closed DESAL when Salvador Allende was elected president and moved 80 of its officials and their families to Colombia (Beigel, 2008).

The geometric expansion of university enrolment in the 1950s had led to the growth of the student body, which had become an increasingly important audience for policy makers and university academics. This generation of students had been impacted by the Cuban Revolution (1959), which legitimized the value of political commitment. A new type of activism evolved within Chilean universities, demanding student participation in university councils and enrolment for lower classes. The tendency to sacrifice the present gains for the future (a mentality present in the catholic socialization of the Chilean middle-class) now materialized as a collective demand for a democratic university. 'Militant capital' (Matonti and Poupeau, 2004) spread to higher education, and created the conditions for a Reform movement, which first succeeded in the Catholic University of Santiago.[8]

The occupation of the building in 1967 forced the election of the first lay chancellor, the architect Fernando Castillo Velasco, who was supported by the students. The creation of a participatory government council opened a strong phase of institutional modernization and the Catholic University started to play a relevant role in the Board of Chancellors. A favourable ambience for critical thought stimulated the autonomy of the university from the Church along with a new concept of 'excellence'. A new radical academic ideal started developing around the idea of 'autonomy', which was understood as the right of the university to have its own government, establish its own scientific methods and set the lines of its academic development (First University Council, 1971). A survey carried out between 1971 and 1972 shows the self-perception that the lecturers of the Catholic University had constructed with regard to the objectives of the 1967 occupation. When asked what the central goal of the reform was, the lecturers interviewed pointed out: Improvement of academic and/or professional training, democratization and connection with the 'national reality' (Avalos, Paves and McGinn, 1974: 176).

The reformists fought against the former conservative Catholic university, which they considered a reproducer of knowledge and the established order. The model scholar was one capable of understanding the 'national reality' and who contributed to its transformation. The reform was aimed at the transformation of the university's structure in order to give priority to scientific research. In the next few years, academic life was organized to strengthen the link between teaching and research. Several interdisciplinary centres were created in the orbit of the new chancellor. These recruited prestigious scholars who had supported the occupation and were the heralds of the institutional transformation. Among them, social scientists played a key role. Compared to other research institutes, these centres had more hierarchy and resources, along with an influence in the Superior Council.

A particular feature of this movement at the Catholic University was the fact that the politicization inspired the professionalization process, by supporting scientific research and modernization. By 1965, the number of lecturers at the Catholic University was 931, and 12.1 per cent of them held full-time positions. In 1968, the number of lecturers rose to 1,117 and the percentage of full-time lecturers reached 17.46 per cent. Three years later, the faculty had grown even more and the full-time positions reached an impressive

52.2 per cent of the total (Avalos and McGinn, 1974: 162; Krebs, 1988: 805). The Catholic University received increasing fiscal contribution during the Christian Democracy's government, a tendency that was reinforced with Allende's administration. In 1967 it represented 41.4 per cent of the total budget, and by 1973 it reached 79.4 per cent (Krebs, 1988: 705).

Meanwhile, the University of Chile and University of Concepción had been through similar 'student-quakes'. The main trends of the academic field were changing. The centres in the orbit of the United Nations—such as CEPAL and FLACSO—also received exiles and started to develop new critical foci. Young social scientists replaced the previous generation in the direction of these centres and stimulated inter-institutional circulation. 'Chile' became the privileged object of analysis for national and foreign social scientists settled in Santiago. Knowledge about the 'national reality' became the standard for 'academic excellence', which the agents vindicated in the interdisciplinary research centres.

In all academic domains new programmes at the postgraduate level were developed. Until then, the postgraduate diplomas of the faculty were minimal and they had mostly been obtained abroad. In the University of Chile, by 1967, lecturers with a doctoral degree constituted 4.7 per cent of the faculty, and those with a Master's degree, 7.3 per cent (Schiefelbein, 1968: 44 and 122). The situation at the Catholic University was different, due to the social background of the students and the weight of private capital during the institutionalization stage. By the beginning of 1970, more than half of its lecturers had done postgraduate studies outside Chile, and one-third held a Doctoral or Master's degree (Avalos and McGinn, 1974).

During the Reform movement, the Board of Chancellors kept working to stimulate the modernization of the system. In view of the considerable increase in the demand for higher education, a commission was constituted in 1969 to create a national admission test, called *Prueba de Aptitud Académica* (Academic Aptitude Test).[9] The commission was presided over by the Director of Student Selection and Registers of the University of Chile and representatives from the other universities. This test was implemented since 1970 and was intended to evaluate specific knowledges and competences for different scientific areas (Krebs, 1988: 705). The policies of the Board were strengthened by increasing public expenditures for higher education. By 1968, the fiscal contribution to private universities ranged between 60 and 80 per cent of their total budgets. According to Schiefelbein, by then, the separation between state and private universities in Chile was 'artificial' (1968: 17).

INSTITUTIONAL AUTONOMY AND INTELLECTUAL ACTIVISM UNDER SALVADOR ALLENDE'S GOVERNMENT (1970–73)

The university reform movement played a central role in the growth of an intellectual activism which was extended to the political arena, leading to the formation of the Movement of Unitary Popular Action (MAPU) and a leftist tendency emerged within the Christian Democratic Party in power. This movement fractured the government's base of support and consolidated the Popular Unity which, as a coalition made of communists and socialists, won the 1970 election. Allende's presidency began in a cheerful climate, built by massive enthusiastic demonstrations in favour of the democratically elected socialist programme. There was a progressive extension of the militant capital in every social space. International observers and experts from different parts of the world arrived in Chile, reinforcing its already cosmopolitan atmosphere.

Stimulated by increasing fiscal resources, the Catholic University constituted a strong sector which was in demand with lecturers and researchers. During Allende's presidency, it maintained high levels of academic production and its graduate programmes gained increasing prestige. It continued the process of professionalization and development of scientific research at the new interdisciplinary centres. Compared with Table 8.2, Table 8.3 shows the growth of full-time positions. A wide circulation of these researchers onto the other network occurred. Agreements were signed between social sciences centres from Catholic University regional centres and public universities, for teaching, collaboration and organization of seminars and conferences.

Meanwhile, the University of Chile was highly convulsed and its Rector was aligned with Allende's political opposition. Several conflicts ended up fragmenting the faculty and the student movement. In fact, by 1972 the Faculty of Economics was split in two: the Facultad de Ciencias Económicas y Administrativas (West centre), and the Facultad de Economía Política (North centre). Struggles between Christian Democracy—in charge of the chancellorship—and the Popular Unity—in power in the national government—affected the institutional autonomy of the University of Chile and an 'ex-

Table 8.3: Teaching Positions in Catholic Universities, 1971–2

Type of position	Universidad Católica de Valparaíso, 1971 (%)	Universidad Católica 1972 (%)
Full-time lecturers (36 hrs/week)	29	52.24
Half-time lecturers (18 hrs/week)	0.0	11.44
Part-time lecturers	71	36.32
Total	100	100

Source: Compiled by author on the basis of: Avalos, and McGinn, 1974: 159–62; Krebs, 1994: 805.

ternalization of the reward system' (Brunner and Barrios, 1988) took place in academic practices.

The particular situation of the University of Chile during Allende's administration indeed changed its leading role in the higher education system and new hierarchies arose in the Board of Chancellors and the Catholic University took over the presidency. But it is convenient to distinguish the situation of the rest of the universities in a historical perspective, objectifying a strong auto-perception of the past, very prominent among Chileans, that was built after the military coup. According to the survey carried out by Brunner in 1985, three out of four scholars interviewed believed that towards 1960s/1970s, theoretical and ideological divisions took precedence over any other professional interest and that institutions were organized according to political orientations (Brunner, 1986).

As we have seen, at the Catholic University, research activities were increased after the occupation of 1967 and the administrative structure changed in order to stimulate interdisciplinarity and new academic units replaced former Faculties. The testimonies gathered prove that classes evolved normally after the occupation of 1967 and there was a clear separation between militant practices such as student assembly and teaching courses. The proceedings of the Superior Council show that until the beginning of 1973 decisions and polemics had a logic of their own, involving university positions, publications, theoretical or methodological trends. Disputes still took place over academic assets, mainly valuable to the academic world: The interpretation of social reality through the writing of reports and books, the creation of categories of analysis, surveys and empirical research.

At FLACSO, a severe internal crisis occurred around 1969: New social scientists took over directive positions and chairs in postgraduate programmes and Marxism were introduced in debate. Simultaneously, the Institute for the Coordination of Social Investigations (ICIS = Instituto de Coordinación de Investigationes Sociales) was created, headed by José

Sulbrandt and Sergio Bagú, propelling scientific research, and historical studies. All this promoted new academic publications and FLACSO's integration into the Chilean academic field.

On its part, the Board of Chancellors continued working on the coordination of university activities and proposing new regulations. In January 1972 a project called National University System was launched, based on federated universities and presided over by a 'National University Council' in charge of authorizing university budgets. In June 1973, this Council was debating a bill for a university organic law (Krebs, 1988: 706).

The fact that Sociology was more related to politics than other disciplines, especially during the period 1967–73, has been usually mistaken for its 'de-professionalization'. However, according to Devés Valdes, Sociology was a considerably constituted discipline and it was clearly a different practice than political essayism (Devés Valdés, 1998: 16). Although a portion of social scientists abandoned academic activity to devote their time to political-partisan activism, or to join the Allende administration, the great majority continued with their pledged commitment to an academic capital. This capital had been reconverted during the 1960s and it was reasonable for social scientists to consider as valuable the combination of professional dispositions with a political engagement, in order to make a contribution (in real time) for social change.

FINAL NOTES ON THE RELATION BETWEEN INSTITUTIONAL AUTONOMY AND ENDOGENOUS KNOWLEDGE PRODUCTION

We have seen how the Chilean state gradually acquired a more predominant role in the direction of the country's economic, social and cultural development; particularly since 1954 in fostering higher education and scientific research.

This sustained public policy enabled the university system to reinforce institutional autonomy, modernizing academic structures and procedures. The fact that part of the academic elite was composed of foreign scientists, the majority coming from South American military coups, favoured an independent intellectual activism rather than a concentration into political parties.

In a democratic and reformist environment, institutional autonomy and financial autarchy offered a prestigious space and a dynamic atmosphere for the development of new scientific approaches. The Dependency focus, marginality theory and underdevelopment studies arose, therefore, as a result of its presence at the crossroads of a set of institutional conditions and an extended intellectual engagement to overcome Latin America's peripheral condition, 'Chile' became an active object (of analysis) and subject (of change); a creative laboratory, autonomous from mainstream theoretical currents.

Both the governments of the Christian Democracy and that of the Popular Unity 'let universities do', on the grounds that they were autonomous and had to solve their own problems internally. They did not interfere in the reforming processes, although they encouraged their own partisans to fill positions within the new distribution of university power (Brunner, 1988: 3). Far from co-opting intellectuals, the state financed the social sciences and the creation of a militant criticism directed against the very bases of the transforming projects of the progressive governments of the region (Brunner, 1989: 5).

Academic autonomy was reinforced in the Catholic University after 1967 because it was strongly supported by fiscal resources, but was also in charge of the intellectual priorities and assignations of academic prestige. In fact, by the mid-1960s many Chilean officials of the UN resigned their posts to integrate universities. Most of the foreign scientists located at international organizations took an active part in the interdisciplinary centres created during the University Reform. As a result of this crossroads of institutional autonomy and intellectual activism, the two formerly separate academic networks became highly integrated. A set of formal and informal mechanisms stimulated these exchanges: the multiple institutional membership of a great part of the academics; informal networks and study groups of South American exiles located at different institutions; inter-institutional agreements between international agencies and Chilean universities; specialized publications; professional associations such as the Latin American Sociological Association; and relevant international conferences, such as the Third World Forum, held at Santiago in 1972.

During this period, the international context offered a favourable atmosphere for the diffusion of Chile's socialist experience and this fact inspired an interest in new critical trends that emerged in regional centres and research institutes located in Santiago. Dependency Analysis had an important reception in the Third World and dependentists reached international audiences. In this phase of the history of the Latin American social sciences, knowledge production significantly reduced foreign references and created endogenous concepts and methodological approaches. However, translation to other languages was scarce and the reception was marginal within the academies of central countries. Besides, this regional academic circuit lived briefly due to the destructive effect of the *coup d'etat* of September 1973. Chile lost its dominant place and the axis of the regional circuit shifted to Mexico, along with a good number of the South American scientists; the second academic exile wave of the region.

After the extension of military regimes in the Southern zone, the circulation of Marxism and Dependency Analysis diminished, and a process of 'de-institutionalization' of the social sciences was performed in the higher education system and undergraduate programmes were closed and many academics were forced into exile. By the mid-1980s, these were reopened by democratically elected governments, but quickly suffocated by Neo-liberal policies in the 1990s. This historical instability has extended or contracted institutional autonomy according to a set of factors, principally the changing role of the State. The crisis of Neo-liberal governments was followed by new policies that supported teaching and scientific research in public universities. This has reopened the discussion on academic dependence and career-building in peripheral countries. All of which points out an important shift towards a recovery of the intellectual dynamism that was reached in the past.

NOTES

1. The author wishes to thank Chirashree Das Gupta (ADRI, Patna) and Kathinka Sinha-Kerkhoff (ADRI, Ranchi) for their valuable comments on this paper.
2. Latin American structuralism is one of a family of structuralisms. This school of thought attempted to explain international economy as a structure of unequal relations. Unlike other kinds of Structuralism, one of its particularities was the historical approach based on Colonial Studies and long-term overview of economic production. See Love (1999).
3. During the late 1950s there was a competition between many countries for the leadership within the organization. Particularly interesting is the battle between Brazil and Chile to install the headquarters of the Latin American Faculty of Social Sciences (FLACSO), which was finally placed at Santiago, in 1957. Cf. Beigel, Fernanda (2009) 'La FLACSO chilena y la regionalización de las ciencias sociales en América Latina (1957–73)', in *Revista Mexicana de Sociología, México*, 71 (2): 319–49.
4. In 1948, OAS created the Inter-American Economic and Social Council and asked ECLA to find a 'formula' to establish the limits of both organizations and avoid 'duplication'.
5. Schiefelbein observes, however, that this growth partly took place at the expense of the growth of other sectors included in the budget of the Ministry of Education, which registered a slower growth.

6. The commission's survey showed that of an amount of 1400 subjects belonging to the 106 graduate programmes developed at the University of Chile, more than three hundred were repeated at least once (and up to 42 times in the case of Chemistry).
7. In 1966, 130 of the 272 existent organizations performed some kind of scientific research (pure or applied), and most of them had been created in the previous ten years (Bases, 1966: 50).
8. Militant Capital is a set of 'know-how' or dispositions related to collective action, such as skills to organize demonstrations, assemblies or building occupations. The concept relies on Bourdieu's framework but has been developed by Frédéric Matonti and Frank Poupeau (see references).
9. This universal pre-selection system is still effective in Chile today.

REFERENCES

Avalos, P. and N. McGinn (1974), in Ernesto Schiefelbein and Noel McGinn (eds.), *La Universidad contemporánea. Un intento de análisis empírico*, Publicación no. 29, Santiago: Corporación de Promoción Universitaria.

Bases para un plan de desarrollo de la Universidad de Chile (1966), Santiago: Editorial Universitaria.

Beigel, F. (2008), *La conexión Santiago: transferencias académicas en las redes Jesuitas (1950–73)*, Buenos Aires: CLACSO.

——— (2009a), 'La FLACSO chilena y la regionalización de las ciencias sociales en América Latina (1957–73)', in *Revista Mexicana de Sociología México*, 71 (2): 319–49.

——— (2009b), 'Dependency Analysis: The Creation of New Social Theory in Latin America', in Sujata Patel (ed.), *The International Handbook on Diverse Sociological Traditions*, London: Sage.

Bell, D. (1985), *The Social Sciences Since the Second World War*, New Jersey: Transaction Books.

Bourdieu, P. (1984), *Homo Academicus*, Paris: Seuil.

Brunner, J.J. (1988), *El caso de la Sociología en Chile: Formación de una disciplina*, Santiago de Chile: FLACSO.

——— (1986), 'Factores que inciden en la especialización temática y en el desarrollo de la sociología en Chile', *Docu-mentos de Trabajo*, no. 302, Santiago: FLACSO.

——— (1989), 'Ciencias Sociales y Estado: Reflexiones en voz alta', *Material de Discusión,* no. 118, Santiago: FLACSO.

Devés Valdés, E. (2003), *El pensamiento latinoamericano en el siglo XX: Desde la CEPAL al neoliberalismo (1950–90), Tomo II*, Buenos Aires: Biblos.

——— (1998), 'El desprestigio de las ciencias sociales: Sociología y polìtica en Chile 1950–73 en Mapocho', *Revista de Humanidades y Ciencias Sociales*, no. 44.

First University Council (*Primer Claustro Universitario*) (1971), Santiago: Universidad Católica.

Garretón, M.A. et al. (2005), 'Social Sciences in Latin América: A Comparative Perspective (Argentina, Brazil, Chile, México and Uruguay)', in *Social Science Information*, vol. 44 (2 and 3), London: Sage, pp. 557–93.

Gazmuri, C. (1999), *Notas sobre las elites chilenas 1930–99*, Instituto de Historia, PUC: Santiago de Chile.

Guia Informativa delas Universida des Chilenas (1965) Consejo nacional de Informatión y Documentation, Santiago: Consejo de Rectores.

Informe Pnud (1981), *Desarrollo y Educacion en America Latina*, UNESCO, Cepal, Pnud, Informes finales (4 vols.).

Informe La Educación Superior En America Latina y El Caribe (2006), *La metamorfosis de la educación superior*, Iesalc-UNESCO, Caracas: Metrópolis.

Krebs, R. (1979), 'Historia del Consejo de Rectores en sus 25 años de vida', in *25 años Consejo de Rectores de las Universidades Chilenas, Santiago.*

Krebs, R. (1994), *Historia de la Pontificia Universidad Católica de Chile (1888–1988)*, 2 tomos, Ediciones Universidad Católica de Chile, Santiago de Chile.

Love, J. (1999), 'Las fuentes del estructuralismo latinoamericano' (The sources of Latin American structuralism), in Jorge Lora and Carlos Mallorquín (eds.), *Prebisch y Furtado: El estructuralismo Latinoamericano* (Latin American Structuralism), México: UAM, pp. 17–32.

Maio, M.C. (2007), 'Une programme contre le racisme au landeimain de la Seconde Guerre Mondiale', in *60 Ans d'histoire de l'UNESCO*, Paris: UNESCO.

Matonti, F. and F. Poupeau (2005), 'Le capital militant. Essai de définition', in *Actes de la recherche en sciences sociales*, no. 155, Paris: Seuil, pp. 5–12.

Miceli, S.O. (2001), *História das Ciencias Sociais no Brasil*, vol. 2, Sao Paulo: Editora Sumaré.

Peixoto, F. (2001), 'Franceses e Norte-Americanos nas Ciencias Sociais Brasileiras (1930–60)', in Sergio Org. Miceli, *História das Ciencias Sociais no Brasil*, vol. 2, Sao Paulo: Editora Sumaré, pp. 477–531.

Reyna, J. (2005), 'An Overview of the Institutionalization Process of Social Sciences in Mexico', in *Social Science Information*, London: Sage, vol. 44 (2 and 3), pp. 411–72.

Schiefelbein, E. (1968), 'Un intento de analisis global de la universidad chilena', in *Revista Plandes*, vols. 28–9, Santiago de Chile, pp. 5–159.

Subercaseux, B. (2004), *Historia del libro en Chile (alma y cuerpo)*, Santiago: LOM.

Szymanski, A. (1973), 'Las fundaciones internacionales y América Latina', in *Revista Mexicana de Sociología*, vol. 35 (4), pp. 801–17.

Trindade, H. (2005a), 'Social Sciences in Brazil in Perspective: Foundation, Consolidation and Diversification', in *Social Science Information*, London: Sage, vol. 44 (2 and 3), pp. 283–357.

——— (2005b), 'Ciencias sociales: instituciones e autores estratégicos no intercambio Franco-Brasilero', in Carlos Benedito Martins (ed.), *Diálogos entre Francia e o Brasil: Formación e co-operación académica*, Recife: Massangana.

CHAPTER 9

Anthropology at the University of the Philippines: Examining Institutional History and Academic Dependency in a South-East Asian University[1]

CARLOS P. TATEL, JR.

INTRODUCTION

This is an exploratory study on the relationship between institutional history and the nature of academic dependency among South-East Asian centres of higher learning. My paper aims to underscore the benefits of analysing institutional histories of academic disciplines in understanding the processes of 'coping' with academic dependency. The gist of this paper stands on the premise that the academe of the South has been long 'dependent' on its Northern counterparts, given the colonial relationship that has existed between the two in modern history. As a working definition for this essay, 'academic dependency' connotes that knowledge production is largely conducted in the institutions of higher learning in the North, i.e. the wealthy, industrialized nations, while academics of the South—consisting of developing nations and former colonies of the West—simply imitate, apply or validate knowledge produced in the North. I will argue here that the Department of Anthropology at the University of the Philippines (UP) has had issues with 'academic dependency', especially with regard to how this department relates to the intellectual tradition of the US. As the department reached its 90th anniversary milestone in 2007,[2] reassessing this 'dependency' status is a crucial institutional agenda. While it may be tempting to conclude that anthropology at UP has simply imbibed the Western, predominantly American, anthropological tradition, a closer look at its institutional history would reveal pockets of academic resistance and a major academic upheaval (largely as a result of the intellectual and nationalist ferment in the UP social science scene that reached its height in the 1970s to the 1980s) as a means of grappling with academic dependency.

'Dependency' is interpreted here as less of a monolithic concept than a phenomenon embellished with resistance, appropriation and, even, syncretism. Thus, 'coping' is viewed here as a dynamic construct that not only documents the 'survival strategies' to withstand Western academic and intellectual imperialism, but more importantly, mirror the independence and agency of the academic South by engaging the borrowed theories as well as innovating on the established methodologies of the North. These points I wish to elaborate with an examination of the institutional history of the anthropology department at UP—the oldest in the Philippines and, arguably, the pioneer anthropological unit in the whole of Asia.

I write here primarily as a 'historian of anthropology' and being a relatively new member of the UP Department of Anthropology gives me the much needed 'distance' from the past while allowing me at the same time to have a closer view at certain processes and situations. Thus, I could only give personal interpretations of events and situations and could not claim that my version is 'the official' one. Official histories of institutions do carry an inherent tendency toward providing a chronological sequence of its 'growth' and 'development'. And though my position as a member of the department makes me part of that 'official history', maintaining an independent stance adds to an objectivity that is so elusive in any historical writing. My study explores the relationship between academic institutional history and colonial dependency and how a particular academic unit strived not only to deal with dependency but, more importantly, to move beyond it by establishing its own independent academic discourse. As anthropology is increasingly recognized as a discipline that is undergoing shifting politics of representation and knowledge production (Moore, 1996: 1), the academic anthropological discipline through more than a hundred years, brought about diverse cultures and traditions of doing, researching and teaching anthropology. Needless to say, this work is towards the direction of examining non-Western anthropologies and to study an academic institution is one concrete way to do this.

Talastasan is a local term that has been integrated in the Filipino academic vocabulary which defines what the Filipino social scientists, for more than three decades (beginning in the 1970s), hoped to envision for the Philippine social sciences—a *nagsasariling talastasan* (roughly, an independent discourse) within which the Filipino academics use concepts and apply methods that are found in and specific to his/her culture, society and history. Under this rubric, the Filipino scholar uses and promotes the national language (though not overlooking the importance of regional languages) as a medium of scholarly communication and exchange that would popularize social sciences among the general Filipino public. It could be said that throughout the decades, the UP Department of Anthropology has had varying degrees of engagement with *Talastasang Pilipino* (Filipino discourse) as exemplified by the Filipinization of its own name—*Agham Tao*.[3] This paper does not claim, however, that the department has already declared 'independence' from the academic North using this concept—instead, it will elucidate the various contexts under which academic dependency was ingrained in the anthropological tradition of UP and the various ways UP anthropologists have grappled with the situation.

Ultimately, this paper hopes to open up a wider research

area aimed at assessing anthropological traditions in South-East Asia. Though cross-cultural studies in South-East Asia by South-East Asians are not common, there have been pockets of local scholarship that deal with 'regional anthropology' in South-East Asia. It may be useful to note here that, among South-East Asian anthropologists, the Philippines is being recognized as one of the first academic 'anthropologies' outside the Western institutions of higher learning (Shamsul, 2004: 286; Magos, 2004). A quick view of a regional history of academic anthropology indicates a salient difference between the Philippines and the rest of South-East Asia: in the former, academic anthropology is associated with the assimilationist programme of American colonialism, while in the latter, academic anthropology emerged largely in the context of post-colonialism, a time when most of the modern South-East Asian nations were just coming out of Western colonial bondage. One common strand among them, though, aside from a common colonial experience with Western imperialists, is the idea that anthropology has contributed to the formation of a modern South-East Asian nation state.

Thus, the investigation of the institutional history of such an important discipline like anthropology is an interesting project that could enrich the common past and culture of South-East Asian peoples, as well as shed light on the role of the anthropological discipline in the development of South-East Asian scholarship today and in the future. By labelling anthropology as an 'academic institution', this essay distinguishes a 'department of anthropology' from the kind of anthropology carried out by colonial states in South-East Asia during the major part of the colonial period. The edited series, *Anthropology and Colonialism in Asia and Oceania* (Bremen and Shimizu, 1999) underscores this point by elucidating the complex nature of the relationship between state anthropology and colonialism across South-East Asia. Therefore, to critically examine an academic institution provides a new dimension to this intellectual dependency analysis—that academic social science disciplines have always had the dual role of advancing knowledge and, at the same time, providing an arena of a fruitful power struggle between colonial forces/ agendas and movements toward indigenization.

Rather than a statement of a 'declaration of independence', this paper is more of a challenge to the current generation of 'homegrown' anthropologists to finally break out of academic/ colonial bondage. Though I focused on UP alone, I will point out that similar narratives of dependency might be seen across institutions of higher learning in South-East Asia. For example, the University of Malaya (UM), being the first university in Malaysia, may resemble the story of UP: the UP founded by the Americans, the UM by the British; UP was founded under a colonial regime, so was UM; UP celebrates its centennial in 2008, UM has already reached this milestone in 2005. The story has a similar plot in other areas such as Indonesia which also experienced a kind of 'state anthropology' under the Dutch colonial regime. As Indonesia became independent after the Second World War, anthropology departments sprung up from different national institutions of higher learning. Anthropology, along with other social sciences provided the thinking for the young Indonesian nation struggling to recover from the effects of colonialism (c.f. Agustin, 2008).[4] Overall, colonial relations between 'the West' and its former South-East Asian colonies provided the impetus for the Americans, British, Dutch, and perhaps, the French in developing their respective anthropological/ethnological traditions in their former colonies. Taking off from this point, it is interesting to note how anthropological departments in South-East Asian universities may have also shaped public opinion and consciousness. How would the differences in their anthropological traditions influence the nature and development of anthropological discourse in the said countries? Perhaps by showing the nature of anthropology at UP, it can serve as a fitting model for other former SEA colonies to analyse the concept of academic dependency.[5]

TOWARDS A HISTORIOGRAPHY OF THE UP DEPARTMENT OF ANTHROPOLOGY

Beginning in the 1960s, many articles, published and unpublished, have been written on the history of the department (Lynch and Racelis, 1961; Zamora, 1965 and 1974; Melendez and Caccam, 1967; Castro, 2006; Tatel, 2007), the history of anthropology in the Philippines (Tangco, 1940, as cited in Evangelista, 1971; Panopio and Bennagen, 1985; Bennagen, 1983, as cited in Abaya et al., 1999; Abaya, Lucas-Fernan and Noval-Morales, 1999; Magos, 2004), the history of the department in the context of the history of Philippine anthropology (Tan, 2004 and 2008) as well as some related histories of social science disciplines that provide pertinent information about the department's history (Ramos, Hernandez and Portugal, 1987; Jocano et al., 1994; Rolda and Panopio, 1984). When viewed alongside the general histories of the University of the Philippines (Craig, 1910; Jamias, 1962; Alfonso, 1985; Aquino, 1991), the history of the department of anthropology is like a fabric that completes the woven cloth that is the University of the Philippines. Moreover, the insights and oral recollections of some current and former members of the faculty and staff as well as professorial lecturers (Abaya, 2007; Tan, 2007; Castro, 2007; Jocano Jr., 2007; Cabanilla, 2007; Barrameda, 2007; Dalisay, 2007; Mangahas, 2007; Longacre, 2007; Salazar, 2007; Racelis, 2007; Del Rosario, 2007)[6] help make the picture clearer: the department in the post-Beyer era has been moving towards an increasingly multidisciplinary anthropological discourse, while hanging on to a four-field framework to the discipline, a somewhat Americanist anthropological approach—namely: biological anthropology, cultural/social anthropology, anthropological linguistics and archaeology—that allows the viewing and investigation of culture and of the people from a holistic perspective and methodology. The department's academic nature makes it one of the very few anthropological units in the Philippines (and in the world, for that matter) that hold this mode of anthropological inquiry.

I looked at academic dependency at UP by reconstructing the development of anthropological pedagogy in UP as it evolved through time. Through a review of different types of sources corroborated by oral accounts of selected past and present faculty members, I examine academic dependency in a very concrete and material context—anthropological theories, ethnographic methods and the Philippine situation is reflected in the department's own curriculum, faculty interests and knowledge production. Certain types of sources prove to be crucial: first, available official documentary records such as the annual UP General Catalogue and Announcements (1911, 1917, 1925, 1948, 1958–9, 1964–5, 1968–9, 1972–3), the College of Social Sciences and Philosophy (CSSP) General Catalogue (2006), Official Statements on certain pressing issues and secondary sources like published historical essays by UP professors on the history of UP and of the Department of Anthropology. Second, oral historical accounts by some senior faculty members (active, retired and those no longer connected with the department), as well as alumni and contemporaries. Finally, I was able to get hold of some photographic data on activities and field schools, but these need more time to complete. Personally, still the best general source for the official institutional history of the department, from the beginning up to the 1960s, as far as methodology and content are concerned, is the essay by Josephine Caccam and Pedro Melendez (1967), a fitting contribution to the *festschrift* for Prof. H. Otley Beyer—a collection edited by the then department chair, Mario Zamora. The two above-mentioned writers were lucky to have personally interviewed Marcelo Tangco—one of the first 17 students of anthropology under Beyer.[7]

ROOTS OF ANTHROPOLOGY IN THE PHILIPPINES

During the early twentieth century, anthropology, as an academic discipline, was undergoing a major intellectual shift: the challenge of 'historical particularism' against the established 'cultural evolutionism' of the late nineteenth and twentieth century. As in the case of the department of anthropology at UP, this particular knowledge production from the West and its corollary academic discourses shaped the Filipino anthropologists take on culture, race and identity of Filipinos. The overall historical context of the birth of the UP Department of Anthropology suggests a close link with the general vision of American colonialism in the Philippines. This had far-reaching effects in the Philippines and in the US. The ideology as well as methodology of the American anthropological 'tutelage' of Filipinos were informed by a confluence of factors: American economic interests, Euro–American ethnocentrism, American concepts of 'manifest destiny' and nation-forming 'frontier theory', the popular notions of race and socio-cultural evolution, their passion and belief in the 'white man's burden', and by the recent experiences of grand international fairs and expositions such as the 1893 World's Columbian Exposition in Chicago[8] and the controversial 1904 St. Louis Exposition in Missouri (Fermin, 2004; Jocano, Marquez and Caguimbal, 1994). Indeed, the American colonial regime benefited from the prevailing academic theories and perspectives then in vogue in the West; as a result, this mobilized intellectuals, especially anthropologists, which paved the way for the emergence of a Philippine Studies Program at the University of Chicago in the 1950s. Specialists on the Philippines were trained there and they contributed in the building and consolidating of a body of literature on the culture and history of the Filipinos. Ethnology, physical anthropology, and eventually, archaeology, played crucial roles in the performance of 'ethnological surveys' by American cultural investigators sent out into the field to do research.

As a prelude to anthropology's institutional birth and growth within UP, it is important to mention the activities of late nineteenth-century Filipino intellectuals, better known as the *Ilustrados*, who have conducted detailed ethnological studies, an assessment of their own country and people in order to create a body of knowledge about Filipinos—a Filipiniana heritage, that would provide an alternative narrative and analysis of the *La Patria Filipina* and her people. Unfortunately, some present-day Filipino scholars sometimes regard the cultural and historical aspects of *Ilustrados'* work as secondary only to the latter's political and social ideas. On the other hand, a closer examination of their collective historical, natural and cultural studies may qualify them as precursors of the anthropological field in the country. This was done around the time when the basis of anthropology as a formal field of academic inquiry was still being laid down in Europe by pre-nineteenth-century *philosophes* and positivists.

Following this line of thought, Jose Rizal should be remembered not only as a martyr and national hero but also as one of the foremost scholars of Filipino pre-hispanic culture, history and society. In 1890, he annotated the 1609 memoirs of Antonio de Morga,[9] proving many positive and important aspects of Filipino society at the time of the Spanish arrival in the Philippines in the sixteenth century. While in Dapitan as an exile, between 1892 and 1896, he conducted several studies in the Filipino languages, collected specimens of natural history and finally, even conducted some surface exploration of the island—identifying stone implements that could be of archaeological significance for the country. Meanwhile, there were published and unpublished scholarly works by noted Filipino intellectuals in the nineteenth century that are worth mentioning as well. Their works contained valuable materials on the archaeological, pre-historic, ethnographic, historical and cultural knowledge about the Philippines and the Filipinos: e.g. Vigan-born but Tondo-raised Jose Burgos (one of the martyr-priests in the triumvirate GOMBURZA; he had about nine college degrees and could well be the first Filipino archaeologist),[10] Vigan-born Isabelo de los Reyes,[11] doctor and scholar T.H. Pardo de Tavera (who became the first official Director of the Philippine National Library),[12] Pedro Paterno (more than being remembered as the mediator between the *Republica Filipina* and the Spanish government at the Pact of Biak-na-Bato, he was also an esteemed Philippine scholar).[13] These scholars could very well be the predecessors of today's Filipino anthropologists, archaeologists and pre-historians. It is a pity that when the ancestry of Philippine archaeology is discussed, foreigners—Spaniards and Americans—are usually mentioned. Rarely is the importance of the works of the *Ilustrados* given due credit.[14]

Meanwhile, several Europeans, naturalists and travellers, had already visited the Philippine islands long before the arrival of the Americans. Their mission was to 'collect' specimens for their respective museums and institutions, aside of course from their unofficial role as travellers and observers of native and colonized peoples. Most notable among them are the following: the German Feodor Jagor (Jagor, 1873/1965; Evangelista, 1971: 99)[15] who visited the country in 1860, the Frenchman Alfred Marche, who arrived in 1881 to collect specimens for the *Musée de l'Homme* (Marche, 1887/1970),[16] and J. Montano and Paul Rey who conducted cave explorations from 1878–88 (Evangelista, 1971: 100). Unfortunately, some writers, probably unaware of the publications and activities of the *Ilustrados*, believe that the activities of Marche spurred the beginning of anthropological history in the country.[17] On a different note, the ethnologist and historian Zeus Salazar (2006), commenting on the historical context of the roots of anthropology in the Philippines, says that the Filipino *Ilustrados* and European visitors shared a common characteristic, i.e. both were not formally trained in the science of anthropology, which was still in process of being defined as a formal scientific inquiry in the West. In a way, both were proto-anthropologists—only because their respective activities were not in consonance with the standard anthropological tenets that we know and observe today. Nevertheless, Salazar notes that one good thing about the *Ilustrados* is that they were skeptics in the sense that they were out to prove something—specifically, to prove that the Spaniards were wrong about many of their assertions about pre-hispanic Filipino culture and society.

Americanist anthropology filtered into the Philippine cultural scene at the turn of the twentieth century. Indeed, Western anthropology was still in its formative stage—yet already poised to set down a well-defined scientific tradition. Imbued with popular notions of race coupled with the dominant framework of uni-lineal cultural evolutionism attributed to the British anthropologist Edward B. Tylor and the American Lewis Henry Morgan, the U.S. colonial government in the Philippines embarked on a major ethnological survey of the major Philippine ethnic groups focusing mainly on the mountain-dwelling non-Christian Filipinos (thus, artificially and arbitrarily separating them from the 'pacified' Christian and lowland Filipinos of Luzon, Visayas and Mindanao). One colonial government agency that proved to be crucial in this respect was the *Ethnological Survey* which later became the Bureau of Non-Christian Tribes (BNCT) (Jocano, Marquez and Caguimbal, 1994; Rodriguez, 2004; Solheim, 1971). David P. Barrows, who happens to hold a PhD in Anthropology, supervised the programme of the bureau along with Dean C. Worcester, a Zoology professor from the University of Michigan (Kramer, 2004; Fermin, 2004) and a controversial fellow who was instrumental in the staging of a Philippine carnival at the 1904 St. Louis Exposition—arguably, the most popular attraction at that infamous international exposition (Fermin, 2004). This bureau would prove to be a vital agency during the American colonial regime in the Philippines, having supplied much of the cultural and racial justification for American presence in the country. This observation is buttressed by a cursory view of the *National Geographic Magazine* (1905, 1911, 1912, and 1913)[18] showing how Worcester, along with other colonial administrators like David P. Barrows and William H. Taft contributed to the 'imaging' and 'representation' of the Filipino—as seen through the lens of the West. Their work as well as the programmes and projects of their respective agencies contributed to the colonial gaze towards Philippine indigenous groups that focused mainly on the differences and uniqueness among various groups instead of elucidating underlying common cultural heritage. As what can be gleaned from their published photographs and ethnologies, they had created an image of a native 'noble savage', one that willingly embraced 'American civilization and culture'.

INSTITUTIONAL HISTORY/INTELLECTUAL HISTORY

The year 2008 marks the centennial of the University of the Philippines—considered as the premier institution of higher learning in the Philippines. It was established by the Americans in 1908, during the first decade of the American colonial regime in the Philippines. The first academic departments and institutes were likewise established by American educators—in fact, they were well-known academics in some of the leading educational institutions in the US, and thus became pioneers in different academic fields in the Philippines. It can be argued that the UP Department of Anthropology, in many ways, during the early phase of its existence, served the technical and professional needs of American colonial bureaus and agencies. The American pioneers in UP trained Filipino students who later became outstanding scholars as well. Buttressed by the latter's postgraduate degrees from the West, mainly from American universities (with strong Philippine studies programmes), they pursued scientific, cultural, social and historical studies that mirrored and copied Western theories and methodologies. A very strong link between the UP and the US institutions of higher learning was established and this continued even after colonialism was officially over. If it is any indication of 'tutelage', masked as continuing education of the Filipino academics, American anthropologists were hired as visiting professors and conducted ethnographies on the Philippines which were met with mixed reactions by Filipino scholars—some agreed with their assumptions and some vehemently objected and criticized their interpretations.

Eventually, a group of Filipino scholars championed for an indigenization or localization of well-entrenched foreign theories and methodologies. Particularly in certain social science departments where they advocated for more fitting theoretical models that would suit the cultural sensibility and historical particularity of the Philippine nation wanting to 'de-colonize' and 'Filipinize' itself. A succession of heated academic debates and polemics followed; stimulating intellectual discourses took place in the university. Such discussions, led by UP scholars, who also had received their training abroad, opened the possibility of creating a truly Filipino academic *talastasan*, by the Filipinos and among the Filipinos themselves.

The UP Department of Anthropology is one academic unit in the university that clearly reflects the above-mentioned narrative. Officially founded in 1917 and being one of the oldest departments in the field of social sciences in the Philippines, the UP Department of Anthropology plays eyewitness to the development of UP intellectual history in particular, and of Philippine social sciences, in general. The celebration of the centennial of the department itself is within reach—2017—hence, to come up with institutional history that will chronicle not only the administrative growth but also assess the evolution of Filipino scholarship in the social sciences, becomes imperative.

The UP Department of Anthropology has always been

known as the unit established by Prof. H. Otley Beyer who was considered by many as the father of Philippine archaeology and anthropology. Thus, the search for and creation of an independent and original Filipino anthropological framework is still on-going, as the current generation of UP anthropologists continue to grapple with local culture and Western orientation in anthropology. At the background of this effort is the Western intellectual tradition under which they are trained, and the Filipino people to whom they want to be of service. Ultimately, the department of anthropology can be seen as a microcosm of the history of the anthropological discipline in the country. But this is something to be desired in the future; the more pressing and bigger objective here in this paper is to provide a case wherein the relationship between institutional history and academic dependency can be explored so as to provide a model through which other South-East Asian centres of higher learning can also be analysed.

INSTITUTIONALIZING ANTHROPOLOGY IN UP

Indeed, the department was founded during the early years of American colonization of the Philippines—its history is intimately linked with the life and career of an American, Prof. Henry Otley Beyer, a geologist by training, who arrived in the country in 1905, employed as an ethnologist by the Office of Ethnological Survey of the Bureau of Education under David P. Barrows, former Dean of the graduate school of the University of California (Craig, 1910). Beyer pioneered anthropological/archaeological research in UP and steered the department from the time when he taught the first anthropology course in 1914, to its formal establishment in 1917 and until his retirement in 1954. He was succeeded by Marcelo Tangco, who is considered the first formally-trained Filipino physical anthropologist. Beyer was invited to UP by the first UP President, Murray Bartlett, to teach anthropology and eventually, to head the newly organized academic unit in 1917;

thus, finally separating it from the Department of History, which was then headed by the well-known Jose Rizal biographer, the American Austin Craig.

It cannot be denied that the beginnings of the UP Department of Anthropology are closely connected with the professional career and personal story of Beyer in the Philippines. It will be shown later in this essay how the life of the department depended upon the decisions that Beyer made as an individual scholar and as a department chair. Beyer himself became an institution in UP and in the Philippines. It is said that Beyer's first encounter with the Philippines was in the 1904 St. Louis Exposition when he saw a replica of the Philippine archipelago (Salcedo, 1967: 3). Upon his arrival in the country, his first assignment was in the Cordilleras, among the Ifugaos. Against this backdrop of personal mission and official function, he headed the newly established Department of Anthropology at the University of the Philippines, upon the invitation of the first UP President, Dr. Murray Bartlett (Caccam and Melendez, 1967: 7; Zamora, 1974: 361–2). What happens next is the first half century of Philippine and UP anthropological tradition dominated by an influential academic mentor in the mould of Prof. Beyer. Hence, the post-Beyer Department of Anthropology, when Marcelo Tangco assumed the chair in 1954, would somewhat struggle to come out of the shadow of an illustrious academic. After Beyer, a whole new generation of excellent individual scholars who have, in one way or another, received training or inspiration from Beyer, steered the department in the next couple of decades, notably: Marcelo Tangco, E. Arsenio Manuel and F. Landa Jocano. Despite the presence of very strong individual intellectuals, I would like to believe that the department under the aegis of these vibrant Filipino scholars underwent a major transformation and the institution grew beyond personalities. It created a lasting legacy that promotes academic excellence and values committed to service to the people and the nation using a broader and deeper understanding of their culture and society. The anthropologists they trained would carry the department through the critical, yet defining years, of the 1970s through the 1980s.

ANTHROPOLOGICAL PEDAGOGY AND RESEARCH: 1914–1954

It was in 1914 when 'Anthro 1', the first anthropology course and probably the oldest existing anthropology subject in UP and in the Philippines, and probably in Asia as well—was first taught by Beyer under the aegis of the Department of History (Ramos, Hernandez and Portugal, 1987). During his first three years of teaching as an 'Instructor' (UP General Catalogue and Announcements, 1917), Beyer was the only one teaching this introductory course that already contained a four-field approach to the discipline: physical anthropology, cultural anthropology, linguistics and archaeology.

In the 1917 General Catalogue, one would find the course description of 'Anthropology 1':

> *Anthro 1*: General Anthropology—A general introduction to the whole subject of anthropology, its history, aims and methods; physical anthropology, archaeology, ethnology, ethnography and language.

As soon as the Department of Anthropology was formed in 1917, Beyer assumed the rank of 'Assistant Professor' (UP General Catalogue and Announcements, 1917) and he eventually set out to recruit a number of teachers to beef up the faculty ranks. Encarnacion Gonzaga was hired as an 'Assistant', and Cecilio Lim was taken in with the rank of an 'Instructor' during the school term 1917–18 (Caccam and Melencez, 1967: 9). Marcelo Tangco, a member of the first batch of anthropology students in UP, was handpicked by his former professor to replace Gonzaga, who, unfortunately, was able to teach at the department for only a year. Additional recruitment that followed provided the much needed personnel for the department. In addition, it reflected the emerging research interests in the department; so we could say that pedagogy developed alongside the research agenda of the department during that time. Clearly, new courses were instituted to respond to the growing and widening of the anthropological discipline in the country, while reflecting also the intimate relationship between the young anthropological institute and colonial agencies such as the Bureau of Non-Christian Tribes under the Secretary of Interior.

To demonstrate this point, the catalogue of 1917 listed some more courses including the two below which were offered to students specifically to train them in a career in field anthropology. The courses were instituted under the guidance of the Secretary of Interior of the Philippine colonial government:

Anthro 7: The Social and Economic Life of the Mountain Peoples of the Philippines (Prerequisite: Anthro 1).

Anthro 8: The Government of Primitive Peoples.

Coming from the Department of English, Hazel Clark Taylor was made lecturer from 1918–20 to teach folklore. Meanwhile, John M. Garvan was recruited as instructor due to his field experience among the Manobos of Mindanao (Caccam and Melendez, 1967: 9). Faculty development was the major thrust of the department as Tangco was sent to the United States in 1921 to pursue higher studies. He came back in 1925 with a master's degree and began concentrating on the area of physical anthropology—a field that he would pioneer in UP (and in the Philippines for that matter), so that by the 1950s, after the Second World War, anthropology at UP was simply known as either archaeology or physical anthropology. For most of his teaching career, anthropology courses relating to this subject matter as well as topics such as human biological evolution came to be known as the 'home turf' of Tangco as he was the only faculty member formally trained in this field (aside from the fact that he was the only one teaching it). Nevertheless, Beyer and Tangco shared teaching responsibilities, especially the handling of *Anthro 1*. Tangco had even produced an unpublished textbook or sourcebook entitled, 'An Outline of Lectures in General Anthropology' (1931) which was, at that time, the only textbook in the Philippines for an introductory course in anthropology. The stature and training of Tangco as the only physical anthropologist in UP and in the country, was mirrored by the state of anthropology in UP then: *Anthropology 1* was a required course for 'Pre-Med' (preparatory programme for prospective medical students) students under the Bachelor of Arts of the College of Liberal Arts (CLA) curriculum. Furthermore, the following anthropology courses in the 1917 catalogue indicate a strong link with the biological and physical sciences:

Anthro 9: Racial Anatomy of the Philippine Peoples.
Anthro 14: Research in Criminal Anthropology.

In the UP Catalogue through the 1920s, more and more courses were offered in the field of physical anthropology. Some courses carried overt racial themes:

Anthro 203: Racial Anatomy of the Philippine Peoples.
Anthro 205: Research in Criminal Anthropology.
Anthro 108: Physical Anthropology.
Anthro 109: Criminal Anthropology and Race Mixture.

While Tangco was doing postgraduate work in the US, another former Beyer student was taken in as lecturer, Eduardo E. Palma. Palma did not stay long, however, and in 1924 (Caccam and Melendez, 1967: 10), Ricardo E. Galang, was hired as lecturer to fill in the position of Palma (Caccam and Melendez, 1967: 10). In 1925–6, Beyer and Tangco were the only full-time faculty members at the department, supplemented only by Galang and Tomas Maglaya as lecturers. Galang, having finished his MA in 1923 with a major in anthropology, was the first anthropology graduate of UP (Manuel, 1970: 207–8).[19] Within the first decade of the department's existence, connections and collaboration with other established departments in UP were observed such as the recruitment of English professor, Dean Spruill Fansler, the American who is said to have started the tradition of folkloric studies in UP, to give some lectures in folklore.[20] Two more lecturers came into the fold: Engracio Guazon who arrived in the academic year 1934–5, and Mariano Abogon who taught from 1936 through 1938. As a whole, the department was basically an academic unit of two—Beyer and Tangco—only assisted by lecturers whom Beyer had personally recruited.

With the reorganization of the College of Liberal Arts in 1921 that saw the creation of new departments and the fusion of existing ones, sociology was combined with anthropology and Beyer served as its chair. Hence, the department came to be known in the official records as the Department of Anthropology and Sociology (Caccam and Melendez, 1967) until 1951, when the former separated permanently from the latter. This means that for about three decades, faculty members who were sociologists by training and scholarly persuasion interacted and worked very closely with anthropologists. Meanwhile, this practice of putting together the disciplines of sociology and anthropology in a single department resonated in other leading Philippine universities such as the Ateneo de Manila University (Quezon City), San Carlos University (Cebu City), Silliman University (Silliman) and Xavier University (Cagayan de Oro City). When their respective departments were also established, sociology and anthropology combined, it was already about half a century after the establishment of the UP Department of Anthropology. Moreover, there are unconfirmed reports that Marcelo Tangco was instrumental too in the creation and establishment of a department of sociology in UP. Thus, when a symposium was organized in honour of Tangco in March 1966, the Department of Sociology and the Sociology Club of UP co-sponsored the event with the Department of

Anthropology, UP Anthropological Society and the Institute of Asian Studies (Bernardo, undated: 1).[21]

Pedagogy was not only circumscribed to UP but also continued to grow beyond the university. Aside from the department, Beyer headed his own institution, the Museum and Institute of Ethnology and Archaeology, a research and collection unit which he founded even before the beginning of his UP years. Consequently, when he became chair of the department, this was attached, rather unofficially, to the department as well. The history of this museum is hazy and needs further research and merits a separate write-up because its identity is separate from the department itself. Nevertheless, it is clear that as of 1967, the Beyer's museum was still in existence because Mario Zamora was the 'officer-in-charge' of this unit a year after Beyer's death in 1966 (Zamora, 1967).

The landmark publications of Beyer were, most notably: *Outline Review of Philippine Archaeology by Islands and Provinces* (1949),[22] *Philippine Tektites: A Contribution to the Study of Tektite Problem in General, in the Light of both Past and Recent Discoveries* (1961),[23] and *The Philippine Saga: A Pictorial History of the Archipelago since Time Began* (1947, with Jaime C. De Veyra).[24] Clearly, these were products of Beyer's tremendous individual scholarship and efforts at networking; but in all of these, Beyer took the reputation of UP with him and that made him more than just a UP anthropologist but a 'public intellectual', to use the present-day label. The first book mentioned, until now, is the only comprehensive survey of archaeological sites in the Philippines, from the early 1900s to the 1940s. Whenever a site would be excavated or explored by contemporary archaeologists in the Philippines, that book would serve as the starting point of an investigation. The second one revealed his geological interests with the study of tektites, but he related it to the archaeological and cultural dimensions of these extraterrestrial materials. Finally, the concept of 'waves of migration' as a complete and comprehensive theory for the peopling of the Philippine archipelago became popular and well-entrenched in Philippine historical texts.

These scholarly efforts by Beyer outside of his teaching chores in the university, not to mention managing and maintaining of a museum at Watson building, Aviles St. in Manila,[25] may be considered part of the research and extension services by a UP faculty member—a trait that is well entrenched in the UP academic community. Furthermore, these are reflections of an internal academic development within the Department of Anthropology. It gives an idea of the general direction of scholarship and nature of pedagogy being undertaken by the department. Beyer, in particular, after having devoted some time to ethnological studies, turned to archaeology; and when he did, he had given the rest of his precious academic life to studying Philippine and regional prehistory (Far Eastern Prehistory Congress). As already mentioned, he chaired the joint Fourth Far-Eastern Prehistory Congress and Eight Pacific Science Congress in 1953.

Attending to archaeology and prehistory was of paramount importance, especially at that time when archaeological sites were discovered here and there due to massive development projects in the Philippine islands and provinces (Beyer, 1947). Most notable of the sites is the Novaliches Dam construction project which produced excellent stratigraphic layers dating back to the Iron Age (Caccam and Melendez, 1967: 2; Beyer, 1947; Solheim, 1971). At this time, from 1917 up to the first decade of the post-Second World War era, archaeology and prehistory occupied a major portion of the relatively short curriculum (UP Catalogue, 1917, 1923, 1927, 1933, 1936, 1948, 1949, 1955, 1957, 1959):

Anthro 10: Philippine Archaeology (begun 1916).
Anthro 204: Philippine Archaeology (begun 1923).
Anthro 101: Archaeology of Malaysia (begun 1926).

Looking at the profile of the first postgraduate students of

Anthropology provides interesting insights on the diversity of interests and geographic extent of not only the topics tackled but also of the origins of the students themselves (Manuel, 1970: 207–8, 266–77; Caccam and Melendez, 1967: 11):

Ricardo E. Galang, 'Analysis of Racial Types Among Christian Filipinos' (1923).

Thomas Huisiang Lin, 'A Study in Chinese Customs of the Past' (1928).

Generoso S. Maceda, 'The Dumagats of Famy' (1932).

Francis X. Lynch, 'A Typological Study of the Neolithic Stone Implements of the Rizal-Bulacan Region of Luzon in Comparison to Those from Other Parts of the Philippines' (1949).

Walter Kenneth Miles, 'The Prehistory of the Philippines: A Review of Fact and Theory as Developed During the Past Half-Century of Research Study' (1953).

E. Arsenio Manuel, 'A Lexicographic Study of Tayabas Tagalog' (1954).

William T. Ward, 'A Preliminary Survey of the Economic and Social Life of the Mortlock Islands' (1955).

Ricardo Galang and Generoso Maceda, though separated by about a decade, were the first two Filipino postgraduate students of Anthropology at UP during the pre-Second World War era. Arsenio Manuel, who graduated in 1954, was the first Filipino anthropology graduate of the post-War period. Meanwhile, the presence of foreign students such as the Chinese Thomas Linn, Americans Frank Lynch, Walter Miles and William Ward and the geographic diversity of their studies, spoke well about the kind of anthropological training at UP. One may also get a sense of the culture of 'mentoring' as exemplified by Beyer as the professor of these students. Thomas Huixiang Lin, after receiving his Master of Arts in Anthropology in 1928 under the supervision of Beyer, went back to his native mainland China to pioneer ethnological and archaeological studies there (Bahay Tsinoy exhibit, 2007).[26] If the presence of foreign students were any indication of the prestige and reputation that the department had acquired through the first few decades of its existence, then the department had been firmly established as one of the foremost anthropological teaching units in the region. Following Lin were Americans Frank Lynch and Walter K. Miles who all finished their MAs in 1949 and 1953 respectively.

The department has been an institutional leader as well, but this leadership was anchored on Beyer. Nevertheless, it reached another milestone with the holding and sponsoring of the Second Far-Eastern Prehistory Congress in Manila in 1934 (Solheim, 1971: 10) and as the primary organizing body of the joint Fourth Far-Eastern Prehistory Congress and Eighth Pacific Science Congress in 1953 in Quezon City. The UP Department of Anthropology, at about this time, was already playing a leadership role in regional anthropological and archaeological research (Beyer, 1953).

Moving forward to the latter part of the first half century of the department's existence, a review of the courses from 1914 until the time of Beyer's retirement in 1954 would show that the department was evolving from a highly biological and physical sciences and archaeological, pedagogical and research tradition to include a more socio-cultural approach. Thus, the UP Department of Anthropology within the first 50 years of existence, had already established itself firmly as a 'four-field' anthropological unit.[27] From 1916–17, courses in socio-cultural anthropology covered the following: general regional ethnography, language, economics and the museum. The decade of the 1920s saw new offerings: folklore studies, and special problems courses. By the 1930s up to the 1940s, basically the same set of courses was retained and, at the same time, some of the course titles were modified. Some of these even had clear objectives to provide alternative approaches with regard to some practical situations in society. As the department grew and changed, so did the curriculum. We will see here the emergence of certain courses that emphasized the generation of basic knowledge about the

Filipino and his/her origins. Attempts would be made to connect the Filipino with other peoples in the region with the study of languages, folklore and material culture. Nevertheless, the courses would still reveal remnants of age-old concepts such as 'race' and exotic views of cultures (UP Catalogue, 1917s–50s):

Anthro 2: Ethnography of Eastern Asia and Oceania (begun 1916).
Anthro 9: The Indo–Oceanic Languages (begun 1916).
Anthro 11: Special Problems in Philippine and Oceania (begun 1916).
Anthro 12: Special Problems in Asiatic Anthropology (begun 1916).
Anthro 17: Folklore of Eastern Asia and Oceania (begun 1920s).
Anthro 201: Special Problems in Philippine and Oceanic Anthropology (begun 1920s).
Anthro 202: Special Problems in Asiatic Anthropology (begun 1920s).
Anthro 101: Archaeology of Malaysia (begun 1926).
Anthro 102: Ethnography of Eastern Asia and Oceania (begun 1926).
Anthro 117: Folklore of Eastern Asia and Oceania (begun 1926).

Anthropology, during the days of the old College of Liberal Arts, was really known as a 'bio-cultural' discipline. In fact, it was listed as a 'Pre-Med' course for students who wished to pursue medicine afterwards. When a college-wide divisional scheme was implemented in 1957, anthropology was listed in both categories (UP General Catalogue, 1958–59: 128–30):

Division of Biological Sciences

Botany
Psychology
Zoology
Anthropology

Division of Social Sciences

Anthropology
Economics
History
Philosophy
Political Science

Psychology
Sociology and Social Welfare

An interregnum followed during the War years, but it is said that Beyer was still able to continue his work despite the Japanese Occupation of Manila. A certain Tadao Kano, an ethnologist in the service of the Japanese military, took interest in Beyer's valuable collection and that contributed a lot in saving the museum from damage during the Battle of Manila (Caccam and Melendez, 1967: 13; Quirino, 1958).

The year 1952 was another important point in time for the department, though largely through the efforts of Beyer and his Research Assistant, Wilhelm G. Solheim II. The latter carried out what could be the first 'field school' in the history of the University of the Philippines: the archaeological excavation of the Batungan Caves in Masbate Island. According to Solheim himself, Beyer provided much of the financial needs of this summer archaeological training. It was Beyer who also suggested this site because he wanted to have additional data for his synthesis of Philippine prehistory. Those who participated in the first field season were Walter K. Miles, Ricardo Angeles and Alfredo Evangelista. Solheim, during the second season of the field work, and this time working on his own, went back to the site with the support of the Wenner-Gren Foundation for Anthropological Research. This time, E. Arsenio Manuel, another Research Assistant of Beyer who was also with Solheim in San Narciso, Tayabas in 1951, came over to help.

BROADENING OF THE ANTHROPOLOGICAL FIELD: FROM THE ACADEMIC PEDESTAL TO ACTION ANTHROPOLOGY (1960s–90s)

If during its first half century of existence the department saw very prominent personalities dominating Philippine anthropology, then the following two to three decades saw greater diversity within the department as more professionals and practitioners filled up its teaching positions. Seasoned anthropologists and luminaries, nevertheless, continued to serve but the young turks came in with their alternative intellectual modes and varying political convictions. Not taking for granted the basic research that the department was already known for, the department headed towards a people-centred anthropology—one that provided practical and just solutions to social and national problems and issues. Similar to what happened to students from other departments as well, many of its students and graduates during the Martial Law years became active in the underground movement as well as in non-governmental organizations (NGO). During the late 1970s to the 1980s, the department was also swept by the indigenization/Filipinization movement in the UP social sciences—a major intellectual upheaval that aimed to rid UP and the Philippine social sciences of Western ideology and perspective. A linguistic turn was in the offing, as *Agham Tao* was also used as an alternative name. However, the original name of the department was maintained, but *Agham Tao* somewhat caught on among some faculty members who still use the term to appropriate the Western discipline into the context of the Filipino.

Clearly, the next three decades of the department was a far cry from the pre-War academic unit that was dominated by towering figures in the persons of Beyer and Tangco; in the post-Beyer/Tangco era, the department organized and sponsored numerous activities that were made possible by a collective effort by the faculty members and staff who saw the value of collectivity and the practicality of establishing links and fostering collaboration with other scholars and units within and outside UP. The department metamorphosed from a passive knowledge producer to a dynamic social institution.

The 1960s saw subtle but meaningful modifications in the courses that reflected a major shift in global anthropological trends and scholarship: one, the introduction of '*Anthro 5*: Peoples of the Philippines'[28] and '*Anthro 124*: Peoples of

Eastern Asia and Oceania'; and two, the changing of the phrase, 'Eastern Asia/Far East' to 'South-East Asia'. The use of the terms 'Peoples' and 'South-East Asia' in lieu of 'Racial Types', 'Mountain Peoples', 'East Asia' and 'Far East' suggests a more culturally sensitive, politically correct and historically situated study of the Filipinos and their geographic context. The curriculum reflected this dynamism as it showed how the department grew and matured in terms of pedagogy and research:

Anthro 114: Archaeology of Eastern Asia and Oceania (begun 1960s).
Anthro 124: Peoples of Eastern Asia and Oceania (begun 1960s).
Anthro 164: Folklore of East Asia and Oceania (begun 1960s).

We will see here the seeming tussle between the 'old school' and new perspectives in anthropology, and even reflecting changing global configuration of geo-politics as observed in the replacement of 'Eastern Asia' or 'Far East' dominantly used before the War, in favour of, for example, more politically correct terms like, 'South-East Asia'.

The research agenda of the department clearly changed with the arrival in the 1960s of U.S. trained Filipino anthropologists—it paved the way for a more relevant anthropology for Filipinos in the 1970s. These scholars who had just received their PhDs from the Philippine Studies Program of the University of Chicago[29] created a niche in Philippine anthropology. This was largely supported by American funding agencies and scholarship programmes like the Fullbright, Rockefeller, Ford, etc. Filipino scholars like Moises Bello, Alfredo Evangelista, F. Landa Jocano, E. Arsenio Manuel and even Americans Frank Lynch and Robert Fox were virtual 'who's who' in the Philippine academic and cultural scene. Thus, unlike Beyer, their mentor and predecessor, they veered away from diffusionism as a theoretical framework and followed a new tradition dominant in the Philippine Studies Program of the University of Chicago: the Structural-Functionalism of Radcliff-Brown and continued by the head of that programme, Fred Eggan, professor of anthropology at the same university. In Cornell University, on the other hand, another Filipino anthropologist got his PhD: Mario Zamora—the sociologist-turned anthropologist who would lead the UP Department of Anthropology to new heights in the post-Beyer era.

The close link of the department to anthropology departments in the US, including the special programme of Philippine Studies at Chicago can be argued to be a continuation of 'tutelage' of the Filipinos in the American educational system and by the same token, 'tutelage' in the American anthropological tradition. US academic institutions provided the venue for UP scholars to get their doctoral degrees and reach a critical mass of trained Filipino anthropologists. As soon as they got back, they headed the department (and other institutions) for the succeeding years.[30]

The chairmanship of Zamora from 1963–71 is worth noting as it produced numerous projects that consolidated the role of the department as a leading teaching unit as well as a research institution in anthropology in the country. His administration encouraged cross-fertilization of disciplines—history, music, folklore, psychology, medicine, linguistics, archaeology, education, philosophy, economics and mass communication[31] —they all found convergence in the anthropological discipline. It was during this time that links with fellow UP scholars were encouraged, not only to lecture at the department but also to participate and collaborate in departmental projects and activities. Venues and opportunities were created that fostered cooperation and collaboration among the faculty members. Meanwhile, it tapped contributions from other Filipino anthropologists outside UP, which further broadened the field and the department's networks. A cursory view of the publications authored or edited by Zamora would give us a sense of the state of anthropology at the time, i.e. popularization of anthropology and making the discipline fit into the larger context of ongoing academic researches in UP and in the Philippine social sciences. In a landmark publication edited by Mario Zamora and Zeus Salazar, *Anthropology: Range and Relevance*, anthropology is treated as a wide-ranging and relevant discipline important in the study of Filipinos. It is interesting to note too, that the first anthropological paper written in Filipino was published in this volume—predating what would be the intellectual and nationalist ferment in the UP social sciences of the 1970s and 1980s.

During the dynamic academic leadership of Zamora, the years 1964–6 proved to be momentous for three main reasons. First, the *Memorandum of Understanding* between the University of the Philippines (represented by the University President, Carlos P. Romulo) and the National Museum (represented by the Museum Director, Galo B. Ocampo). This agreement allowed professional and scholarly exchange between the UP anthropology faculty and the National Museum personnel. As both are understood to have common and shared goals in Philippine anthropology and archaeology, this landmark agreement hoped to foster cooperation and mutual support between the two institutions. As a result, the first joint UP–NM anthropology field school was held in 1965/70[32] at the Tabon Caves, Quezon, Palawan Island under the supervision of National Museum resident archaeologist Robert Fox. It was the first and formal field school of UP anthropology majors since Solheim carried out the first field training in archaeology in 1952. The succeeding year saw broader scope in the UP–NM field school: Juan Francisco headed the cultural anthropology training in Bolinao, Pangasinan while Manuel supervised another batch of anthropology majors in Davao, Mindanao Island. Second, the *UP Anthropology Society* of anthropology majors was formed. This was the first ever anthropological organization in the country, even predating by 13 years the formation of the first and only professional organization of anthropologists in the country, the *Ugnayang Pang-Agham Tao* (UGAT, Inc.). This student organization (that included graduate and undergraduate students) enjoyed the support and encouragement of Zamora, who may have been its first faculty adviser. Finally, the holding of symposia and conferences in honour of senior and highly esteemed mentors: H. Otley Beyer and Marcelo Tangco. The first one was an international symposium held at Abelardo Hall in UP Diliman in honour of Beyer. Filipino and foreign scholars were invited to deliver research papers in honour of the esteemed and beloved mentor. Several units joined hands in making this possible: the Bureau of Science, the National Museum and the UP Department of Anthropology. The proceedings of this international conference were published in 1967 as a *festschrift* to Prof. Beyer. The second one was a similar conference—this time in honour of Tangco. His own department headed the task of putting this up with the support of the UP Anthropology Society and the Sociology Club of UP. In 1968, the first Symposium on National Integration was organized by the department—foreshadowing a major shift in the research agenda of the department, especially in the 1970s and beyond: the issue of indigenous peoples' rights.

With the reorganization of the CLA into a new College of Arts and Sciences (CAS),[33] anthropology found itself in the division of Social Sciences. This may be a strong indication as to where anthropology was going within the context of the University, i.e. increasingly geared toward the cultural and social sciences; while less and less of the physical and biological. The undergraduate course offerings at this time underwent minor changes, this time providing the basis for the current Anthropology curriculum (UP General Catalogue, 1968–9; 1970):

New Undergraduate Courses

Anthro 137: Culture Change.
Anthro 151: Comparative Religion.
Anthro 164: Folklore of South-East Asia and Oceania.
Anthro 199: Field Methods in Anthropology.

Graduate Courses

Anthro 215: Philippine Archaeology.
Anthro 216: Fieldwork in Philippine Archaeology.
Anthro 221: The Village Community.
Anthro 255: Research in Philippine Custom Law and Political System.
Anthro 259: Seminar on India and South Asia.
Anthro 272: Indian Folklore.
Anthro 276: Field Research in Philippine Folklore.
Anthro 284: Seminar on Problems of Contemporary Culture Change.
Anthro 285: Seminar on Problems in Asian Folklore.
Anthro 291: Special Problems in Asian Anthropology.
Anthro 295: Special Problems in Philippine and Oceanic Anthropology.
Anthro 300: Master's Thesis.

We can see here the emerging new fields within the department: area studies as exemplified by the courses on India and South Asia, and folkloric and village studies as demonstrated by the courses on folklore and non-urbanized communities. Meanwhile, the department research and teaching resources were improved as a result of networking and establishment of good working relationships with other institutions such as the National Museum and funding agencies like the Rockefeller Foundation and the private foundation formed to help sustain research in Philippine anthropology and archaeology, the Research Foundation of the Philippine Archaeology and Ethnology, Inc. In 1967, the department formally opened the UP Anthropology Museum while installing Natividad Noriega, Beyer's long-time assistant, as curator. This was the first museum of its kind in UP and probably in the Philippines. Its initial collections benefited mainly from the old Institute of Ethnology and Archaeology of Beyer during the pre-War years.

In the early 1970s, the great strides made in pedagogy, external linkages and research outputs of the department continued up to the time of its new head, F. Landa Jocano. A newly renovated Anthropology Museum was inaugurated featuring an exhibit on Philippine prehistory.[34] The curriculum was once more updated and revised, this time showing an expanded course offering physical anthropology, archaeology and a new course in applied anthropology. When Manuel became chair in 1974, he instituted the PhD programme in anthropology, thus making the anthropological training at UP complete from the undergraduate to the graduate level.

The agenda of the department from the 1970s to the late 1980s was one that tried not to perform solely the academic role of the institution, but more importantly, it strived to be of service to the Filipino people by bringing anthropology closer to the people—even closer than what Zamora had envisioned in the late 1960s. If the earlier aim was to make the discipline understood by non-anthropologists, the guiding principle this time was to make anthropology work for the people—emancipation from poverty, achieve social justice and protect basic human rights. It must be remembered that during these most trying times—the Martial Law of the Marcos era—the UP anthropologists along with other UP intellectuals firmly believed in the idea that the academe must actively participate in the transformation of society.

This new principle guiding the department had been translated into intellectual production by the faculty. It not only endeavoured to produce esoteric and purely academic knowledge about the peoples' cultures but more importantly to use that knowledge to guide state policies and programmes intended for the betterment of the Filipino nation. Data papers, occasional papers, monographs by the faculty members as well as theses submitted by graduate students covered topics that are applied in nature: health and disease, blast fishing, population education, etc. Increasingly, cultural ecology as a theoretical framework began to permeate anthropological production in UP.

During the last two decades, from the 1980s until the present, the department had to confront critical issues—both institutional and disciplinal. It would take issue on the continuing relevance of anthropology to UP in particular, and to the nation, in general. In all of these, the recurring and underlying theme was to keep and uphold at all times the supposed traditional and historic role of the department as a leading academic unit of anthropology in the country. Moreover, it aimed to maintain the highest intellectual integrity and credibility expected from its faculty and to be of service to the people from whom the anthropologists learned and because of whom anthropology continues to exist. Not a few times has the department had to question, challenge or protest state policies or programmes, especially when these implicated the issue of indigenous peoples or impinged on basic human rights. Faculty members have had to brave through tough times; indeed, they carried their ethical and other urgent cultural issues during the dark ages of the Martial Law and beyond. And this was the time when the holding of conferences and symposia criticizing the government and inviting high profile resource persons that openly criticized the government, were considered to be risky academic ventures.

With Ponciano Bennagen at the helm, the department sought to bring anthropology much closer to the people. It tried to perform what was expected of UP academics and that is to be 'agent[s] of reform, constructive social critics and working with and for the people'.[35] When the rights of the indigenous peoples were at stake for example, the department, along with other UP intellectuals, led the critique against the Tasaday issue and demanded from the people and institutions behind this 'discovery' a sense of ethical and scientific responsibility. About this time also, the department collaborated and worked well with the newly established UGAT. Both undertook projects that by now are milestones not only in the history of the department but also for the university as a whole:

- Forum on the Pantabangan and Chico Dam Project (1978).
- The International Conference on the Tasaday and other Urgent Anthropological Issues (1986).
- First Conference of the Ancestral Domain: Human Rights and the Ancestral Domain (1983).

Within the community of anthropologists UP anthropologists strived hard to set an example by working for the interest of the marginalized sector, as an instrument of social renewal and national transformation. UP anthropologists, regardless of whether they were successful with their mission or not, endeavoured to distinguish themselves from those who did anthropology simply as a profession; they tried to do anthropology as if it were a sacred vocation. Meanwhile, as the key figures in the dynamic decades of the 1970s and the early 1980s left the department to pursue other fields, the institution struggled to keep itself afloat despite internal and external woes besetting it. The four-field approach, which was held for so long as a unique feature of anthropological training at UP, was being challenged more than ever in the light of new theories and movements in both anthropology and archaeology.

Meanwhile, the indigenization/Filipinization of the social sciences was started in the UP academic scene during the 1970s and went on through the late 1990s. Amidst reactions and criticisms from various academics within the university, the movement called for a linguistic turn in the social sciences (i.e. from the dominant use of the English language to the use of the Filipino, the national language, in social science discourse). Led by Virgilio Enriquez at the Psychology Department, Zeus Salazar at the History Department (who, at one time, was Professorial Lecturer at the Department of Anthropology) and Prospero Covar at the Anthropology Department, this linguistic turn symbolized a major paradigm shift in Filipino social science; at first, as a reaction to the seeming 'academic/intellectual dependency' from the West, and later developed into an independent and original social science theorizing for the Filipinos and by the Filipino scholars.

Apparently, the brewing 'values debate' that had been going on within the local anthropological circles since the 1970s (but again, participated in by foreign scholars!) somewhat fanned the flames of the indigenization movement in the academic scene. The proponents of indigenization saw how limited and biased the analysis of the Filipino culture and society would become if these were viewed and analysed from the lens and apparatus of Western theory and methodology. In this connection, *Pilipinolohiya*, a design for graduate studies in the Philippine social sciences that is largely attributed to Covar, found concrete expression in the graduate programme of the College of Social Sciences and Philosophy (Aquino, 1999). Covar's anthropological training had a major input in the formulation of the multi-disciplinary programme. However, it is still a subject of further research to assess how much *Pilipinolohiya* has shaped the UP social science scene. Furthermore, as this graduate programme somewhat lost steam in the mid to the late 1990s by reverting to its English name, 'Philippine Studies Program', it deserves a closer look into how it was able to permeate and influence the anthropological tradition in the Department of Anthropology itself. Nevertheless, Covar's professorial chair lecture in 1993 entitled, *Kaalamang Bayang Dalumat ng Pagkataong Pilipino* (roughly, Local Knowledge on the Filipino Personhood) created a stir in the academic community, which in a way, opened the floodgates of scholarship even wider for more attempts to interpret Filipino identity, personhood, society and psychology using non-Western paradigms—particularly, using units of analyses that are found and experienced in the Filipino socio-cultural context (Covar, 1993).

SOME INSIGHTS FROM A HISTORY OF ACADEMIC ANTHROPOLOGY

Aside from its relevance to the year marking the centennial of the University of the Philippines, the writing of the history of the department of anthropology inevitably leads to the examination of the history of anthropology as an academic discipline in the Philippines. What follows are basically brief personal reflections into the institutional history of the discipline by focusing on how academic dependency became a key factor across time. They can be summarized in three points.

1. *Four-field Anthropology.* Anthropology in UP retains the four-field approach that reflects both its uniqueness among the anthropology faculties in the Philippines and, at the same time, the Americanist tradition in Philippine anthropology. Since the teaching of the first anthropology course in 1914, *Anthro 1*, anthropology in UP has always been a four-field disicipline: physical anthropology, cultural anthropology, linguistic anthropology and archaeology. It demonstrates that the department adheres to the 'holistic' approach that is characteristic of the American anthropological school of thought. Nevertheless, this approach fits well into the Philippine context as 'anthropology as a holistic science' guided most of the important ethnographic production in the major part of its academic history.

2. *Politics of Knowledge Production.* For the first seventy years of the department's existence, knowledge production was largely a question of who produced it and what was it used for. Generally, the question was also true for other social disciplines (for example, history), that have been established under the regime of either American administrators or Filipinos who trained under American scholars. Whether anthropology at UP has or has not produced knowledge independent of the major Western theoretical perspectives during that time, is a case that should be assessed by the bulk of intellectual production. As I have already expounded quite extensively in the past sections of this paper, it appeared that the academe followed the general theoretical trend in the West and local anthropologists seemed to function as researchers who only validated such theories. Two instances may support this: First, Beyer's utilization of the German 'diffusionist' school of

thought in the explanation of important aspects of Filipino culture and history, namely: origins and peopling of the archipelago, the traits and 'racial' differences among its peoples and the rise of Philippine pre-Hispanic societies. His ethnographic investigations as well as archaeological survey of the islands were framed within this theoretical perspective. By collaborating with an eminent Filipino historian in the 1940s, this theory, largely known as the 'waves of migration theory' became well-entrenched in the Philippine academic scene and has been widely cited for explaining the genesis of the Filipino people. Second, there was an emphasis on 'formal training' and this meant getting graduate degrees in anthropology at foreign institutions like the University of Chicago in the US. In particular, the Philippine Studies Program of the University of Chicago is a programme instituted in the 1950s, specifically to produce specialists on the Philippines in order to understand this country better. Many Filipinos who graduated from this programme became leaders of the department in successive years. In their works, they have applied a structural-functionalist approach to anthropological inquiry; a predominant theoretical framework in the Department of Anthropology of the University of Chicago during that time. Moreover, it is noted too that the Filipino scholars abroad largely depended on foreign funding and support coming from state and private agencies: Fulbright, Ford, Rockefeller, etc. While we may think that these things occurred only among Filipino scholars, it is interesting to note that this story has a parallel plot in other countries of the South such as in Indonesia. Widely known as a 'Ford country' (due to Ford Foundation scholarships), their intellectual and academic leaders were also sent to American universities to train in different fields (Agustin, 2008). What is striking is that it happened within the decade of the 1950s which was also the period when most of the Filipino anthropologists were also going to the US to get their degrees.

3. *Research Agenda.* This provided the direction as to where the department was heading at different points in time. Studying the research agenda of the department across various periods gives an idea of the programme of action of leaders as well as members of the faculty. It also shows how some committed individual UP anthropologists had carried the torch in shaking off academic dependency. The general theme of the research agenda revolves around the following:

Engagement with the Indigenous Peoples

This has been one of the most pervasive agendas in the 'teaching, research and extension' activities of the department. The faculty has been involved and has grappled with the issue and concept of the 'IP' perhaps since Beyer's time to the present. Its meaning has evolved from the colonial 'non-Christian tribes' of the early 1900s (which ultimately has its roots in the pre-twentieth-century term *Naturales/indigeno)* to the 'cultural minorities' of the PANAMIN of the 1970s to mean the present-day 'IP' of the National Commission on Indigenous Peoples. The colonial Bureau of Non-Christian Tribes (BNCT)—the agency which produced several landmark ethnologies of different Philippine ethnic groups before Second World War—even had a course instituted in the department specifically to train students who wished to work with the agency.

Ponciano Bennagen, Chairman of the Department from the late 1970s to the early 1980s, and probably the first to have written a Master's thesis in Anthropology in Filipino (the national language of the Philippines), became a delegate to the Philippine constitutional convention of 1986 and has been instrumental in ensuring the protection of the rights of the IP under the state. The 'IP' element is central to the advocacy of 'action anthropology' or 'anthropology in the service of the people' that was dominant from the 1970s to early 1980s. When the Tasadays of Mindanao were branded by the

PANAMIN as the so-called 'stone age peoples' in the modern era, the UP Department of Anthropology, along with the College of Social Sciences and Philosophy and Ugnayang Agham Tao (UGAT) sponsored an international conference in 1986 aimed at providing academic and scientific critiques of the Tasaday claim and demanded ethical and moral responsibility from those who were behind the 'hoax'. Around this time also, the department, in cooperation with different institutions and groups, sponsored other relevant and high profile symposia and conferences that concerned the rights and determination of the future of the IP. This is the legacy that permeates the researches and advocacies of individual faculty members who are still doing applied aspects of the anthropological discipline.

Popularizing Anthropology

Though aimed at 'non-anthropologists', popularizing here does not necessarily mean abandoning meticulous scholarship in favour of the general public. It only aims to make anthropology more relevant to the needs and situation of *kapookang Pilipino* (roughly, Filipino context). In fact, popularizing, at least as far as Mario Zamora, the department chair of the 1960s, is concerned, means broadening the scope of anthropology. A landmark publication he has co-edited with the ethnologist-historian, Zeus Salazar, *Anthropology: Range and Relevance (Anthropology for non-anthropologists)*, included wide ranging contributions from different scholars—both local and foreign—with varying specializations but with only a common interest in Philippine culture and society. The ability of anthropology to embrace all other disciplines, e.g. social sciences, biological/physical sciences, is testament to its 'holistic' nature toward understanding of a particular group of people. Moreover, the book featured research projects in other Asian countries which made it one of the first edited books that featured anthropology in non-Western contexts.

Hence, it is worth noting that Mario Zamora's specialist studies of India demonstrated one of the earliest forms of academic independence by studying a culture outside his own.[36]

Methodologically, popularizing anthropology may also mean utilizing other methodologies in the investigation of human social and biological phenomenon. Institutionally, popularizing the discipline means strengthening links and creating more opportunities for networking. By the time F. Landa Jocano assumed the chairmanship from the early to the mid-1970s, the department had already identified key stakeholders in Philippine anthropology, namely: the scholars, the public, the state and the private sector.

Embedded in the history of anthropology are connections and relationships among various disciplines including biological and social sciences. In the divisional reorganization of the former College of Liberal Arts of UP in the 1960s, for example, anthropology was listed in two divisions: the division of biological sciences and the division of the social sciences. Much earlier, in the 1920s, anthropology was considered part of the courses for the 'Pre-Med' (Pre-Medicine). Beyer, himself, was a geologist before he became an ethnologist/archaeologist. Marcelo Tangco, the first Filipino to get a graduate degree in anthropology in the US, is a physical anthropologist —a known sub-field of anthropology that is inclined toward the biological and the physical sciences.

By the 1970s, the founding of two new organizations proved to be crucial: first, the UP Anthropology Society—the student organization of Anthropology majors. It is the first ever association of anthropology in the country; and second, *Ugnayang Pang-Agham Tao* or UGAT, the professional organization of Filipino anthropologists. For quite some time, this organization had its office at the Department of Anthropology in UP, indicating the leadership role that this department had played in the development of a national anthropological tradition.

In the early 1970s, the first ever joint UP-National Museum anthropological field school in Tabon Caves, Palawan was held. Under the supervision of Robert Fox, this activity was a logical outcome of the official agreement or understanding between UP Department of Anthropology and the NM to jointly 'foster and promote anthropological research in the Philippines'. The latter was instrumental also in putting up the exhibit of Filipino prehistory at the UP Anthropology Museum—a major attraction in the former College of Arts and Sciences in UP at that time. Finally, the current chair, Michael Tan, continues to broaden the scope of anthropology by strengthening the medical anthropology and gender and sexuality fields in the department which has links with medical universities, agencies and NGOs here and abroad.

Filipinization/Indigenization

This is an offshoot of the influential intellectual movement that was dominant in UP from the late 1970s to the 1990s. As a result, the department assumed another name: AGHAM-TAO (or roughly, the 'Science of Human Being'). Nevertheless, it appears to be a result of the individual effort of some faculty members rather than a concerted act of the whole department. Taking the lead role here is Prospero Covar, but he is better known to have developed this indigenization framework within the rubric of *Pilipinolohiya* or the 'Philippine Studies Program' of the College of Social Sciences and Philosophy of UP. The department, generally, preferred striking a balance between adhering to the Western mode of anthropological inquiry that it was used to, and advocating the creation of an independent indigenous/Filipino discourse in anthropology, which was espoused mainly by Covar.

In terms of academic training and production by Filipinos, there have been less and less graduate students in anthropology who go to the North for their PhDs, while there are more and more postgraduate theses and dissertations written in the national language. I think this is a strong indication that the UP Department of Anthropology, carried through by committed individual academics, is gearing up for complete academic independence some time in the near future.

ACADEMIC ANTHROPOLOGY'S MARCH TOWARD ITS OWN CENTENNIAL

It is quite symbolic, perhaps, that when, in 1989, the Cultural Center of the Philippines (CCP) hailed Professor Emeritus E. Arsenio Manuel as the Dean of Filipino Anthropology, the Department of Anthropology at UP was not quite the same institution that he used to know. It has definitely transformed into something richer and more dynamic than the one he saw while he was still a student and Research Associate of Beyer. If it were any sign of the current state of anthropology at UP, Manuel was able to live long enough to reach the period of the current chairman, Michael Tan, in the year 2001. That meant that the 'old tradition' had dovetailed with the 'new era' in which anthropology is beginning to rethink, revise and re-orient many of its earlier assumptions about Filipinos, their culture and society, the nation and the very existence of anthropology. Manuel symbolizes a 'historic moment' in the story of academic anthropology in the Philippines. He still is, by the way, one of the most prolific Filipino anthropologists having around fifty titles under his name when searched in the On-line Access Catalogue (OPAC) of the UP Main Library. His era of 'academic tutelage' by the Americans contrasts strikingly with a department of 'homegrown' social scientists who, despite being several generations down the academic family tree, strive to engage this tradition of academic dependency by breaking into and participating in the indigenization movement of Philippine social sciences. Having the public interest in mind, Filipino anthropologists are more sensitive to the politics of theorizing from within and make the academe sensitive and accessible to the general Filipino public.

As a number of antiquated course offerings today reflect the colonial and American anthropological heritage in UP, the present-day department endeavours to create and promote new fields and dynamic areas of studies which do not aim to replace Western models but put them in a better perspective—contextualizing data and interpreting social phenomenon based on the people's own cultural categories and modes of thinking. Already well into the ninetieth year of its establishment, the present department has the rare benefit of hindsight to see what good or bad things have happened in the past; more than ever, it is in the best position to step back to see the bigger picture. It is a great challenge for this institution to come up with pedagogical principles and research agendas relevant in today's world and appropriate for the near future. The present era is rather auspicious and just as historic: The twenty-fifth anniversary of the establishment of the College of Social Sciences and Philosophy (the precursor of which is the College of Arts and Sciences); and the year of the university's centennial. With the marking of the ninetieth anniversary of the founding of the department, this noble institution is yet to pass another crossroads in history. When it reaches its own centennial a decade hence, the department would hopefully break the shackles of aca-demic bondage. This era is a defining moment that the UP Department of Anthropology should take advantage of.

NOTES

1. This paper is based on and expanded from an unpublished paper written by the same author entitled, '90 Years of Anthropology at UP: A Brief Historical Sketch (1917–2007)', presented in the workshop held in Patna. I acknowledge the support of the UP Department of Anthropology for the research and writing of this paper. The contributions of current and former faculty members of the department are acknowledged. Special thanks to the

department Chair Michael Tan for supporting this research from the start. I am also grateful to Zeus Salazar, Nestor Castro, Soledad Dalisay, M.C. Barrameda, Mary Racelis and Rosario del Rosario for providing their insights and support for this research. Many thanks also to Israel Cabanilla, Felipe Jocano Jr, Maria Mangahas, Eufracio Abaya, Rosa Castillo and some UP Anthropology Society alumni for their personal opinions and memories about the department's history. Faculty from other departments and units also provided the inspiration and shared some useful information: Mary Jane Rodriguez-Tatel, Michael Charleston Chua, Milagros Guerrero, Milagros Laurel and Wilhelm Solheim II. Special mention to M.C. Barrameda, Soledad Dalisay and Catherine Liamzon for proof-reading/editing this material; as well as to Irene Agbayani who was my student assistant during the latter part of the research. Finally, thanks to the members of my Anthropology 111 class of the 1 Semester 2006–7 who served as the staff of the exhibit, 'Lalim: Paghuhukay sa Pamanang Arkeolohikal ng UP Departmento ng Antropolohiya'. The exhibit buttressed the data regarding some aspects of the history of the UP Department of Anthropology. All the shortcomings of this research are mine and the opinions and interpretations expressed here do not represent the official standpoint of the said academic institution.

2. A few sources, however, point to 1914 as the date of the founding of the Department of Anthropology at UP. However, the present author maintains that the year 1917 was the official and the most reliable date of its establishment.
3. *Agham* means science; *Tao* means human.
4. Retno Agustin was an Indonesian Graduate Student Fellow in 2008 at the Asia Research Institute (ARI) at the National University of Singapore. Her comments were buttressed by information provided by other Indonesian fellows at ARI. Nevertheless, this is an interesting area that could be further elaborated upon in the future.
5. Based on a cursory survey of official websites of South-East Asian Universities, the following institutions can be part of a regional study: Universiti Putra Malaysia (UPM), the National University of Malaysia, founded in 1965; National University of Singapore (NUS), founded in 1905 (according to a website); Gadjah Mada University; the oldest university in Indonesia, established in 1965. All of the above-mentioned are some of the leading universities in South-East Asia and, thus, may have social science faculties or

anthropological departments that can be studied in the same way as I have studied the UP Department of Anthropology.

6. Most of them are informal personal communications.
7. Caccam and Melendez (1967) cite the 'Report of Records' as their source. Following is the complete list of the first batch of *Anthro 1 students*: Celedonia Agrava, Aurelio P. Arguelles, Sulpicio Bellocillo, Jose Cabalquinto, Jose M. Hilario, Sancho de Leon, Ramon P. Locsin, Ponciano Lorena, Arsenio E. Martir, Marcelo Mondoñedo, Rufino L. Montañano, Teofilo Palencia, Vicente Quinto, Domingo Recio, Marcelo Tangco, Dominador Velasco and Gregorio Velasquez.
8. This was earlier displayed in the 1892 Columbian Exposition in Madrid.
9. See Jose Rizal's annotation of Antonio de Morga's work, *Sucesos de las Islas Filipina* (1890). (See also the translation from Spanish by Encarnacion Alzona, 'Events in the Philippines', which came out in 1969 during the centenary celebration in honor of Jose Rizal).
10. Cf. E. Arsenio Manuel (1955), *Dictionary of Philippine Biography*. Examples of work by Jose Burgos on Pre-hispanic Philippine culture and society: *Estado de Fiipinas a la Llegada de los Españoles* (1864), Manila; *Estudios Sobre la Vida del Filipino Pre-historico* (1866), Manila. [There is a published version with a slightly different title: *Estado de Filipinas antes de la Llegada de los Españoles*, Cebu: Mayo, 1941. Copyright by P.D. Delfin, printed by Barba Press, Cebu; *Estudios sobre la Arqueologia de Manila a la Llegada de los Españoles* (1871), Manila.]
11. Example of his works on the culture and society of the Filipinos: *El Folklore Filipino* (1889), Imprenta de Sta. Cruz, Manila; *Historia de Filipinas* (1889), Imprenta de D.E. Balbas, Manila; *Historia de Ilocos* (1890), Establecimiento Tipografico 'La Opinion', Manila; *Paleografia: Filologia Visaya* (1889), Tipo-Litografia de Chofre, Manila; *Filipinas: articulos varios sobre etnografia, historia, costumbres del pais* (1887), J.A. Ramos, Manila, *La Religion Antiqua de los Filipinos* (1909), Imprenta de El Renacimiento, Manila.
12. Cf. E. Arsenio Manuel's *Dictionary of Philippine* Biography (1955), Filipiniana Publications, Quezon City; Salcedo, 1967: 1; The following are some of T.H. Pardo de Tavera's works on Philippine prehistory and culture: *Contribucion para el Estdudio*

de los Antiguos Alfabetos Filipinos (1884), *El Sanscrito en la Lengua Tagalog* (1887), *Las Costumbres de los Tagalos de Fiipinas, sedun el Padre Plasencia* (1892), *Biblioteca Filipina* (1903), *Reseña Historica de Filipinas desde su Descrubimiento hasta* 1903 (1906) among others.

13. Example of his works on Philippine pre-Hispanic culture and society: *La Antigua Civilisacion Tagalog* (1915), Tip. Linotype del Colegio de Sto. Tomas, Manila.
14. Also part of the on-going study by Tatel (2007) is: 'Lalim: Searching for the Early Filipino Archaeologist and Pre-historian', Concept Paper Manuscript.
15. Cf. Fedor Jagor, *Travels in the Philippines*, translated edition (1965). Filipiniana Book Guild, Manila.
16. Alfred Marche, *Luzon and Palawan*, translated edition (1970) by Filipinia Book Guild, Manila (tr. Carmen Ojeda and Jovito Castro).
17. Evangelista (1971: 98–100) noted that Beyer (1947: 205–6) and Solheim (1952: 62; 1953: 154) listed only one important archaeological investigation carried out in the Philippines before the arrival of the Americans in the Philippine islands—and that is by Alfred Marche who arrived in 1881 and published his works in 1887. When he noted other people who conducted archaeological activities, such as Feodor Jagor in 1869, J. Montano and Paul Rey in 1878–81 and Jose Rizal in 1894, he described them as not having produced significant findings. Meanwhile, Mijares (1998) simply echoed Evangelista's adherence to Beyer and Solheim's view of the beginnings of Philippine archaeology.
18. Cf. Tatel, Carlos Jr. P. (2004), 'The Non-Western Peoples as Filipinos: Mediating Notions of Otherness in the Photographs of the National Geographic Magazine in the early twentieth century. Paper presented at the 4 International Convention of Asia Scholars (ICAS 4) in Shanghai, People's Republic of China, August 2004.
19. Thesis title: 'Analysis of Racial Types Among Christian Filipinos'.
20. But this is not to overshadow the earlier and much more important studies by Filipino *Ilustrados* such as Isabelo de los Reyes, T.H. Pardo de Tavera and Jose Rizal. Nevertheless, stories have it that during Fansler's time, the systematic recording and massive recollection of Philippine was made with the help of UP students themselves who were culture bearers themselves and had roots in provinces outside Manila (Interview with Milagros Laurel of

the UP Department of English and Comparative Literarture, July 2007).

21. Nevertheless, this piece of information must be corroborated with the 'official' history of the UP Department of Sociology.
22. This is the major reference for archaeologists who are going to excavate sites within the archipelago. Cf. Beyer (1949), 'Outline Review of Philippine Archaeology by Islands and Provinces', in *The Philippine Journal of Science*, 77 (3–4), July to August, Bureau of Printing, Manila.
23. Another study was made earlier on the Tektites: *The Relation of Tektites to Archaeology*, National Research Council of the Philippines, University of the Philippines, Quezon City.
24. Manila: Evening News, *Criticisms on the 'Waves of Migration Theory'*. This is also laid out in several sources such as Scott (1994), *Barangay: Sixteenth-Century Philippine Culture and Society* (Introduction). Ateneo de Manila University, Quezon City.
25. This is from a personal communication with Dr. Wilhelm G., on the Solheim II Bahay Internasyunal, 14 July 2007.
26. Cf. Museum Text about Lin Hiuxiang, *Bahay Tsinoy: A Museum of the Chinese in Philippine Life*, Intramuros, Manila (visited in August 2007).
27. These subjects have undergone changes as well; some of the course titles were modified, while some were abolished in the process.
28. This is *Anthro 123* in the present curriculum.
29. This is established in the 1950s. Cf. Fred Eggan (1953), 'A Report on the Philippine Studies Program at the University of Chicago, Newberry Library and Chicago Natural History Museum', in *Fourth Far Eastern Prehistory Congress and Anthropology and Anthropology Division of the Eight Pacific Science Congress; Abstracts and Messages*, Organizing Committee, Quezon City.
30. Interestingly, in 1956, the Philippine Studies Program headed by Fred Eggan at the University of Chicago, sponsored a conference entitled, 'Mindanao Studies'. The contributors were virtual who's who in Philippine anthropological scene at that time: Harold Conklin, Felix Keesing, Charles Frake, etc. Incidentally, this conference—belonging to a series of international conferences on the Philippines organized by Americans—pre-dated the graduate course in the department, 'Anthropology 279 (Special Problems in Mindanao)' by twenty-seven years in terms of focusing on Mindanao as an area of study.

31. Table of contents: Mario Zamora and Zeus Salazar (eds.), *Anthropology: Range and Relevance (A Reader for Non-Anthropologists)*, Kayumanggi Publishers, Quezon City, 1969; Mario D. Zamora, *Cultural Anthropology: Its Dimensions, Its Limitations, Its Applications*, MCS Enterprises, Inc., Manila, 1972 and Mario D. Zamora and Robert Lawless (eds.), *Anthropology for Non-Anthropologists* (General Education Journal No. 12, Second Semester 1966–7).
32. The official year has yet to be established by the author.
33. This will become the present College of Social Sciences and Philosophy (CSSP), College of Science (CS) and College of Arts and Letters (CAL) in 1983.
34. This resembles the exhibition theme of the previous main exhibit of the National Museum and the current exhibit of the Asian Center, UP Diliman.
35. Anonymous (1977), 'The UP Department of Anthropology: 1914–77', p. 7 (unpublished manuscript).
36. During the Academic Dependency workshop in Patna, India (2008), an Indian scholar called my attention to Mario Zamora's possible contributions to the development of anthropology in a major Indian university.

REFERENCES

Primary Sources

Documents

UP General Catalogue and Announcements (1911, 1917, 1925, 1948, 1958–9, 1964–5, 1968–9, 1972–3).

UP Diliman General Catalogue (2000–3).

Document of Understanding Between the National Museum's Division of Anthropology and the University of the Philippines' Department of Anthropology, 28 August 1964, Quezon City.

General Inventory of Dr H.O. Beyer's Collection Now Housed in The Museum of Anthropology, University of the Philippines (Natividad Noriega, compiler).

Statement on the Tasaday Controversy, UP Department of Anthropology, 3 December 1987, UP Diliman.

Statement (on the Tasaday Issue), Ugnayang Pang-Agham Tao, Inc. (UGAT, Inc.), 15 September 1986, Faculty Center 3053, UP Diliman.

Student Handbook, Sociology-Anthropology Department, Siliman University, Dumaguete City.

Interviews

Interview with Dr Zeus A. Salazar, 65 Gomburza St., Area 1, UP Campus, Diliman, Quezon City, February 2006; SM City Food Court, October 2007.

Interview with Dr Soledad Natalia Dalisay, Faculty Center, June 2006.

Interview with Prof. M.C. Barrameda, Faculty Center, October 2006.

Interview with Dr Mary Racelis, Institute of Philippine Culture, February 2007.

Interview with Dr Wilhelm G. Solheim II, Balay Internasyunal, October 2007.

Interview with Dr Rosario del Rosario, UP Gender Office, December 2007.

Interview with Ms Retno Agustin, Asia Research Institute, National University of Singapore, July 2008.

Secondary Sources

On the History of Anthropology in the Philippines and the History of the UP Department of Anthropology

Abaya, Eufracio, Ma. Luisa Lucas-Fernan and Daisy Y. Noval-Morales (1999), 'Shifting Terms of Engagement: A Review of the History of Anthropology', in Virginia Miralao (ed.), *The Philippine Social Science in the Life of the Nation*, Quezon City: Philippine Social Science Research Council.

Abaya, Eufracio (2007), Anthro 278 class lecture (Special Problems in Philippine Cultural Anthropology), 2nd Semester, Academic Year 2006–7.

Anonymous (1977), 'The UP Department of Anthropology: 1914–77', unpublished manuscript.

Castro, Nestor T. (2006), 'Kasaysayan ng U.P. Departamento ng Antropolohiya', unpublished manuscript.

Evangelista, Alfredo (1971), 'The Philippines: Archaeology in the Philippines to the 1950', in *Asian Perspectives*, 12: 97–104.

Jamias, Cristino (1962), 'The University of the Philippines: The First Half-Century', in *Diliman Review* (U.P. Golden Jubilee Special Supplement) Quezon City: University of the Philippines Press.

Jocano, F. Landa, Lilia Marquez and Mamerta Caguimbal (1994), 'Ethnology in the Philippines: A Brief History', in *Problems and Methods in the Study of Philippine Indigenous Ethnic Cultures (A Preliminary Overview).*

Lynch, Frank and Mary R. Hollnsteiner (1961), 'Sixty Years of Philippine Ethnology', in *Science Review*, 2 (11).

Magos, Alicia P. (2004), 'Towards Indigenization: Responses, Challenges and Experiences in the Philippines', in Shinji Yamashita, Joseph Bosco and J.S. Eades (eds.), *The Making of Anthropology in East and South-East Asia*, New York and Oxford: Berghahn Books.

Melendez, Pedro at Josephine Caccam (1967), 'The U.P. Department of Anthropology: 1914–65', in Mario D. Zamora (ed.), *Studies in Philippine Anthropology (In Honor of H. Otley Beyer)*, Quezon City: Almar-Phoenix.

Panopio, Isabel S. and Ponciano L. Bennagen (1985), 'The Philippines', in *Sociology and Social Anthropology in Asia and the Pacific*, New Delhi: Wiley Eastern.

Rolda, Realidad Santico and Isabel S. Panopio (1984), *Cultural Anthropology: Philippine Perspective*, Quezon City: Katha Publishing Co., Inc.

Salazar, Zeus A. (2006), 'Ang Kasaysayan ng Agham Tao/Antropolohiyang Pilipino', unpublished manuscript.

Tangco, Marcelo (1940), 'Anthropology and the Philippines: A Sketch of the History of Anthropology in the Philippines', in *The Philippine Social Science Review*, 12 (3): 189–211 (cited in the *Bibliography of Evangelista*, 1971).

Tan, Michael L. (2004), 'Past Present: Reflections on Philippine Anthropology in the 21 Century', unpublished manuscript, CSSP Faculty Workshop.

——— (2008), 'Philippine Anthropology in a Post-Anthropology Age', *Rafael Palma UP Centennial Lectures: Marangal at Kritikal na Pananaliksik para sa Bayan, 1908–2008,* Palma Hall Audio Visual Room, 27 February 2008.

Tatel, Carlos P., Jr. (2007), '90 Years of Anthropology at UP: A

Historical Sketch (1917–2007)—Concept Paper', unpublished manuscript (On-going research project, UP Department of Anthropology).

Zamora, Mario D. (1965), 'The UP Anthropology Department and Research', in *The UP Research Digest* (January), pp. 31–3.

OTHER SOURCES

Alfonso, Oscar (ed.) (1985), *University of the Philippines: The First 75 Years (1908–83): A Diamond Jubilee Publication*, Quezon City: University of the Philippines Press.

Aijmer, Goran (1997), 'Why Should Anthropologists Bother About the Past: The Force of Anthropology in History', in *Anthropology in History and History in Anthropology*, South China Research Center, Division of Humanities, The Hong Kong University of Science and Technology, Kowloon, Hong Kong.

Aquino, Belinda A. (1991), *University Experience: Essay on the 82 Anniversary of the University of the Philippines*, Quezon City: University of the Philippines Press.

Aquino, Clemen C. (1999), 'Mula sa Kinaroroonan: Kapwa, Kapatiran at Bayan sa Agham Panlipunan', *Professorial Chair Paper*, UP Diliman: CSSP Publications.

Barrows, David P. (1901), 'Instructions for Field Volunteers', *The Bureau of Non-Christian Tribes for the Philippine Islands, Circular Information*, Washington: The Museum of Ethnology, Natural History and Commerce.

——— (1905), 'Educating the Filipinos', *National Geographic Magazine*, 16: 46–9.

Beyer, Henry Otley (1949), 'Outline Review of Philippine Archaeology by Islands and Provinces', in *Philippine Journal of Science* 77 (3–6).

——— (1953), 'Prehistory Abstracts and Messages: Introductory Notes by the Organizing Chairman', in *Fourth Far-Eastern Prehistory Congress and Anthropology Division of the Eight Pacific Science Congress Abstracts and Messages*.

Bennagen, Ponciano (1976), 'Kultura at Kapaligiran: Pangkulturang Pagbabago at Kapanatagan ng mga Agta sa Palanan, Isabela', Master of Arts (Anthropology) Thesis, College of Arts and Sciences, University of the Philippines, Diliman.

Bremen, Jan van and Akitoshi Shimizu (eds.) (1999), *Anthropology and Colonialism in Asia and Oceania*, Great Britain: Curzon Press.

Craig, Austin (1911), 'Short Paper on Philippine University', in M.M. Norton (ed.), *Builders of a Nation: A Series of Biographical Sketches*, Manila, Philippine Islands.

Covar, Prospero R. (1993), 'Kaalamang Bayang Dalumat ng Pagkataong Pilipino', Professorial Chair Lecture, CSSP, UP Diliman: Faculty Conference Hall.

Fermin, Jose D. (2004), *1904 World's Fair: The Filipino Experience*, Quezon City: University of the Philippines Press.

Kramer, Paul (2006), *The Blood of Government: Race, Empire, the United States and the Philippines*, Quezon City: Ateneo de Manila University Press.

Manuel, E. Arsenio (1970), *Dictionary of Philippine Biography*, Quezon City: Filipiniana Publications.

Mendoza, Lily S. (2002), *Between the Homeland and the Diaspora: the Politics of Theorizing Filipino and Filipino American Identities: A Second Look at Post-Structuralism-Indigenization Debates*, New York: Routledge.

Mijares, Armand (1998), 'Philippine Archaeology in Retrospect', in Victor Paz (ed.), *HUKAY: Bulletin of the University of the Philippines Archaeological Studies Program* 1 (1): 16.

Moore, Henrietta L. (1996), 'The Changing Nature of Anthropological Knowledge: An Introduction', in Henrietta Moore (ed.), *The Future of Anthropological Knowledge*, London and New York: Routledge.

Noriega, Natividad (1971), *UP Museum of Anthropology Guide-Brochure* (Data Paper No. 3), University of the Philippines-Diliman, mimeographed publication.

Nunag, Angelito (2007), 'Living the War Years: Everyday Life of the Tondeños during the Japanese Occupation', On-going Masters' thesis in History (manuscript), University of the Philippines, Diliman.

Ramos, Elsie S. and Elizabeth Anne Hernandez and Pamela Grace L. Portugal (1987), 'Kasaysayan ng Departamento ng Kasaysayan (1910–58)', Undergraduate History thesis, Department of History, UP Diliman.

Rodriguez, Mary Jane B. (2004), 'Reading a Colonial Bureau: The Politics of Cultural Investigation on the Non-Christian Filipinos', paper presented at the 4th International Convention of Asia

Scholars (ICAS 4), Shanghai, Peoples Republic of China, August 2004.

Panopio, Isabel and Realidad Santico-Rolda (1988), *Sociology and Anthropology: An Introduction*, Manila: Goodwill Trading.

Ronquillo, Wilfredo P. (2004), 'The Contributions of Wilhelm G. Solheim II to Philippine Prehistory and Archaeology', in Victor Paz (ed.), *South-East Asian Archaeology: Wilhelm G. Solheim II Festscrift*, Quezon City: UP Press.

Salcedo, Juan, Jr. (1967), 'H. Otley Beyer: Anthropology and the Philippines', in Mario D. Zamora (ed.), *Studies in Philippine Anthropology (In Honor of H. Otley Beyer)*, Quezon City: Almar-Phoenix, pp. 1–5.

Shamsul, A.B. (2004), 'Anthropology, Identity and Nation Formation in Malaysia', in Shinji Yamashita, Joseph Bosco and J.S. Eades (eds.), *The Making of Anthropology in East and South-East Asia*, New York and Oxford: Berghahn Books.

Solheim, Wilhelm G. II (1971), 'H. Otley Beyer', in *Asian Perspectives*, 12: 1–18.

——— (1964), *The Archaeology of Central Philippines: A Study Chiefly of on the Iron Age and its Relationships*, Manila: Bureau of Printing.

Taft, William Howard (1905), 'The Philippines', *National Geographic Magazine*, 16: 361–75.

Tatel, Carlos P., Jr. (2005), 'The Non-Western Peoples as Filipinos: Ethnic Representation in the *National Geographic Magazine* of early 1900s', paper presented at the 4th International Convention of Asia Scholars (ICAS 4), Shanghai, Peoples Republic of China, August 2004.

——— (2007), 'Lalim: Searching for the Early Filipino Archaeologists/ Prehistorians', Concept Paper Manuscript.

Worcester, Dean C. (1911), 'Field Sports Among Wild Men of Northern Luzon', *National Geographic Magazine*, 22: 215–67.

——— (1912), 'Head-Hunters of Northern Luzon', *National Geographic Magazine*, 23: 833–930.

——— (1913), 'Non-Christian Peoples of Philippine Islands with an Account of What has been Done for Them under the American Rule', *National Geographic Magazine*.

Zamora, Mario D. and Robert Lawless (eds.) (1967), *Anthropology for Non-Anthropologists*, College of Arts and Sciences, UP, Quezon City.

Zamora, Mario D. and Zeus A. Salazar (eds.) (1969), *Anthropology: Range and Relevance: A Reader for Non-Anthropologists* Quezon City: Kayumanggi Press.

Zamora, Mario D. (1974), 'Henry Otley Beyer, 1883–1966', in *American Anthropologist*, 76 (2): 361–2.

——— (ed.) (1967), *Studies in Philippine Anthropology (In Honor of H. Otley Beyer)*, Quezon City: Alemar-Phoenix.

CHAPTER 10

Evidence, Temporality, Analytical Frameworks: Categories, Writing Procedures and Academic Dependency

MARIO RUFER[1]

INTRODUCTION

This is an article about disciplinary procedures, social narratives, and the construction of 'H'istory as a productive and repressive discourse. This has to do with authors, locations, editorial and circulation politics, specific symbolic apprehensions of gnosis and knowledge and global impulses. Author: almost my whole academic life and objectives have to do with academic dependency. In a relatively peripheral academic centre (Córdoba), Argentina, and holding a BA in History, I decided to pursue an MA in African Studies, but in Mexico. I thought that—as a result of intuition at that time—learning about other places in the 'global South' (and from those places) could encourage a change in a disciplinary regime so rooted in Western epistemologies and methodologies. History in Latin America (and in particular in Argentina) is only now incorporating reflections from post-colonial studies, subaltern epistemologies and 'post-occidental' perspectives in the core of its narrative construction. A conviction that was (and is) the basis of that decision of mine: if we think that history as a discipline can offer a critical approach to a radical present, we need to de-naturalize the experiences of its conception, imagining and writing.

'De-naturalization' is not a new claim in terms of disciplinary approaches, but there are two salient facts we must mention in this regard: (1) Historians are still attached, generally, to forms, methodological protocols and ways of evidence construction that arose in 'Europe' and still considered as a 'sovereign theoretical subject' (Chakrabarty, 2000); (2) Even when historians try to dismantle or unravel the paths of this 'dependency' on European forms of 'translating the past'—this refers to much of post-colonial writing on historiography—we must accept that these 'new protocols' came from US-based and European academia, from scholars teaching and writing there, which configures a peculiar geopolitics of knowledge. That is to say: this constitutes a new form of epistemic asymmetry or at least a new form of knowledge/power validation, which is operating at the core of 'subaltern analyses' in academic work (Palermo, 2007). This does not mean that we must generalize or dismiss the kind of radical reflection and new imaginations in these fields of history-writing, coming from 'the North'. However, it is important to recognize at least two issues here:

1. The assumption put forward first by Dipesh Chakrabarty (1999) and later by Walter Mignolo (Walsh, 2002: 17–43) among others, about why southern scholars must read, know and quote European historians or critics, can now be inversely displaced. If you are speaking about subalterns or post-coloniality or even about reorganization of knowledge, many of the authorized voices come (this means those voices that are written down and published and produced) from the North.[2]
2. As many intellectuals working in 'the South' such as Edgardo Lander (2004: 259–83) or Javier Sanjinés, (Sanjinés, 2002: 157–74) were saying (and also Walter Mignolo of course, an Argentinean literary critic working at Duke University, but with a strong connection with Latin American scholars (Mignolo, 2000: 9–53), we must pay attention to the 'plus' of authorization in knowledge

coming from (northern) located places of production and publication (but not consumption). Even if in Latin America we 'know' about intellectual productions in other 'souths', our access to them is often through a 'northern' channel of validation/authorization/publication. And, even when new studies on the geopolitics of knowledge are present in current studies in social sciences (strongly visible in Latin America) their effects are found mainly in Anthropology, Cultural Studies or Literary Criticism. Interestingly and of upmost importance in this article, History seems to be apart, 'clean' from these challenges: the heterogeneous particularities of historical events, and even the heterogeneous rationalities of social actions in historical terms are considered a coda and figure as the discipline's sub-categories: 'historical ethnography' and 'historical anthropology'; or even seen as the 'anthropological imagination' in history; as if concerning another kind of sensibility, coming from outside history and which could support the real frames of the discipline.[3]

In short, the structure of the discipline as a monument where objectivity can be discussed formally, but never defied in procedures of thinking and writing, is still more or less intact. Above all, History appears as a core including new objects, new evidences, new subjects and new theoretical patterns but adds and criticizes them in already established models of operation. Moreover, when we have fluid theoretical reflections about the imperatives to re-think historical protocols mirrored in the 'European theoretical subject',[4] they rarely transcend theory to see them operating in concrete historical accounts or research projects.

From this point of departure, my question is: How can we deal with alternative forms of production when the 'alternative' is many times formatted in terms of a fixed category socialized by first-world chains of intellectual diffusion? Is a South-South exchange effectively possible in terms of consolidation of projects/discussion and production of knowledge from south(ern) institutional locations? If the answer were yes, and taking into consideration these general 'geopolitics of knowledge' described above, what are precisely the 'disciplinary politics of knowledge' we must discuss in history, in terms of teaching and doing research from southern positions/institutions/real locations? Is there an empirical form 'to see the alternative'—often produced (formatted, or formulated as a *cargoistic* pattern) by the North?[5] Theoretical approaches are still operating as a fixed core of procedures (with strong criticism coming from different places, of course, but which are still, as this article is, in a seminal position of critic-proposition).[6] As we are already told, the apparition of theory in the Western division of thought labour (as different from empiricism) was not only to impose a single framework (geopolitically localized) from where thinking objects and conceiving problems were facilitated, but also to delimitate the conditions to know (and think) the social worlds. (Wallerstein, 1995 and Mignolo, 2003).

In order to discuss some points to encourage a flexible model for historians residing in the South(s) but also doing research from/on South(s) (post-colonial/post-occidental locations),[7] I will examine three main points of discussion: (1) The construction of 'evidence', its powerful grammar and its implication for southern intellectual locations; (2) The re-emergence of heterogeneous temporality and its potential for a situated historical discipline; (3) The consideration of analytical units in the historical discourse, involving what I consider as 'memories without warranty'.

EVIDENCE

It has often been stated that the production of historical evidence is an effect of constraint.[8] This does not only involve the consideration of the archive as a form of political knowledge, as an emanation of power already widely analysed.[9] It does also not (only) mean considering 'alternative' sources and methodologies either; also widely discussed (although a pre-disposition towards written sources is still evident in quotidian protocols of historical practice).[10] I would here like to pose two more important factors for consideration:

1. Our attitudes (the historian's that is) to what does constitute historical evidence.
2. The intermingled social and academic pre-dispositions to history (in this case, with regard to what history is and to historical accuracy and liability).

First, even when we (historians) are familiarized with alternative sources as evidence of the past, often we are reluctant to develop other procedures to treat them, and we persist in the canonical tradition of reading them as strategic evidence. In African and also Latin American studies the examples are various. For example, oral histories have to be proven not as tales but as history. Yet, formulaic elements of what constitutes 'truth' in academic (Western) history are still pervading in this case, and historians often try to show that the procedures and logic of, e.g. oral histories are more or less the same as 'evidence' that comes from the archives.[11] The intention of course is to elevate oral histories to the status of truth. But much more complex is to de-naturalize (Western/colonial/modern) attitudes towards why these formulaic procedures support a veritable history. This is not mainly a theoretical (abstract) position. It implies also a reflection on academic attitudes and political commitment. In different essays, historians such as Frederick Cooper (2005: 157 and onwards) and Steven Feirerman (199: 182–216) from African perspectives, and Javier Sanjinés (2005) or David Slater (2004: 167 and onwards) from Latin American ones, have already posed the constraints of 'History' over social forms of dealing with the past. Again, we are not only concerned here with a consideration of other sources, but with knowing how these can be read from other points of departure, agency, and figurations of power. Oral/artistic/performative sources should not be treated as a *coda* to archival sources, but as different articulations of memory. The important thing therefore is to de-naturalize, starting from the point of access and belonging of the intellectual/historian. Moreover, we know that as an organic part of the 'south(s)', we are traversed by a colonial information economy in the procedures of the writing of history (Lalu, 2000: 46–8). This means that the constitution of evidence as a form of domination implies a concrete bias in the forms of conjuring up, using and representing the past. Again, the question is not only to look for other forms of historical evidence, but to ask, from our places of thinking and writing how to empower and authorize these evidences, not as peculiar traces to hold the 'real' sources, but as epistemic dispositions to the past that we must understand.

This still sounds too abstract. But I will try to reflect on my own research activity and concrete (empiric) problems to pose some questions. When I was doing research in Argentina and South Africa (Rufer forthcoming) about attitudes towards recent (violent) pasts,[12] through official and sub-altern/other commemorations, I understood that the concept added by David Cohen, 'the production of history' (Cohen, 1994: xvi and onwards) implies a strong challenge to understand that academic history is only one piece of 'the voices of the past'.

I will try to explain further. In Argentina, one disruption took place through the construction of new memories of the cruel dictatorship (1976–83): the Indigenous Movement was claiming from 2004 onwards a place in the new museum of memory at the former ESMA (a former clandestine centre for torture and disappearance of people).[13] This was politically unheard of by the state but also by different Human Rights and political organizations. *Stricto sensu*, indigenous people had nothing to do (except in isolated cases) with the opprobrium of dictatorship and forced disappearance of people which mainly concerned young students, workers and middle-class leftist militants, men and women. Why was the indigenous movement asking for this inclusion, this kind of fracture or eruption in the collective arena of political action?[14] Because they consider the 'beginning' of state terrorism not the years 1966, 1974 or 1976 (different implementations of state repression are implied in those dates) but they feel it all started with the 'Conquest of the Desert', the moment when the nation state formation was consolidated with the expropriation of indigenous lands, and the extermination of the indigenous population to 'end with the frontier'. After those events in 1879–85, the history is commonly stated: European immigration, consolidation of Argentina as a strong periphery in the international division of labour. In 2004, when indigenous people started this 'claiming', other events were happening: the Director of the National Museum of History started to criticize these new historical visions of the 'Conquest of the Desert', stating that there was 'no evidence' of the previous population of indigenous people prior to Spanish conquerors in the sixteenth century; that the presentation of the 'Conquest of the Desert' as a genocide, was indeed 'a myth'.[15] History, evidence, myth: A triad of elements constitutive of the discipline and the disciplinary logics of what is 'History' and what is the border of its practice (Cohen, 1994).

However, 'evidence', conceived as a mechanism to prove, needs to be revised. Its revision comes even from the heart of the (Western) disciplinary exercise, but the current practices are difficult to eradicate. In his last intellectual legacy on *History, Memory and Forgetting*, Paul Ricoeur already stated that, 'It is not always forbidden to solve the distance between the representational efficacy of discourse, and the requirements of the event'.[16] In this sense, this distance implies new forms of articulation of evidence. In my interview with one of the main representatives of the Indigenous Movement in Argentina, he stated:

> . . . the thing is not our simple inclusion, as an additive exercise, in a museum as anthropologists usually do. We want to be a part of national history. Not the ones who were murdered—except a few like me [He was referring ironically to the common and effective (but erroneous)

discourse about the disappearance of indigenous populations in Argentina]. That is their history. We have a different one. This one [he extended me a book in *kolla* phonetic]. And this is not a story. This is history, written by a historian. But our historian.[17]

I cannot further elaborate on the consequences of his discourse.[18] However, I wanted to quote this here because of two reasons: (1) The leader was conceiving 'the production of history' as recognition of legislative reason: A book, not a story, written by a historian (the importance of the device, the form and the agent). I am implying that he was trying to show a form of empowered discourse from within the already known forms of historical discourse, and not alternative ones. Why? Because he recognized in me an agent of professionalized history, to whom the past is a kind of discourse with certain amount of defined protocols, he was empowering his discourse with my criteria. (2) He was appointing an implicit re-configuration of temporality (I will return to this in the next section). The strategic use of history and evidence made me reflect on one point: If history is a product of constraint[19] and if evidence in history is a result of the epistemic-colonial economy (which means, is never a neutral procedure), how can we deal with this in our daily work? Furthermore, how can we consider the 'other rests' of sources/evidences (tales, literatures, pictures, art) (Witz, 2003; Fabian, 1996; Comaroff, 1993; Pube, 2004 and Axel, 2001) and also the dispositions to them as constitutive of the forces and relations of power intervening in the conformation of historical discourse? How can we, historians, working on/from 'the South', deal with this 'grammar' of the colonial constitution of evidence-validation-history from our places?

After few minutes of conversation, the leader I was interviewing on that occasion said to me:

. . . first, it is important to recognize an objective fact: In Argentina the population of indigenous people is large in relative terms. Nobody knows it. Why? Because we were culturally invisibilized. Now, we have certain recognition as 'other cultures' [He makes gestures of quote unquote]. But we lack recognition in history. Our culture is not producing documents. Or at least, we produce other things you do not really believe as sources, do you? But now, here, tell me, do you really think that your proofs are real tales about events? Do you really think that yours is real history and that more is needed to tell ours? [he laughed]. . . .

He was adding a perfect distinction to what we inherited from the imperial distribution of knowledge: The passage from the recognition of 'culture' to the recognition of 'history'. But one needs a reconfiguration of the sensibilities of the protocols, procedures and modes of empowerment of historical evidence (Achúgar, 1998).

Another clarification is needed: As a critical discipline, history needs to revitalize not only the contingency of its own modes of production of discourse (Chakrabarty, 1999), (this is to say, recognize connivance with the formative constitutions of colonial modernities and national cultures) (Dube, 2004: 106 and onwards) but also its aspirations as a politics of recovery. My point here is that we must promote from south(s) an epistemic commitment for restitution: not only a so-called restitution of the 'voice of silenced peoples', but also a historicity of strategies of adaptation, negotiation and contestation of epistemic forces of power/knowledge.[20]

Probably, one of the possible measures with which to cope with epistemic dependency towards the constitution of evidence in history (once the restitution of alternative sources is more or less an already achieved goal in academy) is to make these contingencies evident in the process of writing, assuming that the protocols of historical truth are always being re-made, and that binaries like oral/written sources, tales/historical accounts, magic/secularized thinking are not only imposed categories but are also operative and constitutive of social worlds. We cannot assume a priori a strict bias of what is history for them (e.g. indigenous people) and what it is for us. This is mainly because in post-colonial societies (and in Argentina especially, because there is no recognition of colonial relations pervading the national/modern history), we can thus ossify and naturalize differences. After all, they were trying to show me that they have a history of exclusions in the nation: what Barrio was trying to tell me was: 'I do not want to show our own forms of history, but I want to empower our version of historical stitching of time, different from hegemonic ones.' In other words, Barrio knew that recognition of different cultural procedures of history writing can also be a form of naturalizing the asymmetries of power.

My point of view is that it is now necessary to revise procedures and attitudes towards the past and its forms of evidence. In this sense, one of the most important things is as Jeffrey Olick, Diana Drake Wilson and Leslie Witz (Olick, 2003; Drake Wilson, 2000 and Witz, 2003) stressed: that we need to consider debates in 'public space' as an important source for dealing with the past. Public space, understood in its widest sense and not only in Habermas' perspective but as a concrete spacialization of debates to transcend from opinion to *doxa* in different moods. The writing of history is, as de Certeau stated many years ago, a scientific procedure with modes of operation where the very evolution of narration is obliterated. This displays the colonial attitude towards knowledge formation. Why? Foremost, because it occludes different contentions and makes it impossible to stay with contradictions. If we are considering different post-colonial societies with a confluence of sensibilities towards the past, and where commemorations, historical narration and private/communal/familiar productions of history are unstable chains of meaning, far from giving a linear rationality to 'tropos'[21] and 'poetics', we need to provide intelligibility to these contentions. Museums, memorials, monuments, communal commemorations and rituals need to be considered not only as a form of public memory in the new 'boom' of memory studies. They must be seen as 'spaces' representing concrete contentions in history-writing in post-colonial societies. In this case, historians cannot only 'see' different comprehensions of historical time and events; also 'the re-positioning of authority' is present in those contentions (Achúgar, 1998). Who is articulating what, where, when and with what kind of artefacts of evidence (Shohat, 2000) must be included not only as the 'methodological difficulties' chapter of a dissertation, but as the constitutive modes of historical thinking in a post-colonial foundation for the discipline.[22]

However, staying with contradictions does not mean that we have to consider a fragmentary history. This is my last point in this section. Considering the fragment as a source and as narrative condition is of course a great epistemic advance in history, the fragment as a trace that can throw light in present analyses. But it needs also epistemic surveillance: The fragmentary reason, imperative of post-modern Euro-Americanism and present in the cultural turn (Slates, 2004), sometimes implies a kind of condescending attitude towards cultural difference, and a de-politicization of objects, research lines and historical writing in general. Fragment must be considered as a form of operating all the time in history, to contribute to a more 'detailed' and ethnographic account of the constitutive and unstable processes of figurations of power/domination/resistance.

TEMPORALITY/TEMPORALITIES

Time can be considered as a functional and operative illusion structuring all societies. In this sense, the ways to represent time are really complex. As Giacomo Marramao (2002) posed, Western linear 'representation of time' is only a stage in Western 'meaning of time': the stage of Hegelian 'mundanization', the conversion of repressive attitudes of Christian time into repressive time of secular organization of memory, into disposition of modernity/the figuration of the nation.

Even when, again, it was Michel De Certeau who insisted on the imaginary of secular/linear time as a symbolic articulation of (Western) modernity, and not as an intrinsic characteristic of history, the disposition towards history is to fix sequences in analytical units and a temporal homogeneous framework. Historians from Latin America (Abercrombie, 1998) and through classical works on African Studies (Diouf, 2000 and Lonsdale, 1989) were trying to recover 'ethnic temporalities' and historically particular reproductions of time in post-colonial societies. Plural conceptions of time and diverse attitudes toward them are a clear point of departure today. But again, this seems to be a kind of spectre of places 'untouched' by modernity; unsurprisingly, conceptions of time as an attribute of culture, are mainly reserved for anthropological knowledge and analysis (in the Western division of academic work) and not used in historical analyses.

Again, I will pose a concrete departure. It was November 2006 and I was doing fieldwork in South Africa, particularly in Johannesburg. There, we see juxtapositions of ethnicities, subjectivities, historical backgrounds, urban and generational cultures. The place where I interviewed the people was the garden of the Apartheid Museum. This is located at the exit of the museum and is known as the garden of reflection. I was doing some informal interviews with different people and searching for salient features of their perceptions of the museum's representation of history and suddenly a woman who identified as a *Xhosa* and in her mid-1950s, said: 'I knew almost everything. But I really don't understand . . . why they begin with *Apartheid* from 1948 onwards; 1994 really was a break. But . . . 1948? And before? What were we before . . . ?' (Sharpe, 2003: 7). In another interview about the museum, a young black High School girl-student said strongly 'but . . . Has it [the Apastheid] really ended? What was its source?'

Many figurations of time are implied in these questions and in the so-called Indigenous Movement that demand a revision of the dictatorial state's perception of temporality. It is not only a matter of agency or subjective perceptions of time: it implies also how we can deal with the concrete historical experience of time, and with historically transmitted or differently stitched imaginations. This is not only to 'report' another account of history. We, historians, operating with (ultimately) foreign categories, must take these accounts seriously. As Prasenjit Duara has pointed out, modern historical (Western) narratives could not eliminate the different manifestations of being and time, but the proximity of history to modernity did not facilitate the emergence of a language allowing the recognition and negotiation of all that has been repressed and dispersed (Duara, 1995). In that sense, if there is in fact a repressive connection between the modern nation and history, and if linear time is a condition of possibility for the realization of modernity-as-anxiety, we must accept that Western colonizing history has repressed connections between events and social forms of producing imaginations over time. My aim here is not only to say it (again), but to propose a kind of possible programmatic statement to deal with it at (southern) universities and (southern) history writing.

In Argentina at least, our analyses have a concrete potential: there is a connection between different perceptions of temporality with a reformulation of one event (state terrorism). One of the hypotheses formulated again and again by some scholars—the need to study the last series of military violence and repressive technologies in Argentina as the casual, peculiar, but not exceptional history of the nation state (cf. Rufer forthcoming: 227–9)—was posed with concrete performative actions by the Indigenous Movement. This is not only a counter-reading of time. On the contrary, there is an implicit reformulation of the organic foundations of national narrative in that assault to time. The naming of the Conquest of the Desert as 'state terrorism' can be a theoretical mistake in classic terms of political science. But of course, indigenous representatives were absolutely aware of that. It was important to show that violence and the denial of the 'other' was a constitutive procedure 'functional' but also 'foundational' of the nation state. This is to say, pushing back 'state terrorism' to the end of the nineteenth century, was also a form of pushing the colonial foundations of law (in Benjamin's terms) to the core of present, current, modern history. This is not only a means of re-reading of time, but also a re-signification of the patterns of national history: the gestures of our own history not as an exceptional, European spirit in Latin America, but a post-colonial history (which means that there are traces of colonial relationships that we need to see, show, and analyse in the present).[24]

How? Of course, we have the important approach by Partha Chatterjee who makes us think in terms of a 'nation in heterogeneous time', a salient advance from Anderson's statements on (homogeneous) time and the (modern) nation (Chatterjee, 2004). From this viewpoint—if we accept that in history the nation shapes the configuration of 'the modern as a possibility', in Eurocentric terms—we can remake some proposals. Considering time as a vacuum, linear, homogeneous sense of explaining the flow of events seems to be a *sine qua non* condition for the writing of (modern) history. It would be a place for other forms not only to write history, but to empower those writings as valid, liable, visible historical accounts?[25] Probably in this sense we must think of changing time to temporality as a category to de-naturalize, not only in the terms of a so-called philosophy of history (beyond the cultural turn), but in terms of a precision to include it in southern forms of imagining and writing history. Let me explain further. By temporality I mean a category-entity to introduce a political dimension in measuring and considering time: not as a neutral and always here-at-hand framework for history, but a structure of power, a 'grammar' of the discipline: it produces effects in terms of a politic of the present. Looking at what I would like to call 'the politics of temporality' implies the consideration of structuring time as a peculiar dimension for the production and fixation of difference; in this sense, southern historians must be more sensitive to identify that kind of history politics.

Politics of temporality means not only to introduce a variable for 'regimes of historicity' (Hartog, 2003) in the very thinking of historical periods and events as analytical structures organizing historical imagination (which was largely done). Rather, it indicates a political disposition in the analysis of time: how temporalization is considered as a unit for signification, how it legislates historical thinking in a specific frame of domination. Temporality as a political dimension of historical analyses must help to understand why we are still operating with binary dispositions as myth/history, magic/secular, nation/community, how are we (historians as a community) validating categories with strong implications in the diachronic map to construct the same/the other, the warranty of progress/state/nation/development; at the same time these are salient dispositions in the articulation of the archaic/the atavism in the synchronic scenario for 'cultural diversity'—always difficult to attach to and stitch in the historical imagination of the (post) colonial nation.

Now, if we have overlapping temporalities in the account of history[26] what does it mean for 'History'? What are the pathways to think in terms of a 'heterogeneous time' but also a juxtaposed form of conceiving historical time in order to be included in concrete projects of writing history? How can we think that the structuring of state-terrorism in Argentina as an inheritance of nineteenth-century violence is a peculiar form to express a different imagination of violence and the founding ethos of the nation state? How can we project in the concrete historical narration the peculiar and social exigencies that see *apartheid* as a social history in the *long durée* of South African history?

The classic Argentinean historian Tulio Halperin Donghi recognized some years ago that the image of twentieth century's history is fractured, fragmented, puzzled by the very disciplinary attitudes towards a process of fixation of one narrative about secular events (the end of revolution, post-colonialism, and the latest capitalism's cosmopolitan ethics:

'central' and 'peripheral' capitalism) (Teran, 2000: 12). At the same time, Foucault already positioned the concept of *heterotopia* into the historical imagination: fragmented spaces and heterogeneous times assaulted the disaffection to modernity (Foucault, 1984). In some sense, however, those displacements had little impact in the core of the historical discipline. My main point is that, again, to talk about *heterotopia* or heterogeneous times, does not necessarily make historians see the profound implications of power and domination that are meshed in that diversity of 'times'. We do not only need to recognize them. It is necessary to recover them as legitimate ways of imagining; and even more when they are not dealing with any time, but the time of genealogies and elementary structures of violence, in an archaeological perspective.

In this sense, I consider that we must think of history programmes or syllabi 'from south(s)'. As concrete contents, they could include at least three points arising out of what I developed before:

1. De-naturalizing time and its nature as a sign of the modern: communities, ethnicities and nation in relation to time.
2. The present as a historical category: present as a *tropos* and 'imperfect tense'[27] (which means the present not as an obvious here at hand, but a point of departure to structure historical thinking: why here and now southern historians can think the present as a perspective with an epistemic potential to re-conceive the authoritative protocols of history).
3. Historical time as experience: we must include conflictive memories, challenging the established sequence. If we can take the sequence as an object of study (how analytical units—as I will explain further—confirm the frame of history not in a neutral way) we can contribute to a decolonization of the discipline. It is possible to conceive the uses of time as a situational (contingent, powerful, not universal) frame.[28]

FINAL THOUGHTS

The historical discipline depends on analytical units constructed from other contexts and thoughts about them, other relations of power and identity configurations. In this sense, it is not accidental that the new debates on the 'location of culture' and the reconfiguration of identity analyses are not necessarily reflected in the quotidian operations of the writing of history. Already published studies about connivances between empire/nation or colonial/modern formations in Asia, Africa and Latin America (Burton, 2003 and Dube, Banerjee-Dube and Mignolo, 2004) must allow us to put the empiric and methodological bases in order to start a concrete and programmatic practice of the writing of history. I am proposing here some efforts that could be added in order to understand certain questions and concerns about the practice of historical writing/teaching in and from the south(s).

First, we can consider the revision of legitimizing academic practices in the form of liberal theory that institutionalized the discipline, but operating from Eurocentric perspectives on peripheral histories. By these legitimizing practices I mean fixed structures where all 'new objects' must be added (analytical structures as the origin of nation state, Indigenism in Latin America, resistance movements, the *criollismo*, the *mestizaje*, etc). These founding categories (which are important but insufficient to generate a situational politics of history today) do not allow us to see the attempts to debate and widen our analytic horizons. Not only is the temporality of events challenged by other etiologies and experiential approaches. Also, the analytical frameworks are being questioned (though not necessarily directly) at the core of the discipline. The binary divisions such as interior/capital, state/community, urban/rural demand concrete new explorations from a historical perspective. From a critical reading of diverse public constructions of South African memories about apartheid (with a history of deep inner cultural diversity which imposes a necessarily not-consensual, multi-focused reading of any meta-narration), the claims of the Indigenous Movement in Argentina become more logical: they try to re-define the significant units of history (in terms of the origins of the violent nation state which puts it here and now, as a post-colonial history which is something completely unaccepted in core Argentinean historical debates).

Second, a central point of demanding more sensibility in the practices of creating teaching syllabi of history and also in research programmes is a sense of incompleteness of historical thinking, as a history-in-process (and not 'Progress'). Here we must reflect on the need for a 'recovery of particularities'[29] (which means a different perspective from the recovery of 'subaltern voices', popular sectors, relegated agents as essences). The recovery of particularities refers to an epistemologically open attitude towards historical representations, contingencies, contradictions, asymmetries of power and validation processes: to identify, empower and authorize peculiar sensibilities to understand time and event (also to see the appropriation and operation of modern/Western thinking-categories at the core of history writing of 'remote' places/'un-modern' territories. The continuity between the violence at the very foundations of the nation state and the last dictatorships could be seen as an absurd misconception from the point of view of traditional historiography (and also from that point of view, it could be conceived as a kind of 'folkloric understanding of history' to be added as ethnographic material in some anthropological frame). However, from a peculiar perspective of historical situation, from the perspective of those who experienced the violence entailed in the foundation of the nation state and its technologies of eradicating difference (or alterity), such history-writing assaults the present (and the place of the assaulted in it) and demands a re-interpretation of historical experience (and its forms of transmission).[30]

I take here again the argument by Achúgar on the 'relocation of authority' in discourses on memory/history/past accounts. Such relocation must give place to a 'memory without warranty' in the historical discourse. If history can remake the protocols of social inquiries in the forms of socializing, teaching and writing, we can contribute to a 'history without warranty' (Dube, 2004). This then would be the epistemic key to a post-foundationalist but Southern kind of sensibility of history: showing the contradictions, the various pluralities and disagreeing accounts on past events as a constitutive framework of a de-colonized conception of the historical experience, capable of showing the repressive strategies and creative imaginations of the past. All this could be a strategy to uncover the relations of forces, power, iteration and performative potential that history writing entails. The first and *sine qua non* condition would be the real crossing of disciplinary boundaries. Above all, the strategies for distribution of scientific knowledge respond to an imperial/colonial logic which continues to be reproduced by nation state institutions all through the 'global South'. Yet, we will have a clearer map of relations of power and domination in post-colonial spaces only if we are also capable of democratizing the ways to show, narrate, authorize and explore that past(s) and the subjects of its production.

NOTES

1. I thank Kathinka Sinha-Kerkhoff, Anjan Ghosh and Fernanda Beigel for their generous comments on this paper.
2. It is worthwhile to mention here a recent revision of Bachelors and Masters syllabi in social sciences at different universities in Mexico. At least 85 per cent of the basic bibliography is related to European authors and European topics formulated in terms of what Immanuel Wallerstein called 'the geo-imperial distribution of academic labour and knowledge production'. This is not new, but supported by a surplus of legitimacy in the construction of problematic spectrums, even in the discussion of the very logic of social sciences operating

by discovering problems and contradictions at 'local' and 'social' arenas (as Karl Popper had it). Cf. División Editorial, *Desafíos para la docencia universitaria*, Universidad Autónoma Metropolitana, México, 1999, pp. 134–6.

3. See the important arguments expressed in this regard by Saurabh Dube, dealing with history, theory, historical anthropology and the very dispositions of writing. Saurabh Dube, *Historias Esparcidas*, México: El Colegio de México, 2007, pp. 35–45.
4. I am referring here to Dipesh Chakrabarty, 'Postoclonialismo y el artilugio de la historia . . .', op. cit.
5. The Argentinian anthropologist Rita Segato has reflected on this topic, seeing how 'alterity' is sometimes produced and strategically used by the nation state (different from historical alterities ['otherness'] resulting from subjectivization processes in social-historical arenas), and how 'transnational political identities' are often guided by a fixed, a pre-established 'script': what constitutes an 'authentic Indian', for example. She suggests: 'If we are not aware, the best allegory to the rights of minorities in the globalized world will be represented by the transformation of the *Barbie* doll who, faced with the criticism made to the Anglo–Saxon pattern of beauty she imposes, was later on presented with ethnic clothes and darker skin. However, the bone structure we can guess under the skin is the same.' See Rita Segato, 'Identidades políticas/alteridades históricas: una crítica a las certezas del pluralismo global', in *La nación y sus otros. Raza, etnicidad y diversidad religiosa en tiempos de las políticas de la identidad*, Buenos Aires: Prometeo, 2007, pp. 37–70.
6. Again, I am not referring here to other (subaltern, non-classic, alternative) constructions of objects and sources (which of course fortunately exist) but to the procedures on how we authorize, fix and legitimize the rules of operation regarding these objects, evidence and sources in the process of writing, distributing and socializing academic knowledge. Cf. Catherine Walsh, Freya Schiwy and Santiago Castro Gómez (eds.), *Indisciplinar las ciencias sociales. Geopolíticas del conocimiento y colonialidad del poder*, op. cit.; Zulma Palermo, 'Es posible descolonizar la universidad?', op. cit.
7. The word 'post-occidental' was put in motion by Walter Mignolo. Briefly: He thinks that it is not possible to homogenize historical experiences from South(s) in Latin America, South Asia or Africa

as simply post-colonial. The colonial difference is a trace all through them, but the historical specificity and dispositions on colonialism are not only temporally different. In Latin America, there is a sense of being 'West' as a 'differed' condition, as a kind of mirroring of the historical experience. In history, de-naturalizing this differed condition constitutes an important challenge. See Walter Mignolo, 'La colonialidad a lo largo y a lo ancho: el hemisferio occidental en el horizonte colonial de la modernidad', in Edgardo Lander (ed.) (2000), *La colonialidad del saber: euro-centrismo y ciencias sociales. Perspectivas latinoamericanas*, Buenos Aires: Clacso, pp. 65 ff.

8. See among others, Gayatri Chakravorty Spivak (2000), 'Post-structuralism, Marginality, Postcoloniality and Value', in Diana Brydon (ed.), *Postcolonialism: Critical Concepts in Literary and Cultural Studies*, London & New York: Routledge, pp. 57–84; Premesh Lalu, 'The Grammar of Domination and the Subjection of Agency: Colonial Texts and Modes of Evidence', in *History and Theory*, 39 (4), December 2000, pp. 45–68.
9. We must refer here to the tension at the very core of European philosophy addressed by Derrida, who takes the archive as 'commencement' (point of departure to analyse the past) and as a legislative disposition (what we have as legitimate to prove the past). Here lies one of the most important debates since structuralism in historiography, with different hermeneutic approaches. Then, 'arche' and 'commencement' operate as an enclosure to define what past is (not was). To Derrida, this enclosure act is only a desire, a claim, not a definitive effect. Jacques Derrida, *Archive Fever: A Freudian Impression*, Chicago: University of Chicago Press, 1996. To see this referred to a concrete case (TRC in South Africa) see Brent Harris, ' "Unearthing" the "Essential" Past: The Making of a Public "National" Memory Through the Truth and Reconciliation Commission (TRC), 1994–8', MA thesis, University of the Western Cape, Cape Town, 1998, unpublished, pp. 1–9.
10. Cf. Peter Burke (2000) [1997], 'La historia como memoria colectiva', in *Formas de historia cultural*, Madrid: Alianza Editorial, pp. 65–85.
11. There is an important debate here, known to scholars familiar with debates on 'oral tradition' and 'oral history'. The Africanist and historian David W. Cohen has some doubts regarding the

claims made by Jan Vansina in his famous work on the 'oral tradition' as history that legitimizes and the use of oral African sources to classify and re-construct a truthful past. Reflecting on the different nature, purposes and strategic-present uses of oral discourse, David Cohen utilizes the concept 'production of history' in order to open-up the debate to not only sources but mainly to the act of its production, conception, contingencies and uses (which means, an important reflection on the political side of the production of historical knowledge). Cf. Jan Vansina, *Oral Tradition as History*, Madison: Wisconsin University Press, 1985; David W. Cohen, *The Combing of History*, Chicago: University of Chicago Press, 1994. However, Cohen's work was often received by historians as 'too anthropological', and he was thought of as 'not very aware of the necessity of truth in history' and ultimately 'as too post-modern'; as if a discussion on the political nature of production and socialization of academic knowledge could 'endanger' a kind of immaculate truth again, in Derrida's terms, lying behind sources, beyond 'commencement'. What really is in danger, I argue, is the important idea that in social sciences 'truth' and 'politics' never are totally separate domains. See Mario Rufer, *La nación en escenas. Memoria pública, poder, poscoloi-nalismo*, México: El Colegio de México, forthcoming.

12. This research specifically refers to the links between public memory and forms of inclusion/exclusion of agents in history, taking as focal points the *Apartheid* and the last military dictatorship in South Africa and Argentina, respectively. My aim was to demonstrate that through the productions of the history of these periods and through the disputes between different agencies, we can (and we should) read wider forms of exclusion from historical narrations and from national projects. But the main point is that these forms of exclusions and biases are also present in the new 'boom' of memories of these periods.
13. ESMA is the acronym for 'Escuela de Mecánica de la Armada' (Mechanics School for the Army). This military school functioned as a clandestine centre for detention and torture of people during the last military dictatorship in Argentina. Through a government agreement, the Space for Memory and Human Rights (a museum) was officially created there in 2004. This has had an important impact because one of the hallmarks of Nestor Kirchner's

Government (2003–7) was the recognition by the state of the cruel genocide between 1976 and 1983, and the official intervention by a strong politics of Human Rights for the first time since 1983. Cf. Mario Rufer, *La nación en escenas*. . . , op. cit., cap. 4.

14. See for this discussion, Raymundo Mier (2000), 'Apuntes para una reflexión sobre comunicación y política', in *Versión*, no. 10, pp. 59–105.
15. Cf. Mario Rufer, 'Monuments, Museums and Re-articulation of Nation: Pedagogies, Performances and Subaltern Apprehensions of Memory', *Intercultural Communication Studies* (ICS), vol. XVI (2), 2007, 158–77.
16. Paul Ricoeur, *La memoria, la historia, el olvido*, tr. Agustín Neira, México: Fondo de Cultura Económica, 2004 [2000], p. 341. Of course, this is a long discussion in the historiography of the Western tradition. It is important, however, to recognize here the importance of the creation of procedures for enlarging the visibility of other forms to solve the gap between fact and representation. Here, evidence is not only a constitutive part of history, but also of the (Western/imperial) power relations innate in the daily practice of narrating history. In the case of Europe, Ricoeur, De Certeau and Hayden White stressed (from different standpoints) something else than the text as a (fictional) artefact constructed by figures of languages. They also favoured the visibility of contingent procedures intervening in the writing of history as part of the epistemic problems of the discipline. Cf. De Certeau, Michel (1979), *La escritura de la historia*, ed. Universidad Iberoamericana, México, 193 [1975]; Hayden: White, *El contenido de la forma*, Paidós, Barcelona.
17. Interview with Mario Barrio. Pompeya, Buenos Aires, 1 November 2005.
18. I develop it carefully in Mario Rufer, *La nación en escenas*, op. cit.
19. This is the point of departure for all Foucauldian analyses. See also Saurabh Dube, 'Introducción', in Saurabh Dube (ed.), *Pasados poscoloniales*, México: El Colegio de México, 1999; Ranajit Guha: 'La prosa de contra-insurgencia' in Saurabh Dube (ed.), *Pasados poscoloniales*, México: El Colegio de México, 1999. Online version at http://www.clacso.org/wwwclacso/espanol/html/libros/poscolonialismo/poscol.html

20. Here I mean that the famous discussion on Spivak's 'Can the Subaltern Speak?', which generated an important amount of debate.. Even when it is still important to recall this work, it needs other directions. It does now allow us to understand that we can de-essentialize subalternity/domination by unravelling the contradictions of history in contingent groups. Here, the study of procedures about what is truth and how we can find more than one truth about an event is an important point of departure. Cf. Gayatri Chakravorty Spivak, 'Can the Subaltern Speak?' in Bill Ashcroft (ed.) (1995), *The Postcolonial Studies Reader*, New York: Routledge.
21. Here I refer to the Latin word *tropo* (sing), which is mainly used in narrative discussions about history. Cf. Hyden White (1973), *Metahistory: The Historical Imagination in Nineteenth-Century Europe*, Baltimore: Johns Hopkins University Press.
22. This is the basic theoretical foundation of my Ph.D. dissertation. Cf. Mario Rufer, *La nación en escenas. . .* , op. cit.; specifically: 'Introducción: poder, memoria, producción de historia', pp. 11–80.
23. I am not trying to cover up here the complex topic, e.g. 'apartheid temporality' and its broader implications. I only put some question marks on its apparently secure and established a priori, in order to increase analytical and historical reflection. For a more detailed discussion on this, see Mario Rufer, *La nación en escenas . . .* , op. cit., pp. 75–85.
24. This is at the core of our own (scientific/academic) perceptions of the self.
25. In the case of Africa, Johannes Fabian (among others) introduced those questions in order to deal with other forms of historical imagination, writing an ethnography of a Congolese local historian (and painter), Tshibumba Matulu. Fabian's work is an excellent example of an ethical critique of the 'evidence' concept and also of a new imagination of articulating sequences, narrations and nodes of meaning. Unsurprisingly, again, Fabian's work is being read mostly by anthropologists and rarely included in history courses. Broadly, it is being analysed in terms of 'cultural reproduction' of 'alternative imaginations' of history, and not necessarily as other forms of evidence which contribute to the creation of a new 'historiographic operation', or to

understand more deeply its productive power/knowledge relations. Cf. Johannes Fabian, *Remembering the Present...*, op. cit.

26. Thomas Abercrombie (1993), *Pathways of Memory and Power...*, op. cit., Janet Hoskins, *The Play of Time: Kodi Perspectives on Calendars, History, and Exchange*, Berkeley: University of California Press. Again, as we can see, I am quoting almost only anthropologists or analysts with a strong ethnographic approach.
27. Premesh Lalu, 'The Grammar of Domination and the Subjection of Agency...'. Lalu refers to a peculiar quality of the present: a situational one, but also a contingent condition to define epistemic practices.
28. The narration of a specific case-study could help to understand these operations of 'time' and 'present' as a fixation for analytical categories: when I attended a congress organized by History departments in Mexico two years ago, I presented a paper on the appropriations of official (state) memories by the Argentinean Indigenous Movement in Argentina and by black sectors in South Africa. First, I submitted my paper under the panel 'Recent History and its Problematics'. The coordinator wrote to me to say that my paper was an interesting piece of research, but that it was not recent history; actually it was ethno-history. However, at the Ethno-History panel, they considered it more appropriate to submit the paper to the panel on 'Theoretical and Methodological Problems'. I see this as an example of the fragmentation of historical thinking at the core of its own functioning as an academic discipline.
29. I have taken this expression from Saurabh Dube, *Historias Esparcidas*, op. cit., pp. 42 ff.
30. Here, I cannot explain nor develop all my arguments, but of course this does not imply that I surpass the deeply peculiar historical foundations and technologies of recent military regimes. The only thing I want to remark here is the peculiar narrative of violence, plundering and the disappearance of national subjects taken as a continuity (of course, also important to take as a manifestation during the time of a left-wing state government).

REFERENCES

Abercrombie, Thomas (1998), *Pathways of Memory and Power: Ethnography and History Among an Andean People*, Madison: University of Wisconsin Press.

Achúgar, Hugo (1998), 'Leones, cazadores e historiadores: a propósito de las políticas de la memoria y del conocimiento', in Santiago Castro Gómez and Eduardo Mendieta (eds.), *Teorías sin disciplina: Latinoamericanismo, poscolonialidad y globalización en debate*, México: Miguel Angel Porrúa.

Axel, Brian Keith (2001), *The Nation's Tortured Body: Violence, Representation and the Formation of a Sikh 'Diaspora'*, Durham and London: Duke University Press.

Burke, Peter (2000 [1997]), 'La historia como memoria colectiva', in *Formas de historia cultural*, Madrid: Alianza Editorial.

Burton, Antoinette (ed.) (2003), *After the Imperial Turn: Thinking with and Through the Nation*, Durham and London: Duke University Press.

Chakrabarty, Dipesh (1999), 'Poscolonialismo y el artilugio de la historia: Quién habla en nombre de los pasados "indios"?' in Saurabh Dube (ed.), *Pasados Poscoloniales*, México: El Colegio de México.

——— (2000), *Provincializing Europe: Post-colonial Thought and Historical Difference*, Princeton: Princeton University Press.

Chatterjee, Partha (2004), 'A nação em tempo heterogêneo', in Partha Chaterjee, *Colonialismo, modernidade e política*, tr. Flavio Baqueiro Figueiredo, EDUFBA-CEAO, Salvador de Bahia.

Cohen, David W. (1994), *The Combing of History*, Chicago: University of Chicago Press.

Comaroff, John and Jean Comaroff (1993), *Ethnography and the Historical Imagination*, London: Boulder.

Cooper, Frederick (2005), *Colonialism in Question: Theory, Knowledge, History*, Berkeley and Los Angeles: University of California Press.

Derrida, Jacques (1996), *Archive Fever: A Freudian Impression*, Chicago: University of Chicago Press.

Diouf, Mamadou (2000), 'Des historiens et des histoires, pour quoi faire? L'histoire africaine entre l'état et les communautés', in *Canadian Journal of African Studies*, 34 (2).

Drake Wilson, Diana (2000), 'Realizing Memory, Transforming History: Euro/American/Indians', in Susana Crane (ed.), *Museums and Memory*, Stanford: Stanford University Press.

Duara, Prasenjit (1995), *Rescuing History from the Nation: Questioning Narratives on Modern China*, Chicago and London University of Chicago Press.

Dube, Saurabh (1999), 'Introducción', in Saurabh Dube (ed.), *Pasados poscoloniales*, México: El Colegio de México.

——— (2004), 'Introducción', in Saurabh Dube, Ishita Banerjee-Dube and Walter Mignolo (eds.), *Modernidades coloniales: Otros pasados, historias presentes*, Mexico: El Colegio de Mexico.

——— (2007), *Historias Esparcidas*, México: El Colegio de México.

——— (2004), *Stitches on Time: Colonial Textures and Postcolonial Tangles*, Durham and London: Duke University Press.

Fabian, Johannes (1996), *Remembering the Present: Painting and Popular History in Zaire*, Los Angeles: University of California Press.

Feierman, Steven (1999), 'Colonizers, Scholars, and the Creation of Invisible Histories', in Victoria Bonnel, Lynn Hunt (eds.), *Beyond the Cultural Turn: New Directions in the Study of Society and Culture*, Berkeley-Los Angeles-London: University of California Press.

——— (1995), 'African Histories and the Dissolution of World History', in Robert H. Bates, V.Y. Mudimbe and Jean O'Barr (eds.), *Africa and the Disciplines: The Contributions of Research in Africa to the Social Sciences and Humanities*, Chicago: University of Chicago Press.

Guha, Ranajit (1999), 'La prosa de contra-insurgencia', in Saurabh Dube (ed.), *Pasados poscoloniales*, México: El Colegio de México.

Harris, Brent (1998), '"Unearthing" the "Essential" Past: The Making of a Public "National" Memory through the Truth and Reconciliation Commission (TRC), 1994–8', MA thesis, University of the Western Cape, Cape Town, unpublished.

Hartog, François (2003), *Régimes d'historicité. Présentisme et expériences du temps*, Paris: Seuil.

Hoskins, Janet (1993), *The Play of Time: Kodi Perspectives on Calendars, History, and Exchange*, Berkeley: University of California Press.

Lalu, Premesh (2000), 'The Grammar of Domination and the Subjection of Agency: Colonial Texts and Modes of Evidence', in *History and Theory*, 39 (4), December.

Lander, Edgardo (2004), 'Eurocentrismo, saberes modernos y naturalización del orden global del capital', in Saurabh Dube, Ishita Banerjee-Dube and Walter Mignolo (eds.), *Modernidades coloniales: Otros pasados, historias presentes*, México: El Colegio de México.

Lonsdale, John (1989), 'African Pasts in Africa's Future', in *Canadian Journal of African Studies*, v. 23 (1).

Marramao, Giacomo (2002), *Cielo y tierra: Genealogía de la secularización*, Buenos Aires: Paidós.

Mier, Raymundo (2000), 'Apuntes para una reflexión sobre comunicación y política', in *Versión*, no. 10.

Mignolo, Walter (2000), 'Introducción', in Walter Mignolo (comp.), *Capitalismo y geopolítica del conocimiento. El eurocentrismo y la filosofía de la liberación en el debate intelectual contemporáneo*, Buenos Aires: Duke University–Ediciones El Signo.

——— (2000), 'La colonialidad a lo largo y a lo ancho: el hemisferio occidental en el horizonte colonial de la modern-idad'; in Edgardo Lander (ed.), *La colonialidad del saber: eurocentrismo y ciencias sociales. Perspectivas latinoameri-canas*, Buenos Aires: Clacso.

Mignolo, Walter and Freya Schiwy (2003), 'Double Translation: Transculturation and the Colonial Difference', in *Translation and Ethnography: The Anthropological Challenge of Intercultural Understanding* by Tullio Maranhao and Bernhard Streck, Arizona: University of Arizona Press.

Olick, Jeffrey (2003), 'Introduction', in Jeffrey Olick (ed.), *States of Memory: Continuities, Conflicts, and Transformations in National Retrospection*, Durham and London: Duke University Press.

Palermo, Zulma (2007), 'Es posible descolonizar la universidad?' in Walter Mignolo (ed.), *On Decoloniality*, Special Issue of *World and Knowledges Otherwise: A Web Dossier*, vol. 2, dossier 1. http://www.jhfc.duke.edu/wko/dossiers/1.3/documents/formattedZulma-Palermo.pdf, last access 22/11/07.

Ricoeur, Paul (2004 [2000]), *La memoria, la historia, el olvido*, tr. Agustín Neira, México: Fondo de Cultura Económica.

Rufer, Mario (2007), 'Monuments, Museums and Re-articulation of the Nation: Pedagogies, Performances and Subaltern Apprehensions of Memory', in *Intercultural Communication Studies* (ICS), vol. XVI (2).

——— (forthcoming), *La nación en escenas. Memoria pública, poder, poscoloinalismo*, México: El Colegio de México.

Sanjinés, Javier (2005), *El espejismo del mestizaje*, IFEA-Embajada de Francia en Bolivia, La Paz.

Segato, Rita (2007), 'Identidades políticas/alteridades históricas: una crítica a las certezas del pluralismo global', in *La nación y sus otros. Raza, etnicidad y diversidad religiosa en tiempos de las políticas de la identidad,* Buenos Aires: Prometeo.

Sharpe, Colleen (2003), Coming Together: The Role of the Apartheid Museum in Helping Re-negotiate Memory and Identity in Post-apartheid South Africa, Research Report of Master of Arts, Faculty of Humanities, University of Witswatersrand, Johannesburg, unpublished.

Shohat, Ella (2000), 'Notes on the post-colonial', in Fawzia Afzal-Khan and Kalpana Seshadri-Crooks (eds.), *The Pre-occupation of Postcolonial Studies*, Durham and London: Duke University Press.

Slater, David (2004), *Geopolitics and the Post-colonial: Rethinking North-south Relations*, Oxford: Blackwell.

Spivak, Gayatri Chakravorti (1995), 'Can the Subaltern Speak?', in Bill Ashcroft (ed.), *The Postcolonial Studies Reader*, New York: Routledge.

——— (2000), 'Poststructuralism, Marginality, Postcoloniality and Value', in Diana Brydon (ed.), *Post-colonialism: Critical Concepts in Literary and Cultural Studies*, London & New York: Routledge.

Teran, Oscar (2000), 'Tiempos de memoria', in *Punto de vista*, December.

Thompson, E.P. (1078), *The Poverty of Theory and Other Essays*, London: Merlin Press.

Vansina, Jan (1985), *Oral Tradition as History*, Madison: Wisconsin University Press.

Wallerstein, Immanuel (1995), *Abrir las ciencias sociales. Informe de la Comisión Gulbenkian para la reestructuración de las ciencias sociales*, Siglo XXI, Buenos Aires.

Walsh, Catherine (2002), 'Las geopolíticas del conocimiento y colonialidad del poder: Entrevista a Walter Mignolo', in Catherine Walsh, Freya Schiwy and Santiago Castro Gómez (eds.), *Indisciplinar las ciencias sociales. Geopolíticas del conocimiento y colonialidad del poder: Perspectivas desde lo andino*, Quito: Universidad Andina Simón Bolivar.

Witz, Leslie (2003), *Apartheid's Festival: Contesting South African National Pasts*, Bloomington: Indiana University Press.

CHAPTER 11

The Costs and Benefits of Academic Globalization: A Case Study of Ranchi (Jharkhand, India)

KATHINKA SINHA-KERKHOFF

INTRODUCTION

During the 1960s and 1970s research institutions in the state of Jharkhand[1] generally were, by choice more than by force I argue, engaged in empirical work rather than in the production of ideas and theories. More precisely, theory production alone rarely was their main purpose. One should see this I feel, as the outcome of decades-long 'indigenizing' in Indian social sciences (cf. Sinha, 2005 and also Chatterji, 2005). In a conference held in 1968 on 'Urgent Social Research in India', the problem of urgency was looked upon from two points of view: '(1) there are areas or fields of investigation which are of very great theoretical significance; and (2) there are areas where problems connected with national development call for our immediate attention'. It was agreed upon that, 'in India [. . .] it should be the purpose of social scientists working either in the universities or research institutions to contribute to both these fields' (Vidyarthi, 1969: 377). In fact, during the 1970s and 1980s, 'de-islanding' (Prasad, 1981: 209–11) of the social sciences was an important aim for many Indian social scientists, in particular for anthropologists who argued that besides the need for interdisciplinary research, research data had to be communicated to the masses. Therefore, along with 'fundamental research' with theory formation, 'applied social science' that studied 'issue-based problems' or 'cognizable real life problems' (cf. 1999: 3114) were advanced in different parts of India. A consequence of this was that social scientists did normally study their 'own' society in terms of national borders.

Nevertheless, during this time, Indian social science and in particular social anthropology in Jharkhand (then Bihar) did not belong to the 'periphery'. To the contrary, scholars like Lalita P. Vidyarthi and research institutions such as the Tribal Welfare Research Institute in Ranchi, the capital of the state of Jharkhand, were very much part of the international scenario with scholars in India urging for 'more international collaboration' and inviting scholars from 'all over the world' 'representing different disciplines and countries' to study Indian problems in a 'comparative' perspective. Vidyarthi (1969: 377) himself emphasized at the time that collaboration, 'should not be confined to universities but should include all organizations carrying on anthropological and sociological research'. During the conference in 1968, Indian scholars particularly deplored, 'the lack of contact between Indian scholars and their peers in other Asian, and also in African, countries' (Singh, Wood and Vidyarthi, 1971: 97–8). South-South collaborative and comparative research was therefore very much on the research agenda at least in Ranchi.

In 2009, as academic globalization much advanced, one would expect much improvement in this regard. Not so however. What is more, L.P. Vidyarthi's *alma mater*, Ranchi University in the State of Jharkhand, is hardly considered worth visiting. The *Man in India* founded in 1921 by Sarat Chandra Roy and once an internationally acclaimed Quarterly Journal of Anthropology and other journals published from Ranchi such as the *Journal of Social Research* and the *Bulletin of the Bihar Tribal Research Institute*, have either stopped being published from Ranchi, or are struggling for survival. Besides, the works of scholars based in Ranchi are rarely published anywhere. Like other scholars in eastern

India, these scholars tend to prefer empirical work above theoretical research (Behera, 2009) but their work has no takers any longer. Scholars in Ranchi are now relegated to the 'periphery' of the academic world internationally as well as nationally. Their conscious decision to go for 'applied research' which never meant the absence of theory but inductive rather than deductive theory formation is now often considered 'proof' for their 'dependency on Western theoretical thought' or even of their inability to 'think originally'.

If we thus apply the 'centre-periphery continuum or structure of academic dependency' of Syed Farid Alatas (Alatas, 2003, see also Amsler, 2007: 36) to the present-day Indian context one could argue that scholars based in 'the social science powers' are those living in places like Delhi, Kolkata, Hyderabad, Pune and Mumbai, where most of the production of new knowledge and theory building takes place. Other scholars not based in these centres are less visible in international scholarship and academically 'peripheral' and tend to be confined to doing work that is empirical rather than theoretical and that is focused in their own region rather than other regions in India or regions beyond their own country.

Debates on 'peripheral social sciences' have usually focused on colonialism as the main culprit of asymmetric relations between social science knowledges (cf. Amsler, 2007). Others seek to highlight 'global commoditization of knowledge' in order to explain current epistemic inequalities (Poblocki, 2009). Within India too, there are scholars who have pointed to these 'inequalities' among social scientists. Partha Chatterjee for instance underlined 'the colonization of social science by certain metropolitan centres in the country' (Guru, 2002: 5003). Gopal Guru (ibid.: 5003–9), however, sees this division as based on 'cultural hierarchies' rather than on geographical differences and argues that 'Indian social science represents a pernicious divide between theoretical *brahmins* and empirical *shudras*'. Yet whether based on geographical or caste distinctions, the result is the same: An 'epistemological imperialism that empowers non-dalits/tribals [or those located in the academic centres] to launch intellectual expeditions to conquer newer epistemological territories that belong to the dalit/adivasi intellectual universe' (ibid.: 5003). We can easily replace 'dalit/adivasi intellectual universe' by 'Ranchi intellectual universe' and argue with Guru (ibid.: 5004) that in 2009 the, 'Social Science discourse in India is being closely disciplined by self-appointed juries who sit in the apex court [in Delhi or the London University for instance] and decide what is the correct practice according to the canons. These juries decide what is theory and what is trash'.

In this paper I take a closer look at the 'downfall' of Ranchi as an intellectual centre and thereafter look at the impact of academic globalization on the productivity and quality of work carried out by social scientists residing in the city, taking into account my own experiences as a social scientist affiliated to a city-based research institution (the ADRI) during the last fifteen years (1995–2010). As Altbach (2003: 4) argued, 'there are many aspects of peripherality of the academic profession in developing countries' and I contend that as 'theory-oriented' social science became higher valued than 'empirical' or 'descriptive science' (cf. Poblocki, 2009), social scientists in Ranchi who opted for 'applied science' found themselves at the periphery by the beginning of the 1990s. By this time, academic centrality had shifted not only to other geographical centres but also to different research methods and topics not in vogue among social scientists in Ranchi. From this, I go on to question if and how 'academic globalization' impacts this situation and could bring about an academic 'renaissance' in the city.

The basic idea of academic globalization, Stuart A. Umpleby of the George Washington University in the USA stated during a conference is that 'due to the internet and international travel academics can now easily collaborate with colleagues at universities in other countries, either for teaching or research'. Implicit in this argument is that this baring of collaborative opportunities beyond developing world borders, will reduce the organizational problems associated with the collaborative process within and among developmental spheres (Walsh and Maloney, 2003) and increase the productivity levels of collaborators (Lee and Bozeman, 2005). However, of the few studies that have investigated the relationship between academic globalization and scientific collaboration and increased output levels, almost none have been conducted in the developing world, 'the South' as posed against 'the North'.[2] A notable exception, however, is the work carried out by Duque, Ynalvez, Sooryamoorthy, Mbatia, Dzorgbo and Shrum (2005) in Kenya, Ghana, and Kerala (in India). These researchers warned that, 'It is dangerous to speculate about the effects of the Internet on the production and dissemination of knowledge without close attention to the local context (represented by country or region) and institutional context (represented by organizational type)'. They also pointed to 'the positive, though conditional, influence of the Internet' and concluded that these, 'Productivity and collaboration paradoxes allude to the puzzles generated by contextual conditions that shape differential or negative impacts of new information and communication technologies'.

Taking these findings as starting points, I contemplate in this article the costs and benefits of these two aspects of academic globalization, i.e. increased flows of scholars and increased access of information through Internet. I take my experiences as Director Research in the Asian Development Research Institute (the ADRI) in present-day 'peripheral' Ranchi as a case study.

THE ASIAN DEVELOPMENT RESEARCH INSTITUTE IN RANCHI

The creation of a new state carved out of Bihar in 2000 greatly impacted the status of Ranchi, which became a capital overnight. As a result, the ADRI suddenly found itself located in a capital which attracted new technologies, infrastructure, bureaucrats, politicians, institutions, organizations, new ideas and ideologies and researchers. At the same time, Ranchi is the capital of a state which despite the rise in per capita income since the last eight years remains one of the poorest states in India. The state has abundant natural resources with 40 per cent of the country's mineral reserves. However, diversification in industry, agriculture or the service sector was till date not sufficient to broaden the growth in the economy. Consequently, the fruits of the higher growth are not available to citizens across the state. The state is lagging behind in infrastructure provision, connectivity and social indicators as compared with many other Indian states (Bhandari and Kale, 2009: 14). Also, extreme inequality and poverty is said to be the main reason for anti-state activities on a large scale in the state (the so-called Naxalite problem). The state continuously faces all sorts of political turmoil and good governance remains a far cry.

However, though the state's literacy rates are much lower than those of most other Indian states, in terms of higher education, Jharkhand is doing relatively well both in quantitative as well as qualitative terms. Nevertheless, the institutional framework is devised much more for 'technical' (including engineering, technical, architecture, management, pharmacy and medical courses) than for degrees in the arts and humanities. Besides, in the field of higher education emphasis is on teaching rather than research. Though once part of the centre as discussed below, social science research in Ranchi is now at a very low echelon in terms of productivity and quality.

Nonetheless, Ranchi houses some major institutions such as a university (established in 1960) with a central library with approximately 150,000 books and with a total intake of around 90,000 students. It has hostels (2 for males and 4 for females) and is financially dependent on the University Grant Commission (UGC) in addition to fees by students. The

Faculty of Social Science heads the departments of Anthropology, Economics, Geography, History, Home Science, Philosophy, *Jyotir Vigyan* (Astrology), Political Science, Psychology and Sociology and offers undergraduate, postgraduate as well as MPhil and PhD courses. This university is one of the five universities in Jharkhand (including one deemed university). Furthermore, Ranchi houses affiliated colleges and autonomous institutions such as the Xavier Institute of Social Service (XISS). The latter was established as an institution for Social Service in 1955, got registered in 1973 and offers postgraduate programmes since 1975. Apart from being basically a management institute it also offers development-oriented courses, among others a Diploma in Rural Development. Ranchi also has since 1985 an Indira Gandhi National Open University (IGNOU), a Central University that offers certificate programmes as well as postgraduate programmes. In addition, there is the Tribal Research (Welfare) Institute (including museum) and numerous NGOs, though only a few of them are research-oriented. The ADRI is an example of the latter.

The ADRI was established and registered as a Society by a group of social scientists in 1991. The motivation for starting yet another Institute was not merely to expand social science research, but to emphasize some dimensions of it which were thought to be critical but had received rather limited attention. Included among those dimensions, for example, is to lend social science research a distinct development orientation. ADRI's brochure mentions:

> Even at best, research institutes do not go beyond generating ideas, leaving the consequential task of operationalising them to other social institutions with most of whom their interaction is rather limited. The ADRI would like to go a few steps further by making efforts to deliver its research output to its potential users in a demystified form and spur them to activities. Further, the ADRI would also like to promote social science research that emphasizes development as a social process with wide people's participation which, besides material growth, is also mindful of their heritage and aspirations.

In 1995, the ADRI Society was requested to host a State Resource Centre (SRC) on adult education by the National Literacy Mission (NLM) under the Union Ministry of Human Resource Development. The objective of SRC was to provide organizational, pedagogic and training support to the ongoing literacy campaign in Bihar. When Bihar was divided and Ranchi became the capital of Jharkhand in 2000, the ADRI in Patna (capital of Bihar) reacted enthusiastically. It had already a small office in Ranchi but now hoped it also could function as a separate SRC for Adult Literacy funded by the NLM in New Delhi. The idea was that in turn the ADRI research institute in Ranchi would benefit from such a development. Indeed it did, in some ways. The ADRI research institute in Ranchi is now housed in a spacious building with ample space for in-house seminars and workshops, with a generator, a photocopying machine, internet and other computerized facilities. In terms of human resources the situation has not changed, however, as all but one permanent staff member are on the SRC pay role, i.e. paid by the Government of India, which makes them first and for all accountable for the literacy work in the state. Research work in Ranchi is carried out by non-permanent consultants, short-term affiliated scholars, students from other institutions on (summer-) placement assignments and project-based research assistants.

In some way one is justified to define the ADRI in Ranchi as a centre in the periphery. It is linked up with the central government of India in New Delhi through its SRC and the Research Institute has an extensive international network. Besides, the ADRI in Ranchi is part of ADRI Society with its main office in Patna, the capital of Bihar. The ADRI in Ranchi also functions as a centre field, attracting NGOs and researchers based in more rural environments in the state. Simultaneously, the ADRI is a nodal point for intellectual life within the city. Nevertheless, from an all-India perspective, this research institution in the state of Jharkhand is considered peripheral even more so as it does not receive permanent funding and is not affiliated to the Indian Council of Social Science Research (ICSSR) in New Delhi. There is no flow of money from ADRI but only to ADRI and that not even on a regular basis and of permanent nature. Besides, the institute staff is appointed on project basis only. More importantly, however, ADRI stands for an integration between research and development activities in one wider social agenda and therefore supports 'action research' hoping to stimulate the development of a 'knowledge society'. This foundation places ADRI in a particular position as the many NGOs that Ranchi houses are not supported by a research centre and the research institutions (including the university) are not (any longer) based on 'action research'.

RANCHI FROM A CENTRE OF INTELLECTUAL LIFE TO THE PERIPHERY

During the 1970s and 1980s, Ranchi was known as the home as well as the centre of intellectual life of the 'Father of Indian Ethnography', the late Rai Bahadur Sarat Chandra Roy. The first anthropological journal edited by an Indian, *Man in India*, was being published from Ranchi ever since 1921. Ranchi and its surroundings had a strong tribal presence (locally defined as *adivasis*) and as research was valued as fieldwork based, most of the research institutions at the time were carrying out research among *adivasis* of the region. This fieldwork based studying of 'own society' rather than 'the other' did not, however, marginalize Ranchi intellectuals. In fact, the opposite was true and Ranchi twice housed international anthropological conferences.

If S.C. Roy brought international repute to India by his selection as member of the Council de Honour of the International Congress of Anthropological and Ethnological Sciences, L.P. Vidyarthi's election as the President of the Tenth ICAES and IUAES (1973–8) marked the advent of a 'New Era' in Indian anthropology. From 1898 till his death in 1942,

of a 'knowledge society'. Though Satpathy, Kar and Mohapatra (2009) rightly argue that the extent of the use of computer and Internet in the social science research and teaching is still very low in Jharkhand compared to other parts of India, the use of ITC among students and teachers is widely acclaimed in Ranchi. However, no systematic research has been carried out to test the impact of these new information and communication technologies in Ranchi. Nevertheless, participant observation during the last fifteen years provides some ideas about trends.

Through IT, scholars in Ranchi have certainly become less isolated. If not in reality, the feeling of being marginalized is significantly reduced due to e-mail access. Besides, teachers and students who often complained about lack of or insufficient library facilities, now see their research problems attenuated. Yet, linguistic problems, a lack of training in the use of internet tools and also possibly the general disinterest in research, seem to be responsible for the use of IT for other purposes than research and enhancement of collaborative academic undertakings. As students do not receive guidance in the use of internet for research purpose, the outcome of increased IT use is a serious degradation in the quality of research reporting. Lack of linguistic skills (in English), is also responsible for this. Moreover, as academically marginalized, students often have difficulty understanding concepts and methods current in academic centres and have difficulty to put up with academic domination as represented on internet sites. All this is added to the simple fact that most 'mainstream' academic work is not freely available through the Internet.

More importantly, another trend is observed. Whereas academic globalization has brought more foreign scholars to Jharkhand to carry out fieldwork, it is making 'arm-chair scholars' of students in Ranchi. Scholars from outside the state use the increased information now available through the Internet, to better plan their field visits in the state. They arrive with more field knowledge, better formulated research plans and clearly laid-out travel schedules. What they now 'only' need, they feel, is a 'research assistant' who can guide them during their actual fieldwork. Students in Ranchi on the other hand, replace vigorous fieldwork with new information they acquire through the Internet. This coupled with their inability or lackadaisical attitude to use the Internet for the acquirement of academic knowledge and epistemological purposes, provides space for further inequality between epistemological territories of the centre and the periphery. Moreover, instead of producing their own works, articulating their own concepts and carrying out their own fieldwork, these students desperately in need of jobs, offer to become research assistants of the scholars from outside Ranchi who often have not much time to carry out all the fieldwork by themselves.

The result is the typical divide described by Alatas (2003). The productivity of these 'research assistants' (often post-doctoral scholars) even if of high quantity or quality remains invisible as scholars who employ such researchers publish under their own names only. What is more, judging from citations in works on Jharkhand authored by scholars employed and based in the centres, it is doubtful whether these scholars ever read the output produced in the periphery itself; as of course, quotation of work by scholars who work and live in Jharkhand will not help them to get their work accepted for publication in journals produced in the academic centres. And we all know too well that as Kürti (2008: 33–4) so rightly analysed: 'Citing, or having recognition of one's work by others may have serious repercussions in terms of academic advancement, hiring or scholarliness as defined in various national settings' and 'this is even more serious as the impact factor or citation index are fast becoming the standard of measurement of scholarly work in most countries now'. At the same time, scholars whose work only (or mainly) relies on this locally produced knowledge never see their publications accepted in these journals because they do not address academic discourse in vogue at the centres.

INCREASED FLOWS OF SOCIAL SCIENTISTS IN AND OUT OF RANCHI

Academic globalization has had notable impact on day-to-day life in the ADRI office in Ranchi. The number of scholars from outside the state that visited the office significantly increased during the last nine or ten years. Ranchi is now part of the research agendas of scholars in many foreign countries, perceived from regular visits of scholars from Japan, the USA, Denmark, Austria, Germany, France, the Netherlands, Italy, Spain and the UK. These scholars normally were on 'field-research trips' in the state and the ADRI as a kind of 'compensation' for the services it provided (data provision, infrastructural and forum facilities, centre of affiliation and other much needed research assistance) generally asked them to deliver a lecture related to their own research interests. Many of them, though by far not all, gladly consented to this.

The interest of the local scholarly community in these lectures (in English) was only great if and when the topic concerned (development) matters in Jharkhand. Clearly, scholars in Ranchi (still) only tend to work on matters related to their own state (and Bihar) and support development-oriented research projects. Theory formation is not much valued and conceptual frameworks developed in the centres of knowledge production are often not understood or plainly rejected. Assessing the local impact of such lectures by foreign scholars, it must be said that they never had long-term implications in terms of changes in the local discourses, research themes, methodology and selection of research regions, local productivity or resulted in increased collaborative efforts. More depressing, many scholars in Ranchi would agree with what as Kürti (2008: 32) argued in the case of

East European scholars, it seems 'those who are in positions of power to evaluate our scholarly backgrounds and qualifications' do not only 'question our scholarly traditions but simply believe them to be exercises in futility'.

Undoubtedly, a few scholars from outside the state established 'permanent' ties with some individual local scholars and/or institutions like ADRI or the XISS and the university which became part of their academic network. However, in all these years this kind of scholarly interaction rarely resulted in bringing local scholars to academic centres. Whereas these foreign scholars keep on visiting the state (and the office), for local scholars a visit abroad or even to Delhi is only once in a lifetime chance if ever it happens to them. Unlike their foreign colleagues who visit the city on a regular basis, social scientists in Ranchi have also remained aloof of—and often consciously—theory production, or even application, do not cross-disciplinary boundaries and do not venture beyond Jharkhand (or India) as research region or take up comparative research projects. Clearly, 'the academic divide' has remained, if not increased, despite and partly because of academic globalization.

Interestingly, though mobility of foreign scholars is definitely reflected in the increased number of scholars the ADRI and a few other city-based educational institutions welcomed throughout the years, scholars from within India are rarely seen. Even though an increasing number of Indian scholars study issues related to Jharkhand, neither they nor their institutions seek local institutional support, affiliation or collaboration. What is more, during national or international conferences organized in academic centres such as Delhi for instance no effort is made to invite 'new blood' from Jharkhand. As a result, scholars from outside Jharkhand are recognized experts on 'matters of state', whereas those from within the state and who confine their research interests to Jharkhand only, are 'nobodies' in national and international academic platforms. Even more worrying is the increased brain-drain of scholars from Jharkhand to these centres. Having had an opportunity to study in educational institutions located at the centre, scholars rarely return to Jharkhand to pursue their academic careers.

In a way one can argue therefore that increased scholarly mobility further marginalizes scholars in the periphery. Yet on the positive side, scholars in eastern India have become aware of this marginalization due to academic globalization. Interestingly, the root cause of this marginalization is perceived to be the 'local' rather than the 'global' and the *status-quo* at pre- rather than post-doctoral levels. Scholars in the region point to the fact that the teacher–student ratio in social science subjects is precarious in this part of India, which is one of the lowest and unacceptable by any standard. The vacancies are never filled in and thanks to increased exposure through outside visitors and Internet there is a general feeling among scholars located in eastern India (to which Jharkhand belongs) that in their places 'the standard of social science research and teaching has gone down to the lowest ebb' (Behera, 2009: 15; see also Jayaram, 2003: 199-231). It is felt that research in eastern India (including Jharkhand) is 'repetitive, stereotyped, descriptive and mediocre in terms of quality' (ibid.: 16). More lamentably, Behera a professor at the Sambalpur University in Orissa (another academically peripheral state) adds, most of the PhD theses 'fail to get good publishers because of the sub-standard quality' (ibid.).

This awareness of being marginalized and dependent resulted in the organization of a workshop in Sambalpur in February 2009 during which scholars from Jharkhand, Orissa, West Bengal, Bihar, Andhra Pradesh and Madhya Pradesh contemplated on how 'to improve both substance (i.e. content) and the form (i.e. methodology) of social science teaching and research in eastern India'. Strong emphasis was put on regional networks rather than international academic networks and on exchanges among scholars located within the so-called periphery rather than between the periphery and the centre. It was concluded that in this way and 'If proper educational infrastructure along with an academic network and database in social science research and teaching is created in eastern India, it will definitely retain the intelligentsia and lead to further development in social science' (ibid.: 16–17). Importantly, during the workshop it was the poor quality of education and deficient teaching that were considered as bottlenecks hindering an improved status of social science research in eastern India. In short therefore, academic globalization if anything brought awareness among scholars in states like Jharkhand of their academic dependency and triggered off action for improvement. Development was perceived to come, however, from changes within the local itself (the marginalized periphery) rather than having to be initiated in the centres.

A small empirical study carried out by me in 2008 among fifty university teachers and students and among staffs and students affiliated to the XISS, IGNOU and the ADRI produced similar findings. More than complaints regarding lack of infrastructure or exposure it was the poor student–teacher relations that was addressed by both parties. Besides, all advocated applied social science and few students were interested in a research career as this entailed too much of uncertainty. Internet exposure as well as collaboration with outside scholars was low on their list of priorities. Students who were seriously contemplating further research, rather complained about lack of proper guidance, academic freedom and intellectual excitement in the immediate environment. Teachers' concerns were a different curriculum, updated textbooks and different teaching methods. Increased productivity in terms of research and publications was low on their priority lists. In such a situation, visits by foreign scholars will either have insignificant impact or induce (more) estrangement. Clearly, the interests of the two groups are miles apart.

CONCLUSION

During the next decade, academic globalization defined as increased flows of social scientists and as increased access of information will only increase, one reckons. Eric C. Thompson (2006: 41) rightly pointed out that in order to understand the effects of academic globalization on academic dependency we need a fine-grained, institutional-level analysis in situated regional contexts. In Ranchi, the capital of the state of Jharkhand, as this case study shows, academic globalization has not had much positive impact or could even lead to greater dependency or marginalization of scholars in the state. Benefits could be costs if not streamlined properly. Importantly, the study shows that this streamlining is a local rather than a global responsibility and should start at the level of teaching institutions than at the (post-)doctoral level. It is at this level, collaborative efforts between 'centres' and 'peripheries' on a genuine equal level are urgently needed if we want to bring about an academic renaissance in Ranchi.

True academic globalization should not be a unidirectional process of the periphery to the centre. The centre should also progress to the periphery. I anticipate that within ten years from now, if an increased number of scholars now working in the institutions located in the centres, start teaching in marginalized institutions of knowledge production in Jharkhand, not only will the local be transformed but the centres themselves will become more 'localized'. In this way, we might expect a truly democratic (and original) knowledge production on matters concerning (people in) Jharkhand.

NOTES

1. The Indian state of Bihar was divided in 2000 and its southern districts became part of the new state of Jharkhand.
2. I acknowledge, however, that such a division of geographical space

is no longer valid and that a dissolution and blurring of lines which identified one with the other has made the maintenance of a strict North–South binary difficult (see for this: Hours and Selim 2009: 47–54).

REFERENCES

Altbach, P.G. (ed.) (2003), *The Decline of the Guru: The Academic Profession in Developing and Middle-Income Countries*, New York: Palgrave Macmillan.

Altbach, P.G. (2003), 'Centers and Peripheries in the Academic Profession: The Special Challenges of Developing Countries', in P.G. Altbach (ed.), *The Decline of the Guru: The Academic Profession in Developing and Middle-Income Countries*, New York: Palgrave Macmillan, pp. 1–23.

Altbach, P.G. and T. Umakoshi (eds.) (2004), *Asian Universities: Historical Perspectives and Contemporary Challenges*, Baltimore: Johns Hopkins University Press.

Amsler, S. (2007), *The Politics of Knowledge in Central Asia: Science Between Marx and the Market*, London and New York: Routledge.

Behera, D.K. (ed.) (2009), *Status of Social Science Research and Teaching in Eastern India*, Abstract Volume, National Workshop February 17–19, School of Bio-Social Studies Sambalpur University and Indian Council of Social Science Research, Eastern Regional Centre.

Bhandari, L. and S. Kale (eds.) (2009), *Indian States at a Glance 2008–9: Jharkhand, Performance, Facts and Figures*, Delhi: Pearson Power.

Bremen, J. van, E. Ben-Ari and S. Farid (eds.) (2005), *Asian Anthropology*, Abingdon and New York: Routledge.

Chatterji, R. (2005), 'An Indian, Anthropology? What Kind of Object Is It?', in J. van Bremen, E. Ben-Ari and S. Farid (eds.), *Asian Anthropology*, Abingdon and New York: Routledge, pp. 162–79.

Debnath, B. (1999), 'Crisis of Indian Anthropology', in *Economic and Political Weekly*, 30 October, pp. 3110–14.

Duque, R.B. et al. (2005), 'Collaboration Paradox: Scientific

Productivity, the Internet, and Problems of Research in Developing Areas', in *Social Studies of Science*, vol. 35 (5), Scientific Collaboration, October, pp. 755–85.

Guru, G. (2002), 'How Egalitarian Are the Social Sciences in India', in *Economic and Political Weekly*, 14 December, pp. 5003–9.

Hatekar, N. (2009), 'Changing Higher Education Scenario in India', in *Economic and Political Weekly*, vol. XLIV (38), 19 September, pp. 22–3.

Hours, B. and M. Selim (2009), 'Production of the South: Incongruities and Loss of Meaning', in *Economic and Political Weekly*, vol. XLIV (30), 25 July, pp. 47–54.

Jayaram, N. (2003), 'The Fall of the Guru: The Decline of the Academic Profession in India', in P.G. Altbach (ed.), *The Decline of the Guru: The Academic Profession in Developing and Middle-Income Countries*, New York: Palgrave Macmillan, pp. 199–231.

Kürti, L. (2008), 'East and West: The Scholarly Divide in anthropology', in *Anthropological Notebooks*, vol. 14 (3): 25–38.

Lee, S. and B. Bozeman (2005), 'The Impact of Research Collaboration on Scientific Productivity', in *Social Studies of Science*, vol. 35 (5): 673–702.

Poblocki, K. (2009), 'Whither Anthropology without Nation-State?', in *Critique of Anthropology*, vol. 29 (2): 225–52.

Sahay, V. S. (1981), 'In Search of a Ranchi School of Anthropology', in *Development of Researches in Anthropology in India*, Ranchi Anthropology Series 2, New Delhi: Concept Publishing House, pp. 237–47.

Singh, R.D., E. Wood and L.P. Vidyarthi (1971), 'Urgent Anthropology: Further Comment on Urgent Social Research in India', in *Current Anthropology*, vol. 12 (1), February, pp. 97–8.

Sinha, V. (2005), 'Indigenizing' anthropology in India': Problematics of Negotiating an Identity', in J. van Bremen, E. Ben-Ari and S. Farid (eds.), *Asian Anthropology*, Abingdon and New York: Routledge, pp. 139–62.

Thompson, E.C. (2006), 'Internet-Mediated Networking and Academic Dependency in Indonesia, Malaysia, Singapore and the United States', in *Current Sociology*, vol. 54 (1): 41–61.

Umpleby, S.A. (2007), 'Academic Globalization: The Growth of International Collaboration in Education and Research', Presented at the 11th World Multi-Conference on Systemics,

Cybernetics and Informatics, Orlando, Fl., 8–12 July, available on: www.gwu.edu/~umpleby.

Vidyarthi, L.P. (1968), 'Conference on Urgent Research in India', in *Current Anthropology*, vol. 10 (4), October, pp. 377–9.

Vidyarthi, L.P. and V.S. Upadhyay (eds.) (1981), *Development of Researches in Anthropology in India*, Ranchi Anthropology Series 2, New Delhi: Concept Publishing House.

published in journals and edited books. Her recent publications include *An Autobiography of an Indian Indentured Labourer* (co-edited with Ellen Bal and Alok Deo Singh), (2005) and *Tyranny of Partition: Hindus in Bangladesh and Muslims in India* (2006).

CARLOS P. TATEL, Jr. is a faculty member of the Department of Anthropology at the University of the Philippines-Diliman. He is interested in the study of the interface between history and anthropology in the context of colonialism in South-East Asia. He has published articles on historical archaeology and also indigenous textiles and urban housing projects for the poor. For his current doctoral research, he is investigating the social memory of disaster among residents of a town in Bikol province, Philippines. He is presently co-editing a book concerning the contribution of an anthropological field-school to disaster studies in rural Philippines.

Index